Edward Payson

Mementos of Rev. Edward Payson

Edward Payson

Mementos of Rev. Edward Payson

ISBN/EAN: 9783337714826

Printed in Europe, USA, Canada, Australia, Japan

Cover: Foto ©ninafisch / pixelio.de

More available books at **www.hansebooks.com**

MEMENTOS

OF

REV. EDWARD PAYSON, D.D.

EMBRACING

A Sketch of his Life and Character,

AND SELECTIONS FROM HIS WORKS.

By REV. EDWIN L. JANES,
AUTHOR OF "WESLEY HIS OWN HISTORIAN," AND "CHARACTER AND CAREER OF FRANCIS ASBURY."

WITH

AN INTRODUCTION BY W. B. SPRAGUE, D.D., LL.D.

NEW YORK:
NELSON & PHILLIPS.
CINCINNATI: HITCHCOCK & WALDEN.
1873.

Entered according to Act of Congress, in the year 1873, by

NELSON & PHILLIPS,

in the Office of the Librarian of Congress at Washington.

PREFACE.

ALTHOUGH Edward Payson has been sleeping in the sepulcher nearly half a century, he is still held in veneration by many as a Christian minister of deep devotion, intense earnestness, and unfaltering fidelity. His name to such is yet fragrant, and awakens devout gratitude to God that such a man ever lived, as a model of the true minister, and as an illustration of the Spirit and Power of vital Christianity.

But there are others whose impressions of this remarkable man have, by the lapse of years, become indistinct; and others still, belonging to a new generation, who are without any knowledge of him. It is most desirable, therefore, that one whose character was so pure, and whose ministry was so full of evangelical teaching, and fraught with such marked results, should be kept before the Christian public.

The last edition of his works, published in 1849, being exhausted, there only remains an Abridged Memoir published by the American Tract Society. I am obliged to R. W. W. Rand, Publishing Secretary of that Society, nephew of Dr. Payson, for his cordial concurrence with my work. From this memoir, together with the original biography, I have gathered the facts relating to the Life and Character of Dr.

Payson as recorded in the following sketch, and have, to some extent, presented those facts in the language of the biographer.

In a careful reading of Dr. Payson's Works, embracing his Letters, Diary, and Sermons, I have found very many diamonds of truth burnished into " excessive brightness " by the power of his vigorous intellect and vivid imagination, and have put them in this casket.

Among these selections the minister will find seed-thoughts for the pulpit; the parent, instruction and admonition; the young, earnest counsels; the impenitent, solemn warnings; and the Christian, such views of God and Christ and heaven as cannot fail to inspire the soul with faith, hope, and love.

E. L. J.

INTRODUCTION.

I HAVE consented, by request of my highly esteemed friend and neighbor, the Rev. E. L. Janes, to write a few paragraphs introductory to a work, the parts of which have been selected and arranged by himself, designed as a memorial of the late Rev. Dr. Edward Payson. But for my unwillingness to decline the request of a friend, I might find a reasonable apology for not attempting this service in the fact that I had no personal knowledge of Dr. Payson beyond what I gathered from hearing from him a single sermon. While I was a student in Yale College—I think it was in 1811—I distinctly remember its being noised abroad one evening that Mr. Payson, of Portland, was to preach in one of the Congregational churches, and my curiosity was so much excited by his high reputation that I went to hear him. I remember nothing of the sermon, but I was greatly impressed by the solemn earnestness of the man, and all that I have read and heard of him since has been in harmony with the impressions which I then received. Though I was his contemporary in the ministry for eight years, I do not remember that we ever met during that period, though his name was as a household word among the ministers of New England.

It is the glory of a good man that his usefulness survives him. The influence for good which he has exerted continues to move on, often in nameless and invisible channels, and sometimes receives a fresh impulse from the co-operation of those who revere his memory. Dr. Payson, during his life, was doubtless among the most earnest and faithful of our American clergy; and, as the result of his labors, it is safe to presume that he is wearing a bright crown among the ransomed. But the influences which he originated are still at work, and are destined to continue indefinitely; and it is matter of joy that those are found, even beyond the denomination with which he was connected, who are more than willing to labor to perpetuate them. Dr. Payson's publications, during his life-time, were only a few occasional sermons or addresses, which, though written with uncommon power, and greatly admired wherever they were read, were essentially ephemeral, and quickly passed away. But after his death these were all republished, and about twenty years since three large attractive volumes appeared, the first containing a Memoir of his Life, by the Rev. Asa Cummings, and the second and third, nearly one hundred of his own sermons. These volumes have had a wide circulation, and it is understood that the edition is now quite exhausted. The Rev. E. L. Janes, of the Methodist Episcopal Church, having been deeply impressed by the reading of this work, including the Life as well as the Sermons, and feeling that both are too precious to pass into oblivion, while there is little prospect that they will come to another edition in their present form, has furnished the accompanying outline of his history, and what he deemed the most striking extracts from his discourses. The volume is one of very great interest, and cannot fail to be rendered attractive, by its novelty, even to those who have read the original work.

With all our admiration of Dr. Payson's character, we deem it proper to state that the qualities by which he was most distinguished were closely allied to certain natural endowments which, if not closely guarded, interfere essentially with one's comfort and usefulness. In his nature there was an unbounded earnestness, mingled with somewhat of severity; and while his preaching and his intercourse always exhibited the former, the latter was not always excluded. But his heart overflowed with love to his fellow-creatures, and if, at any time, he became, for a moment, restive and impetuous, he was never satisfied with himself until he had made the most ample restitution.

How great a service Mr. Janes has rendered to the cause of religion by furnishing this volume we may see from its adaptation to remedy certain evils now very patent in the Church and the ministry. That a strain of preaching, much less direct and pungent than that of Dr. Payson, is demanded by most of our assemblies, admits not of question; and that not a small number of ministers, who range themselves with the evangelical class, are disposed to meet this ungracious claim, is equally certain. Let this work, on which Mr. Janes has bestowed so much labor and care, have a wide circulation, and we may expect that the pulpit will give no uncertain sound, and that the Church will come up to a higher point of zeal and fidelity. W. B. SPRAGUE.

FLUSHING, *June,* 1872.

CONTENTS.

PART I.
SKETCH OF PAYSON'S LIFE AND CHARACTER.

	Page
Preliminary Remarks	15
Payson's Parentage	16
Early Developments	17
Early Literary Training	18
Awakened by the Death of a beloved Brother	18
An Experiment	19
His Review of his past Life and Covenant Engagement	19
Worldly Amusements — Rules of Action	19
Makes a Public Profession of Religion	20
Appreciation of his Conversion	20
An Important Step	21
As a Bible Student	21
Earnest Praying and Excessive Fasting	22
Apportionment of Time	23
Impaired Health — Conflicting Emotions	23
Horrible Temptations	24
Only Pastoral Charge	25
Protests Against an Increase of Salary	26
A Successful Rencounter	26
Intense Earnestness	27
Zeal and Fidelity Rewarded by Success	28
Rule in Preparing for the Pulpit	29
Influence Through the Press	29
Conflict with a Lingering Pride of Heart	30
Humility	31
Domestic Character	31
Humor — A Specimen	33
Intense Sufferings	33
Remarkably Sustained by Views of the Divine Perfections	34
Demeanor under Bodily Sufferings	36
Last Scenes of his Life and Labors	36
Confined to the Chamber of Sickness and Death — His Triumph	38
Dying Words to the Young Men of his Congregation	40
Unparalleled Sufferings and Unbounded Joy	41
Last Agony	42
Extract from Payson's Funeral Sermon, preached by Rev. Charles Jenkins	43
Concluding Remarks	44
Payson — Bramwell — Fletcher — Hedding	46

PART II.
SELECTIONS FROM THE WORKS OF EDWARD PAYSON, D.D.

	Page
Blending the Friend with the Parent	49
A Wise Preference	49
The Reason of the Confusion Stated	50
Extract from Payson's First Oration, July 4, 1806	50
Peculiar Temptations and Special Relief	52
Payson's Appreciation of Pious Parents	52
The Scheme of Redemption Glorious	53
A Motive for Choosing Religious Companions	54
Our Old Friend Bunyan	54
Spiritual Pride	55
The Town in an Uproar	55
Both Sides of the Question	56
The Ministers of Christ in a Trying Situation	56
Primeval Harmony	57
The Discord and Jargon of Sin	58
Confidence in God under Trial	60
A Minister a Burden Bearer	60
"Jesus, Jesus is All!"	61
Ardent Desires to Glorify Christ	61
A Brand Plucked out of the Fire	62
"If I could Borrow the Archangel's Trump"	62
A Half-Sleeping, Half-Waking Dream	63
Getting a Wife without Loss of Time	64
Public Prayer a Kind of Devout Poetry	65
A Fault in Public Prayer	66
How a True Embassador of Christ Delivers his Message	66
Three Things Make a Divine	67

	Page
Extempore Preaching	68
Satan's Cunning	69
Meditations on the Priesthood of Christ	69
Professors in Concentric Circles around Christ	70
Growth of Grace in the Heart Illustrated	71
The Thirsty Sinner by the Riverside	71
Love for the Absent One	72
Pardon Impossible without Repentance	73
The Criminality of Sin	73
The Absurdity of Sinners' Excuses	74
A Mediator Rejected	75
A Newspaper, an Almanac, and the Bible	75
God's Image Reflected by his Saints	76
Good Impressions—Illustration	76
The High and Low Seat	77
A Proper Course of Reading for Christians	77
The Son Comforts the Mother	78
Closet Duties—Satan's Devices	79
Weighty Words to a Christian Minister	80
A Proof of Faith in Prayer	82
"Satan has Jumped on to the Saddle"	82
Exalted Views of God	83
Satan's Questions Answered	84
Inscriptions on Immortal Minds	85
The Dying Christian on the Last Summit of Life	85
Happiness in a Surrender of the Will	86
The Happy Cripple	86

CONTENTS.

	Page
An Assemblage of Motives to Holiness	87
An Overflowing Fountain	88
"I Am that I Am"	88
Eternity of God	89
Love of God	89
Folly and Absurdity	90
A Rebellious Will—Illustration	90
An Angel Visitor Astonished	92
The World the Diana of its Inhabitants	92
Our Treatment of the Word of God a Test	93
Neglect of Prayer—Its Practical Import	93
The Sinner's Wish	94
Christian Experience against Infidel Objections	95
Christianity as a Delusion	96
Insufficiency of Human Reason	96
Natural Religion a Failure	97
The Height of Folly and Madness	99
Two Sets of Armor	100
God Meets the Sinner's Excuses	101
A Change of Position—Results	102
Christ a Magnet	102
Adam our Federal Head	103
The Attributes of God Harmonized in Redemption	104
A New Lesson for Angels	105
The Glory that Shines in the Gospel	106
"Glad Tidings! Glad Tidings!"	106
Christ an Unrivaled Friend	108
The Sage and the Pupil	109
The Three Occasions of Christ's Anger	109
The Sufferings of Christ Real	110
The Power of Love	111
Christ's Self-Denial	112
Christ Satisfied	112
Christ's Reception of Penitent Sinners	113
Going on to Perfection	114
Advantages of Possessing Christ	116
The Bible entirely Practical	117
Earnestness in Prayer a Test	117
Symptoms of Spiritual Decline	118
Impatience at not Receiving Answers to Prayer	118
Praise Procures the Divine Blessing	119
The Communion a Funeral Scene	120
Sympathy with Christ as a Man of Sorrows	120
The Grand Law of Nature	121
Man can do what God Requires	122
Covetousness a Pit without a Bottom	122
A Little Court within the Breast	122
Contemplation of Eternity	123
Death the Porter of Paradise	123
Honor and Danger of the Gospel Ministry	123
A Thousand Years as One Day in Heaven	125
"O What Must it Be to be There!"	126
The Bereaved Mother Comforted	127
Doubts Arising from Infirmities Removed	127
"One Broken Wing"	127
How Rich the Poorest Christian	128
And the Lamb is the Light Thereof	129
No Night in Heaven	131
The New Jerusalem and its Inhabitants	131
The Sailor Spoken on his Life Voyage	133
The Bible a Compass, Chart, and Quadrant	134
Drunkard's Rock	134
A Dangerous Whirlpool	135
The Straits of Repentance	135
The Bay of Faith	136
The Highlands of Hope	136
The Sailor at his Evening Watch	137
The Destruction of the World	137

CONTENTS.

	Page
Sir William Jones' Estimate of the Bible	138
Historic Information of the Bible	138
Antiquity of the Holy Scriptures	140
Unsuccessful Opposition to the Word of God	141
Benefits of the Bible to Our Race	143
Divine Origin of the Bible	144
The Bible a Mirror	145
Scripture Precepts—Their Importance	148
Instructive Examples	149
The Bible a Vehicle of Consolation and Hope	150
Consequences Resulting from the Loss of the Bible	152
God's Boundless Empire	153
The Infinite Contrast	154
The Plan of Redemption above Human Conception	155
Folly of Judging of God by our Limited Knowledge of Him	156
The Reasonableness of Faith	157
The World Created for Christ	158
The Human Race Created for Christ	158
A Proof of Christ's Divinity	160
The Cross the Central Object of Creation	161
Introduction of Sin into the World	162
The Broad and Narrow Way	165
How to See our Sins as God Sees Them	166
The Righteousness of Christ—How Obtained	170
Thoughts are Words in the Ear of God	172
Sin an Infinite Evil	172
Everlasting Punishment—Argument	174
The Folly and Absurdity of Pride	175
Why the Remembrance of God is Painful	176
The Eternity of Those who Forget God	177
Various Means Employed to Save Sinners	178
Caprice of Sinners in Judging Christians	179
The Natural Affections Christianized	180
An Important Distinction	181
"He shall See of the Travail of his Soul and be Satisfied"	183
The Happiness of Jesus Christ	185
The Battle and the Victory	186
The Sword of the Spirit in the Hand of Omnipotence	188
The Glory and Majesty of Christ	189
The Prophet's Vision	191
A Revival Scene	192
A Desperate and Fatal Game	193
The Difficulty of Convincing Men of Sin	194
Compassion for the Perishing	195
The Strange Contrast	196
Thanksgiving in Paradise	196
How Christians Should Keep Thanksgiving Day	198
The State of the World at the Second Coming of Christ	200
Christ's Second Coming Described	201
Man Capable of Equality with Angels	204
Man's Capabilities Invest the Cross with Sublimity	206
Motives to Imitate the Angels	207
The Pangs of Remorse in Eternity	208
An Unquenchable Fire	211
Objections to Future Punishment Answered	212
Benefits of the Universal Spread of Christ's Kingdom	215
"For in Him Dwelleth all the Fullness of the Godhead Bodily"	216
Habitually at Ease in Zion	218
The Alarm Sounded	219
Fearful Consequences of Not Punishing Sin	220
Superior Advantages of the Christian Dispensation	222

Contents.

	Page
Despair: Its Nature and Effects	223
God Listening to the Afflicted Penitent	225
All Classes Invited to the Gospel Feast	225
Moral Sublimity of Christ's Invitations	227
Merely Human Instrumentalities Ineffectual	228
How to Prolong the Visits of the Saviour	230
Christ's Absence from the Church	230
The Believer's Foretastes of Heaven	232
The Sufferings of Christ a Proof of his Love	234
A Striking Illustration	236
The Oracles of God	237
The Inquirer at the Oracle	240
Nature and Effects of Godly Fear	243
The Fear of God Controlling the Imagination	244
The Duty of the Church toward Children	244
The Gospel Glad Tidings	245
The Gospel Glorious Glad Tidings	247
An Appeal to Christian Ministers	248
Christ as a Citizen of our World	250
The Meekness and Patience of Jesus in Crucifixion	254
Christ's Mediatorial Kingdom	256
The Progress and Prospects of Christ's Kingdom	257
Christ's Ascension	260
The Human Soul a Palace	262
Satan's Code of Laws	263
Satan's Armor	264
The False Peace of the Sinner	265
The Sinner's Substitute in the Hands of Justice	266
Man Lost to God	267
Man Lost to Holiness and Happiness	268
The Penal Consequences of Sin	269
The Light that Guides us Back to God	270
The Marshaled Hosts	271
God's Highest Claims	272
Goodness of Heart and Greatness of Mind	273
A Startling View of the Sinner's Guilt	274
The Safe Side	276
Repentance a Cause of Rejoicing with God	276
Why the Son of God Rejoiceth Over Repentant Sinners	279
Similarity the Basis of Communion with God	281
In What Communion with God Consists	282
The Christian Joy in Communion with God	284
Reasons for Family Worship	286
The Picture Not Overdrawn	288
Solemn Questions to Parents	290
A Whirlpool	291
The Power of Example Illustrated	293
An Appeal to Baptized Children	293
Children Welcomed to the Fold of Christ	295
Parents Guilty of the Sin of Eli	296
Consequences of Parental Unfaithfulness	298
God's Moral Government Over Nations	299
The Crime of Perjury a National One	300
A Solemn Caution to Young Men	302
Evils Avoided by Early Piety	303
The Sublime Contrast	304
Sound and Important Views for Voters	305
Responsibility of Legislators and Magistrates	307
Mutual Love Between Christ and his People	308
The Happiness of Loving and Being Loved	310
The Infidel Met on his Own Ground	311

Contents.

	Page
Safety of Believing in the Divinity of Christ	312
An Objection Answered	313
The Safe Side	315
"How Can a Man Be Too Religious?"	315
The World We Live In	316
Christmas Thoughts	318
The Certainty of Unseen Things	320
"Holiness to the Lord"	323
The Nature and Claims of Jehovah	325
The Character of Jehovah	327
God's Works of Providence Demand our Praise	328
A Deluge of Blessings	332
Transient Emotions	333
God's Works of Grace Soon Forgotten	334
The Character of Our National Religion	336
The Existence of the World Accounted For	337
"If the Bible Be Not True"	339
The Certainty of a Future Judgment—Argument	343
Christ Coming to Judgment	344
The Persons to Be Judged	345
The Things for Which Men are to be Judged	347
First Object that will Rush upon the Mind at Death	349
Mortal, Yet Immortal	349

MEMENTOES

OF

EDWARD PAYSON, D.D.

PART I.

SKETCH OF HIS LIFE AND CHARACTER.

Preliminary Remarks.

DURING a period of fifty years, embracing the last quarter of the eighteenth century and the first quarter of the nineteenth, the Congregational Church of New England was distinguished by a host of eminent Divines. Dr. Sprague's "Annals of the American Pulpit," Vols. I and II, contain a brief biography (not including those referred to in the foot-notes) of two hundred and eighteen Congregational ministers, whose labors covered more or less of the above period, and who were born in New England; namely, one hundred and two in Massachusetts, ninety-five in Connecticut, fifteen in New Hampshire, four in Maine, one in Vermont, and one in Rhode Island. Of these, one hundred and thirty-three were honored with the titles of D.D. or LL.D., conferred, with rare exceptions, by New England colleges.

It is safe to say, that in no one period in the history of New England were there more talent and enterprise displayed in the cause of education and religion, including the missionary cause, than in the last and first quarters of the two centuries. Men of intellectual might and Christian zeal were found hard at work, not only as pastors, but also as tutors, professors, presidents of literary and theological institutions, missionaries, secretaries, authors, and editors. The most of these devoted men were contemporary with the subject of our sketch, their ministry extending into the nineteenth century, and running parallel with his, for a longer or shorter period.

While the New England hills and valleys were all ablaze with the intellectual and spiritual fires that emanated from school-house and academy, from college and theological seminary, from the pulpit and religious press, there was an evangelical fire burning in Portland, Maine; and so bright was the flame as to attract distant attention, and so intensely did it burn as to consume in a few brief years the devoted man who kindled it. That man was EDWARD PAYSON.

Payson's Parentage.

Edward Payson was born at Rindge, New Hampshire, July 25th, 1783. His father, Rev. Seth Payson, was a man of piety and public spirit, somewhat distinguished as a clergyman, and favorably known as an author. His mother was an intelligent, devoted Christian woman.

Payson attributed his religious character and influence, under God, to the instruction, example, and prayers of his Christian parents. Among the earliest impressions made upon his mind by his mother was, that it was his duty to become religious in childhood.

Payson's Early Developments.

Payson early manifested a remarkable inquisitiveness of mind, which his mother cherished by answering his almost endless inquiries. In the first developments of his moral powers, his infant mind grasped the fact that he was a sinner. He was often known to weep under the preaching of the Gospel when only three years old! He would frequently call his mother to his bedside to answer questions respecting his relation to God and a future world. It was the judgment of his mother that he was converted in childhood. It is believed that he never neglected private prayer while living under the parental roof.

His early mental developments indicated that he would be a man of decision, enterprise, and perseverance. His taste for the sublime was remarkable in childhood. During a tempest he might be seen on the top of a fence, or some other eminence, while the lightnings played and the thunders rolled around him, sitting in composure and enjoying the sublimity of the scene.

He was a very good reader at four years of age, and could transfer the contents of a book to his own mind with remarkable facility. All the books in his father's collection and in the town library, suitable to his age and attainments, were read before he left the paternal home, and made available in his ministry by the tenacity of his memory.

Payson's Early Literary Training.

This was conducted principally by his parents, excepting the studies preparatory to college, which were pursued, in part, at least, at a neighboring academy. He entered Harvard College in 1800, at seventeen years of age, at an advanced standing, and with the reputation of being a magnanimous, honorable, generous youth. Here he was known and respected for the purity of his morals, the regularity of his habits, and his amiable disposition; as also for his mental industry. He had at college the reputation of being a "great reader." His fellow-students, before knowing the rapidity with which he acquired knowledge, and the strength and tenacity of his memory, rallied him as having a machine to turn over the leaves; and, at another time, as having left off taking out books, because he had read all of the thousands in the alcoves of Old Harvard. After graduating, in 1803, he spent three years as principal of an academy in Portland, and commanded the esteem and veneration of his pupils.

Payson Awakened by the Death of a beloved Brother.

In the early part of 1804, the death of his brother was the means of fixing his attention on religion more fully for the rest of his life. In a letter to his mother he writes: "Infatuated by the pleasures and amusements this place affords, I gradually grew cold and indifferent to religion. From this careless frame nothing but a shock like that I have received could have roused me. I hope, by the assistance of divine grace, this dispensation will prove of eternal benefit."

Sketch of Life and Character. 19

An Experiment.

Young Payson made the experiment which most are disposed to make before fully consecrating themselves to Christ, and with this result, as stated by himself: "In the impracticable attempt to reconcile God and the world, I spend my time very unhappily, neither enjoying the comforts of this world nor of religion; but I have at last determined to renounce the false pleasures for which I pay so dear; and this I should have done long ago, but for the advice and example of some whose judgment I respected."

Payson's Review of his past Life and Covenant Engagement.

Under date of July 25, 1805, he writes: "Having resolved this day to dedicate myself to my Creator by a written covenant, I took a review of my past life, and of the numerous mercies by which it has been distinguished. Then, with sincerity, I humbly hope, I took the Lord to be my God, and engaged to love and obey him. Relying on the Holy Spirit for assistance, I engaged to take the Holy Scriptures as the rule of my conduct, the Lord Jesus Christ to be my Saviour, and the Spirit of all grace and consolation as my Guide and Sanctifier. The vows of God are upon me."

Worldly Amusements—Rules of Action.

To one who urged Mr. Payson to go into society and frequent public amusements, he wrote: "Can a man walk on pitch and his feet not be defiled? Can a man take coals of fire in his bosom, and his clothes not be burned?"

In regard to worldly associations and amusements, Payson adopted the following simple rules: 1. To do nothing the lawfulness of which he doubted in any degree. 2. To consider every thing unlawful which indisposes for prayer and interrupts communion with God. 3. Never to go into any company, business, or situation, in which he could not consistently ask and expect the divine blessing. By the help of these rules, he says, "I settle all my doubts in a trice."

Payson Makes a Public Profession of Religion.

He joined the Church at Rindge, under the pastoral care of his father, while on a visit to his parents, during one of his quarterly vacations, Sept. 1, 1805. Soon after he writes to his mother: "As yet I have no reason to repent of the step I took while at home. I have felt wondrous brave and resolute since my return, but I rejoice with trembling. If I know any thing of myself, I shall need pretty severe discipline through life, and I often shrink at the thought of the conflict that awaits me; but I am encouraged by the promise, that my strength shall be equal to my day."

October 6th he writes: "Since my return from Rindge I have hardly known one unhappy moment. I enjoy mental peace, and at times happiness inexpressible."

His Appreciation of his Conversion.

Under the impulse of gratitude, and from a profound sense of obligation, he writes: "'Is not this a brand plucked out of the fire?' Zech. iii, 2. What a just and striking description of every sinner! To snatch a smoking brand from eternal burnings, and plant it among the stars in the firmament of heaven, there to shine like the sun forever! Such a brand am I; a brand yet smoking with the half-extinguished fires of sin; a brand scorched and blackened by the flames of hell! What then do I owe to Him, who entered the furnace of divine wrath, that he might bring me out?"

An Important Step.

In 1806 Mr. Payson resigned the charge of the academy in Portland, and returned to his father's house, where he pursued his theological studies, till he entered the ministry. This step may be regarded as one of the most important of his life. His biographer thinks, had he entered at once upon the work of the ministry, as he contemplated, he had not been the minister that he became. In comparative retirement, with his father for his tutor, and with an illustration of the purity and power of Christianity before him in the lives of godly parents, he was most auspiciously situated.

He appreciated these advantages, and gave himself up to the work of preparation with an exclusiveness and ardor perhaps never equaled.

Payson as a Bible Student.

He seems to have concentrated all his powers upon the acquisition of scriptural knowledge, and the cultivation of Christian and ministerial graces. He entertained the most exalted views of the office of the ministry, and of the qualifications requisite, and sought them with a corresponding zeal.

He regarded himself not so much as a student of systems of divinity, drawn up by men, as a student of the Bible. He regarded these systems with jealousy. Doubtless the works of eminent divines, which he had already read, exerted some influence upon his mind; but in his independence as a thinker, and in his deep reverence for the word of God, he placed them all in subordination to that divine word, embracing that one book as an adequate foundation for his faith, and an infallible guide to duty.

His reading was confined principally to such writings as helped to elucidate and unfold the literal meaning of the Bible. In this manner he studied the whole of the inspired book, so that there was not a verse on which he had not formed an opinion. In this way he acquired an unparalleled readiness to meet every question, on every occasion, whether proposed by a caviler or conscientious inquirer. This ready knowledge of the Bible gave him the confidence of the people, as a man mighty in the Scriptures, to confound and silence gainsayers, and to ornament his discourses with the brilliant diamonds of truth, and to set apples of gold in pictures of silver.

Earnest Praying and Excessive Fasting.

Mr. Payson pursued his studies with almost unceasing prayer, studying theology on his knees, and pleading the promises in a prostrate position, with the Bible open before him.

He added much fasting to prayer. His seasons of fasting were long and frequent, so much so as to injure his bodily health. In after years he saw and lamented his error of fasting too long. But he was at the time a student and candidate for the holy ministry, and desired to comply with the precept,

"Mortify the flesh, with the affections and lusts." He felt that as a servant of Christ he should be the master of his own passions and propensities, and resorted to this scriptural way to gain that mastery.

It is safer, perhaps, to go to an extreme in this direction, than to neglect altogether this essential discipline of the body.

Apportionment of Time.

Mr. Payson was also too severe upon himself in the apportionment of his time, as will be seen by the following arrangement: twelve hours to be given to study, two to private devotion, two to relaxation, two to meals and family devotion, and six to sleep.

Impaired Health—Conflicting Emotions.

Payson's health had now become impaired by his severe regimen, and also by a fall from a horse, so that he writes at different dates: "Was excessively melancholy." "Was oppressed with pride and vanity." "Spent the day in the woods in fasting and prayer, to obtain a mortification of my abominable pride and selfishness." "More gloomy and oppressed than yesterday." "I was greatly oppressed with pride and vanity, which made their attack upon me in inexpressible shapes."

Yet interspersed with these gloomy sentences we find others, describing a deep, happy Christian experience: "God was pleased to fill me with himself, so that I was burned up with most intense love, and panting after holiness." "Never before had such faith and fervency in prayer." "I am as happy as nature could sustain."

Melancholy, at times, overwhelmed him like a thousand monsters, so that his soul was crushed under it. At other times he was "surprised with visits from his blessed Lord, full of sweetness and love." His peculiar mental constitution and physical condition had much to do with these sudden and frequent transitions of religious feeling. Besides his constitutional predisposition to melancholy, his health had been shattered by abstinence, night vigils, and extraordinary exertions. The sentiment of Bishop Horne will apply here: Religion was not the cause of his gloom, but was his refuge in times of depression.

Horrible Temptations.

Payson's peculiar temperament and bodily weakness made him a conspicuous mark for the infernal archer to shoot at. "I thought long since," he writes, "that I had endured every thing horrible and dreadful that was ever felt, heard of, or conceived; but I find that the depths of Satan and the depths of a depraved and wicked heart are not easily fathomed. These unfathomed depths, however, serve to show me more clearly the infinite height and depth of Christ's love!"

At a later period in his history he explains the reason why God permitted him to be so grievously tormented in the past: "That I might counsel and comfort those of Christ's sheep against whom Satan raged violently."

Under date of Dec. 5, 1823, he writes, "I have been sick and laid by for two Sabbaths, but am now able to resume my labors. But, O the temptations which have harassed me for the last three months!

I have met with nothing like them in books. I dare not mention them to any mortal, lest they should trouble him as they have troubled me. Should I become an apostate, and write against the Christian religion, it seems to me that I could bring forward objections that would shake the faith of all the Christians in the world. What I marvel at is, that the arch-deceiver has not been permitted to suggest them to his scribes, and have them published to the world. All the atheistical and deistical objections which I have met with in books are childish babblings compared with those which Satan suggests, and which he urges upon the mind with a force which seems irresistible."

Payson's only Pastoral Charge.

This was in Portland, Maine. He was ordained pastor of the Congregational Church of that place, Dec. 16, 1807. He served the Church with remarkable fidelity and success for twenty years; indeed, lived and died with them and for them. This was the more remarkable as he was so uncompromising in his preaching and intercourse with his people.

His remaining in one charge for a lifetime shows him to have been remarkably free from a worldly and ambitious spirit. It was his prayer that if God had any worldly blessings in store for him he would be pleased to give him grace instead of them, or change them into spiritual blessings. He writes, "I can hardly help praying, sometimes, that he would take away all he has bestowed, so that I shall not sin against such goodness." He felt "to bless God that when his roots began to shoot into and cleave to the earth, he plucked them up before they were too deeply and firmly fixed."

Payson Protests Against an Increase of Salary.

We may readily suppose that, possessing, as he did, so unselfish a nature, his people would never have any difficulty with him about salary. They had difficulty, however, but it came from him in the shape of strong protests against an increase of the salary voted him at the time of his settlement! And although he had calls from Boston and New York, with higher salary and position, he could not be tempted to leave his beloved Portland charge.

A Successful Rencounter.

In carrying out his rule "to make none but pastoral visits, and always to have religion recognized in every social circle in which he mingled," he once had a successful rencounter with a lawyer in Portland who ranked high for wealth and influence, but was skeptical. When he gave his consent to his wife that Mr. Payson might be invited socially to visit them, it was on the condition that he should not converse on religion, nor ask a blessing over his food, nor offer a prayer in his house. But so skillfully did Mr. Payson manage his host that he did ask a blessing, returned thanks, read the Scriptures, and had family prayer, and all at the request of the master of the house! As the critical moment arrived, Mr. Payson inquired of his host, "What writer has said that the devil invented this fashion of carrying round tea to prevent a blessing being asked?"

"I do not know, sir," replied the lawyer, "who it

was ; but we will foil the devil this time. Please to ask a blessing, Mr. Payson."

This reminds us of an anecdote of the Rev. Ezekiel Cooper, who is said to have satirized the fashion of handing round tea in this manner. On an occasion of the kind he was heard to exclaim, "What a poor, helpless creature man is, with a cup of tea in one hand, a piece of cake in the other, and a fly on his nose, and no means of getting him off."

Payson's Intense Earnestness.

Payson's experience, prayers, hopes and fears, joys and sorrows, indeed his whole ministerial life and labors, were marked with an intensity seldom known. "My disposition," said he, "is naturally so ardent that I can enjoy nothing with moderation ; so that I must either be totally indifferent to worldly objects, or else love them to such a degree as to render them idols."

He was very jealous for the Lord of Hosts, and was a living witness of the power of divine grace, and a living reproof to cold and formal professors. The indifference of men to their salvation, and the prevalence of wickedness, made "his heart ache, and his eyes weep." He expostulated, warned, and entreated ; he mourned in secret places, and interceded with God to save the people.

In keeping with this spirit of zeal that burned within him and blazed around him, he highly appreciated revivals—prayed, and fasted, and worked for them, and was never satisfied without a revival state in his Church. He ardently loved the work of the ministry. If he had sufficient strength for the duty, he considered it no favor for a visitor to supply his pulpit. It was like a man proposing to eat up a good dinner prepared for himself when half starved. "Since the failure of my health," he writes, "I preach but three sermons a week!"

On being urged by his people to visit Europe for his health, with the offer of a free passage, he replied, "It would be gratifying to see Old England, but I cannot spare the time."

Payson's Zeal and Fidelity Rewarded by Success.

Payson's success may be attributed in a great measure to his ardent and persevering prayers, and the undoubted sincerity of his belief in what he taught. Though he drew crowds around him, there was nothing of stage effect either in his eloquence or personal appearance—no imposing attitudes or gestures; no extremes of intonation; no affectation. It was a simple uttering of the deep convictions of the heart. It was the eloquence of truth spoken in love. The words seemed to come from his mouth encompassed by that glowing atmosphere in which they left the heart. He was always in earnest, and impressed the fact upon his hearers. "It is a glorious day to live in," said he; "so much to be done. I would not now exchange a place in the Church below for a place in heaven. The longer our time of labor is, the better. There will be time enough for rest."

With such a spirit he could not fail of success. In one year of his ministry his Church received an accession of seventy-three, and in the year of his death seventy-nine. The average number was more than thirty-five a year during the whole of his ministry.

He often performed services for other congregations, and went on missionary tours to places not having a settled ministry, spending several days in arduous labors, and with signal results.

His agency was also felt in raising the tone of piety in all the Churches that could be reached by his influence; and his presence, counsels, example, and prayers, gave shape tone, and energy to many public institutions of his day.

Payson's Rule in Preparing for the Pulpit.

It was his invariable object to introduce so much of the fundamental truths of the Gospel into every discourse, that one who had never heard a sermon before, and should never hear another, might learn from it what is essential to salvation.

His Influence Through the Press.

Mr. Payson was mistaken when he said that God had denied him the honor of doing good with his pen, and of speaking for Christ when silent in the dust.

No man, probably, whose pen was so limited in its work has accomplished so much. "The Bible Above All Price" was the first production suffered to go to press. Myriads of copies have been circulated. His "Address to Seamen" was so effectual at the time of its delivery that nine thousand copies were printed at once, and unnumbered copies since. Also a sermon before the Maine Bible Society, entitled "The Oracles of God," was a popular discourse, but did not reach the extent of popularity or circulation as did those just mentioned. Besides, how full of instruction, influence, and inspiration are the pregnant sentences falling from his pen, as contained in his Diary and Letters, and given to the world in his Biography. Thousands of Gospel ministers have doubtless been made wiser and better men, and have been stimulated to seek a richer experience, and higher devotion to the work of the ministry, by reading the published Sermons, and especially the Biography, of Dr. Payson.

Payson's Conflict with a Lingering Pride of Heart.

"I find," he writes, "scarcely any time to read or study, and am constrained to go into the pulpit with discourses so undigested, my pride is constantly mortified, and though it lies groaning and bleeding under continual wounds, it will not be persuaded to give up the ghost."

In a letter to his mother he writes, "You must not say one word that even intimates that I am growing in grace. I cannot bear it. Every body here, whether friends or enemies, is conspiring to ruin me. Satan and my own heart will of course lend a hand, and if you join them too, I fear all the cold water which Christ can throw upon my pride will not prevent it from breaking out into a destructive flame. As certainly as any body flatters or caresses me, my heavenly Father has to whip me for it, and it is an unspeakable mercy that he condescends to do it. I can easily muster a hundred reasons why I should not be proud, but pride wont mind reason, nor any thing else but a good drubbing. Even at this moment, I feel it tingling at my finger ends and seeking to guide my pen."

Payson's Humility.

In the following extract we find true humility expressed in one of his beautiful figures: "Could I paint a true likeness of Christ, I should rejoice to hold it up to the view and admiration of all creation, and to be hid behind it forever. It would be heaven enough to hear him praised and adored, though no one should care about insignificant me."

In a letter to a candidate for the ministry he expresses himself thus: "Let those who choose to engage in such a race (for worldly distinctions) divide the prize. Let one run away with the money, another with applause; be God's approbation the only prize for which I run."

In alluding to two distinguished characters, who asserted that they were never happy until they ceased striving to be great, he writes, "My heart saw it and consented to it, and now I am comparatively happy."

In reviewing his life in this same spirit of humility, he could say, "I have done nothing myself; I have not fought, but Christ has fought for me; I have not run, but Christ has carried me; I have not worked, but Christ has wrought in me; Christ has done all."

His Domestic Character.

He at one time expressed a fear of marrying, lest, from his ardent temperament, he should love a wife too little or too much. Nor would he be anxious about the selection, nor waste his Master's time in seeking one, confident that he should certainly have a good wife if God saw best. He did marry wisely and well, and we here give an extract showing that his heart was as true to his companion as it was, in a higher sphere of affection, true to Christ and his Church.

He writes on board of a vessel sailing up the Delaware in sight of Philadelphia, "The prospects on the banks of the river were delightful and cheering every moment. The day was fine and the swiftness of our motion was agreeable, and, to crown all, I saw God in his works, and tasted his goodness in every thing. I thought of you almost every moment, and nothing but the presence of yourself and the children was wanting to make me as happy as I could be in this world. Every one on board is in a bustle, and I am standing away in one corner talking with my best, dearest earthly friend. You, at the distance of five hundred miles, have more attractions for me than the whole city of Philadelphia, which is spread out before me. Kiss the children for me, talk to them about me; love me as I do you. I love you far better than I did when I wrote the last letter to you before our marriage."

The qualities of a tender husband, and of a faithful and affectionate father, were uniform in their action, and were daily manifested in his household in a manner that showed the intense interest he felt in the religious welfare of his family and domestics.

He had both religion and good sense enough not to be a vain and foolish father, but avoided that doting partiality for his children which causes so many parents to hold the reins of parental discipline with a lax hand. Here is a specimen in which with keen humor he takes off the vanity of doting parents.

"As to baby," he writes, "she is the greatest genius and the greatest beauty in these parts. Suffice it to say, that she has four teeth; stands alone; says 'Pa' and 'Ma;' 'no,' 'no,' very stoutly, and has been whipped several times for being wiser than her father."

Payson's Humor—A Specimen.

After speaking of attacks from other diseases, he writes, "Rheumatism next arrived, eager to pay his respects, and embraced my right shoulder with such ardor of affection that he had well-nigh torn it from its socket. I had not thought much of this gentleman's powers before, but he has convinced me of them so thoroughly, that I shall think and speak of them with respect as long as I live. Not content with giving me his company all day, for a fortnight he insisted on sitting up with me every night, and what is worse, made me sit up too. During this time my poor neck, back, and shoulder, seemed to be a place in which the various pains and aches had assembled to keep holiday, and the delectable sensations of stinging, pricking, cutting, lacerating, wrenching, burning, gnawing, succeeded each other, or all mingled together in the wildest confusion.

"The cross old gentleman, though his zeal is somewhat abated by fomentations and blisters with which we welcomed him, still stands at my back, threatening that he will not allow me to finish my letter."

His Intense Sufferings.

He writes on one occasion, "My flesh trembles and my blood almost runs cold when I look back on what I have suffered. A very large proportion of my path lies through the valley of the shadow of death."

Parts of his body, including the right arm and left side, were singularly affected. They were incapable of motion, and lost all sense of feeling externally, while in the interior parts of the limbs thus affected he experienced at intervals a most intense burning sensation, which he compared to a stream of fused metal or liquid fire coursing through his bones.

Remarkably Sustained by Views of the Divine Perfections.

"God's promises appear most strong, solid, real, substantial: more so than the rocks and everlasting hills. And his perfections! what shall I say of them? When I think of one, I wish to dwell on it forever; but another and another equally glorious claims a share of my admiration, and when I begin to praise I wish never to cease. Let who will be rich, or admired, or prosperous, it is enough for me that there is such a God as Jehovah, and such a Saviour as Jesus, and that they are infinitely and unchangeably glorious!

"*Dec.* 19. Had a most ravishing view of Christ this morning, as coming at a distance in the chariot of his salvation. In an instant, he was with me and around me, and I could only cry Welcome! a thousand times welcome to my disconsolate heart!"

After enumerating some special instances of God's goodness to him, he adds, "But great as are my reasons to love God for his favors, he is infinitely more precious on account of his perfections. Never did he appear so inexpressibly glorious as he has for some weeks past. I have nothing to fear, nothing to hope from creatures. They are all mere shadows! There is only one being in the universe, and that being is God! May I add, He is my God! I long to get to see him in heaven: I long still more to stay and serve him on earth. Rather, I rejoice to be just where he pleases, and what he pleases.

Dec. 16, 1817, he writes, "Never before enjoyed such a sense of his love, or felt so constrained to love him and every thing that belongs to him; especially his word, which I could not forbear kissing and pressing to my bosom. Was perfectly willing to die without leaving my chamber. Had for a long time a melting heart, and came with a broken frame to the feet of Christ weeping aloud, and obtained a full and sweet assurance of pardon."

"*Sept.* 1. While lying awake last night had most delightful views of God as a father; felt that my happiness is as dear to him as to myself; that he would not willingly hurt one hair of my head, nor let me suffer a moment's unnecessary pain. Felt that he was literally as willing to give as I was to ask—seemed, indeed, to have nothing to ask for.

"*Sept.* 19. Last night, while lying awake, had more distinct apprehensions of God's greatness than at any previous time. Realized little of any thing except simple greatness, and this almost crushed me to death. I could not move a limb or scarcely breathe. Could realize more than ever that a clear view of God must be hell to the wicked, for had any sense of his anger accompanied this view of his greatness, I could not have supported it!"

Payson's Demeanor under Bodily Sufferings.

The most agonizing sufferings of body, when exempted from depression of mind, never rendered him the less cheerful and agreeable. His demeanor in these seasons of suffering was often such that he was rather envied than pitied by his family and attendants, being seasons of unusual gayety and cheerfulness, and in which he allowed his playful imagination to throw a brightness npon the gloom of the sick-chamber.

Last Scenes of his Life and Labors.

His last sermon was preached from the text, "The word of the Lord is true." It was not written, of course, but no discourse that he ever wrote was more instructive or eloquent. When speaking of the trials to which the Bible had been subjected by its enemies, never were the mightiest infidels made to appear so puny, insignificant, and foolish. "He who sitteth in the heavens" could almost be seen deriding them.

When describing the manner in which Christians have tried it, his experience aided his eloquence, and added strength to the conviction it wrought in the minds of his hearers. On pronouncing the benediction, he descended from the pulpit, took his station in front of it, and commenced a most solemn appeal to the assembly.

"I now put aside the minister," said he. "I come down among you—place myself on a visible equality. I address you as a brother and fellow-traveler to the bar of God." He then gave vent to the struggling emotions of his heart in a stream of affectionate entreaty, and requested them, mentally and silently, to adopt a series of resolutions touching a belief in and practice of Christianity, which he was about to propose. Though his withered arm hung helpless by his side, yet he seemed instinct with life, and every succeeding resolve was rendered emphatic by a gesture of the left.

One of his last communion seasons is thus described: "His body was so emaciated by long and acute suffering that it was scarcely able to sustain the effort; but his soul, raised above its perishing influence, and filled with a joyful tranquillity, seemed entirely regardless of the weakness of its mortal tenement. His right hand and arm were so palsied by disease as to be quite useless, except that in the act of breaking the bread he placed it on the table with the other hand, raising it as a lifeless weight, until it had performed the service required, as if unwilling that even the withered hand should be found unemployed in the holy work!

Aug. 5. This day he entered the meeting-house for the last time. Twenty years had passed since he entered it for the first time as a preacher: then a trembling youth, now the spiritual father of many hundreds; then just girded for the warfare, now the veteran who had fought the good fight, and was about to resign his commission.

He was supported into the house by his senior deacons, and was privileged to witness the admission of twenty-one candidates into the Church. He only had strength to read "the Covenant" and to say to the Church, "I want you always to believe that God is faithful. However dark and mysterious his dispensations may appear, still confide in him. He can make you happy when every thing else is taken from you."

Payson Confined to the Chamber of Sickness and Death—His Triumph.

He was asked by a friend if he could see any particular reason for this dispensation. He replied, "No; but I am as well satisfied as if I could see ten thousand reasons."

In a letter dictated to his sister, he writes: "Were I to adopt the figurative language of Bunyan, I might date this letter from the land of Beulah, of which I have been for some time such a happy inhabitant. The celestial city is full in my view. Its glories beam upon me, its breezes fan me, its odors are wafted to me, its sounds strike upon my ears, and its spirit is breathed into my heart. Nothing separates me from it but the river of death, which now appears as an insignificant rill, which can be crossed at a single step, whenever God shall give permission. The Sun of Righteousness has been gradually drawing nearer and nearer, appearing larger and brighter as he approached, and now fills the whole hemisphere, pouring forth a flood of glory, in which I seem to float like an insect in the beams of the sun, exulting, yet almost trembling, while I gaze on this excessive brightness, and wondering why God should deign thus to shine upon a sinful worm."

On being asked, "Do you feel reconciled?" he replied, "O that is too cold; I rejoice; I triumph; and this happiness will endure as long as God himself, for it consists in admiring and adoring him. I can find no words to express my happiness. I seem to be swimming in a river of pleasure which is carrying me on to the great fountain. It seems as if all the bottles in heaven were opened, and all its fullness and happiness have come down into my heart. God has been depriving me of one blessing after another, but as each one was removed he has come in and filled up its place. If God had told me some time ago that he was about to make me as happy as I could be in this world, and that he should begin by crippling me in all my limbs and removing from me all my usual sources of enjoyment, I should have thought it a very strange mode of accomplishing his purpose. Now, when I am a cripple and not able to move, I am happier than I ever was in my life before or ever expected to be.

"It has often been remarked that people who have passed into the other world cannot come back to tell us what they have seen, but I am so near the eternal world that I can almost see as clearly as if I were there; and I see enough to satisfy me of the truth of the doctrines I have preached. I do not know that I should feel at all surer had I been really there."

"Watchman, what of the night?" asked a gray-headed member of his Church. "I should think it was about noonday," replied the dying Payson.

The ruling passion being strong in death, he sent a request to his pulpit that his people should repair to his sick-chamber. They did so in specified classes, a few at a time, and received his dying message.

Payson's Dying Words to the Young Men of his Congregation.

"I felt desirous that you might see that the religion I have preached can support me in death. You know that I have many ties which bind me to earth: a family to which I am strongly attached, and a people whom I love almost as well; but the other world acts like a much stronger magnet, and draws my heart away from this.

"Death comes every night and stands by my bedside in the form of terrible convulsions, every one of which threatens to separate the soul from the body. These grow worse and worse till every bone is almost dislocated with pain. Yet while my body is thus tortured, the soul is perfectly, perfectly happy and peaceful. I lie here and feel these convulsions extending higher and higher, but my soul is filled with joy unspeakable! I seem to swim in a flood of glory which God pours down upon me. Is it a delusion that can fill the soul to overflowing with joy in such circumstances? If so, it is a delusion better than any reality. It is no delusion. I feel it is not. I enjoy this happiness now. And now, standing as I do on the ridge that separates the two worlds—feeling what intense happiness the soul is capable of sustaining, and judging of your capacities by my own, and believing that those capacities will be filled to the very brim with joy or wretchedness forever, my heart yearns over you, my children, that you may choose life and not death. I long to present every one of you with a cup of happiness and see you drink it.

"A young man," he continued, "just about to leave the world, exclaimed, 'The battle's fought, the battle's fought, but the victory is lost forever!' But I can say, 'The battle's fought, and the victory is won—the victory is won forever!' I am going to bathe in the ocean of purity, and benevolence, and happiness, to all eternity. And now, my children, let me bless you, not with the blessing of a poor, feeble, dying man, but with the blessing of the infinite God." He then pronounced the apostolic benediction.

Payson's Unparalleled Sufferings and Unbounded Joy.

A friend said to him, "I presume it is no longer incredible to you that martyrs should rejoice and praise God in the flames and on the rack?"

"No," said he; "I can easily believe it. I have suffered twenty times as much as I could in being burned at the stake, while my joy in God so abounded as to render my sufferings not only tolerable but welcome."

At another time he said: "God is literally now my all in all. While he is present with me no event can in the least diminish my happiness; and were the whole world at my feet trying to minister to my comfort they could not add one drop to my cup."

To Mrs. Payson, who observed to him, "Your head feels hot and seems to be distended," he replied: "It seems as if the soul disdained such a narrow prison, and was determined to break through with an angel's energy, and I trust with no small portion of an angel's feeling, until it mounts on high.

"It seems as if my soul had found a new pair of wings, and was so eager to try them that in her fluttering she would rend the fine network of the body in pieces."

Payson's Last Agony.

On Sabbath, Oct. 21, 1827, his last agony commenced, attended with that labored breathing and rattling in the throat which rendered articulation extremely difficult. His daughter was summoned from the Sabbath-school, and received his dying kiss and "God bless you, my daughter." He smiled on a group of his Church-members, and exclaimed, with holy emphasis, "Peace, peace! Victory!" He smiled on his wife and children, and said in the language of dying Joseph, "I am going, but God will surely be with you."

He rallied from the death conflict, and said to his physician, that although he had suffered the pangs of death, and got almost within the gates of Paradise, yet if it was God's will that he should come back and suffer still more he was resigned. He passed through a similar scene in the afternoon, and again revived.

On Monday morning his dying agonies returned in all their extremity. For three hours every breath was a groan. On being asked if his sufferings were greater than on the preceding Sunday night, he answered, "incomparably greater." He said the greatest temporal blessing of which he could conceive would be one breath of air.

Mrs. Payson, fearing from the expression of suffering on his countenance that he was in mental distress, questioned him. He replied, "Faith and patience hold out." These were the last words of this dying Christian hero! Yet his eyes spoke after his tongue became motionless. He looked on Mrs. Payson, and then rested his eyes on his eldest son with an expression which said, and was so interpreted by all present, "Behold thy mother!"

He gradually sunk away, till, about the going down of the sun, his chastened and purified spirit, all mantled with the glory of Christian triumph in life and death, ascended to share the everlasting glory of his Redeemer before the eternal throne!

"His ruling passion was strong in death." His love for preaching was as invincible as that of the miser for gold, who dies grasping his treasure.

Dr. Payson directed this label to be attached to his breast: "Remember the words which I spake unto you while I was yet present with you;" that it might be read by all who came to look at his corpse, and by which he, being dead, still spake. The same words, at the request of his people, were engraven on the plate of the coffin, and read by thousands on the day of interment.

Extract from Payson's Funeral Sermon, preached by Rev. Charles Jenkins.

"I might speak of his gifted intellect; I might dwell on his wonderful powers of combination; on that excursive faculty which, forever glancing from earth to heaven, could gather the universe around him in aid of his illustrations. But to speak on these points becomes not this solemn occasion. He would frown on the attempt. He counted 'all things loss for Christ.' If I may speak of his character, it shall be that character which had so conspicuously the Christian stamp. In this respect, grace made him great. It wrought a deep work in his soul. The predominant features of his whole mind, for many years, were high spiritual views and deep spiritual feelings. These tinged, or rather were the element, of his thoughts and efforts. His natural ardor of temperament doubtless affected not a little his religious exercises. It gave them violence and energy. His seasons of spiritual elevation were heaven brought down to earth; his seasons of religious depression resembled the storms of autumn—sudden, dark, threatening—leaving a serener and purer sky, but betokening that winter is approaching. He was pre-eminently a man of prayer. There was in his prayers a copiousness, a fervor, a familiarity, a reaching forth of the soul into eternity, that was almost peculiar to himself, and that told every hearer that heaven was his element, and prayer his breath, and life, and joy. As a preacher it is easier to say what he was not than what he was. He was eloquent, and yet no one could describe his eloquence to the apprehension of a stranger; it consisted in an assemblage of qualities that could be seen and felt, but not described. He did not preach himself; his subject always stood between himself and audience. Ah! I will not, I cannot, enlarge. Let the thousand voices of them who have been brought to the knowledge of Christ by his ministrations tell what he was as a preacher."

Concluding Remarks.

We have aimed in this sketch so to exhibit the man and minister that his points of character would be at once recognized without special analysis.

We hav eseen him as the precocious child, a good reader and thinker at four years of age; as the penitent boy, weeping under the preaching of the Gospel when only three years old ; as the ardent youth, pursuing his studies with untiring diligence and success ; as the Bible student, attaching to the divine records an infinite pre-eminence over all other books, and seeking, with corresponding reverence and zeal, to enrich his heart and mind with its treasures, and leaning upon the promises like a pilgrim upon his staff, and grasping with a giant faith the perfections of Jehovah, and the plan of redemption as therein revealed. We have seen him as the conscientious Christian, with a nature as sensitive to sin in every form as the tender flower to the breath of winter. We have seen him battling with the rage, and power, and insidious schemes of the tempter to destroy his confidence in God and revealed religion, and in these terrible conflicts foiling his mighty adversary. We have seen him, in his zeal for the glory of God and the salvation of men, devoting himself with intent of mind, and ardor of soul, and effort of body, seldom if ever equaled in the history of the ministry. And blending, as he did, a deep and intense Christian experience, integrity of principle, and simplicity of spirit with dignity of manners, his influence was irresistible in his day. And his gifted intellect and fertile imagination have given to the world those sublime thoughts and splendid imagery which have contributed to perpetuate that influence. We have seen him in death strong in faith, giving glory to God, with the language of victory upon his lips, and the fires of hope blazing in his eye, and the joy of heaven filling his soul.

Payson—Bramwell—Fletcher—Hedding.

In reading the Biography of Payson we have been reminded of Bramwell, whom he resembled in his devotional spirit, struggling mightily with God in prayer for the salvation of sinners, and, like him, putting forth a corresponding effort to save them.

In the higher life we would associate him with the heavenly-minded Fletcher, whom he approximated in the heights and depths of Christian experience, his soul, like that of Fletcher's, glowing with the fires of holiness, for which he panted, and which he gloriously realized.

In his dying triumph he may be associated with his distinguished contemporary, Bishop Hedding. Between these two Christian heroes there was a very remarkable coincidence in their sickness and death, both in regard to the severity of their sufferings and the greatness and grandeur of their triumph.

Payson suffers and dies with such language as this falling from his lips: "Hitherto I have viewed God as a fixed star; bright, indeed, but often intercepted by clouds, but now he is coming nearer and nearer, and spreads into a sun so vast and glorious that the sight is too dazzling for flesh and blood to sustain." Among his last utterances were the words, "Peace, peace! Victory, victory!"

Hedding suffers and dies exclaiming, "God has been wonderfully good to me. His goodness has been overwhelming, overwhelming! I never saw such glory before, such light, such clearness, such beauty! O what glory I feel! It shines and burns all through me! It came upon me like the rushing of a mighty wind as on the day of Pentecost!"

If in heaven, as on earth, congenial spirits seek companionship, we may expect to find Payson talking with Bramwell on the power of prayer, with Fletcher on the beauty of holiness, and with Hedding on the triumphs of faith over suffering and death.

May every reader of this sketch be stimulated by the lofty example it records to aim high in the pursuit of Christian attainments and usefulness, and finally reach that heaven where the immortal spirit of Edward Payson bathes in a sea of glory, and

> "Where saints of all ages in harmony meet,
> Their Saviour and brethren transported to greet;
> Where anthems of rapture unceasingly roll,
> And the smile of the Lord is the feast of the soul."

PART II.

SELECTIONS FROM THE WORKS OF EDWARD PAYSON, D.D.

Blending the Friend with the Parent.

"WERE others blessed with friends like mine, how much greater would be the sum of virtue and happiness on earth than we have reason to fear it is at present. Why cannot other parents learn your art of mixing the friend with the parent? of joining friendship to filial affection, and of conciliating love without losing respect?—an art of more importance to society and more difficult to learn—at least, if we may judge by the rareness with which it is found—than any other; and an art which you, my dear parents, certainly have in perfection."

A Wise Preference.

"I should take infinitely more satisfaction in the conversation of a plain, unlettered Christian, than in the unmeaning tattle of the drawing-room or the flippant vivacity of professed wits. What gives me most uneasiness, and what I fear will always be a thorn in my path, is too great a thirst for applause. When I sit down to write I perpetually catch myself considering, not what will be most useful, but what will be most likely to gain praise from an audience.

If I should be unpopular, it would, I fear, give me more uneasiness than it ought; and if—though I think there is little reason to fear it—I should in any degree be acceptable, what a terrible blaze it would make in my bosom!"

The Reason of the Confusion Stated.

"*January* 15, 1806. If you, my dear mother, can pick out the meaning in the last page, I shall be glad; for in truth it is but poorly expressed. You must have observed that my letters are very obscure; that the transitions from one subject to another are rapid and capricious. The reason of this confusion is, when I sit down to write, forty ideas jump at once, all equally eager to get out, and jostle and incommode each other at such a rate, that not the most proper, but the strongest, escapes first. My mind would fain pour itself all out, at once, on the paper; but, the pen being rather too small a passage. . . . So much by way of apology."

Extracts from Payson's First Oration, July 4, 1806.

"The vessel of our republic, driven by the gales of faction, and hurried still faster by the secret current of luxury and vice, is following the same course, and fast approaching the same rocks, which have proved fatal to so many before us. Already may we hear the roaring of the surge; already do we begin to circle round the vortex which is soon to ingulf us. Yet we see no danger. In vain does experience offer us the wisdom of past ages for our direction: in vain does the genius of history spread her chart, and point out the ruin toward which we are advancing: in vain do the ghosts of departed governments, lingering round the rocks on which they perished, warn us of our approaching fate, and eagerly strive to terrify us from our course. It seems to be an immutable law of our nature that nations, as well as individuals, shall learn wisdom by no experience but their own. That blind, that accursed, infatuation which ever appears to govern mankind when their most important interests are concerned, leads us, in defiance of reason, experience, and common sense, to flatter ourselves that the same causes which have proved fatal to all other governments will lose their pernicious tendency when exerted on our own."

"That virtue, both in those who command and those who obey, is absolutely essential to the existence of republics, is a maxim, and a most important one, in political science. Whether we retain a sufficient share of this virtue to promise ourselves a long duration, you, my friends, must decide. But should the period ever arrive when luxury and intemperance shall corrupt our towns, while ignorance and vice pervade the country; when the press shall become the common sewer of falsehood and slander; when talents and integrity shall be no recommendation, and open dereliction of all principle no obstacle to preferment; when we shall intrust our liberties to men with whom we should not dare to trust our property; when the chief seats of honor and responsibility in our government shall be filled by characters of whom the most malicious ingenuity can invent nothing worse than the truth; when we shall see the members of our national councils, in defiance of the laws of God and their country, throwing away their lives in defense of reputations which, if they ever existed, had long been lost; when the slanderers of Washington and the blasphemers of our God shall be thought useful laborers in our political vineyard; when, in fine, we shall see our legislators sacrificing their senses, their reason, their oaths, and their consciences at the altar of party; then we may say that virtue has departed, and that the end of our liberty draweth nigh."

Peculiar Temptations and Special Relief.

"I have lately been severely tried with doubts and difficulties respecting many parts of Scripture. Reading the other day, I met with this passage, 'For his great name's sake.' It was immediately suggested to my mind, that, as the Deity bestowed all his favors on us 'for his great name's sake,' we were under no obligations to feel grateful for them. And though my heart assented to the propriety of gratitude, my head would not. In hearing my scholars recite the Greek Testament, I am disturbed by numberless seeming inconsistencies and doubts, which, though they do not shake my belief, render me for a time extremely miserable. I find no relief in these trials from the treatises which have been written in proof of the truth of revelation. It is from a different source that assistance is received."

Payson's Appreciation of Pious Parents.

"*April* 20, 1805. MY DEAREST MOTHER: I have just been perusing something excessively interesting to my feelings. It is a short extract from your journal in my sister's letter. Surely it is my own fault that I do not resemble Samuel in more instances than one. What a disgrace to me, that, with such rare and inestimable advantages, I have made no greater progress! However, thanks to the fervent, effectual prayers of my righteous parents, and the tender mercies of my God upon me, I have reason to hope that the pious wishes breathed over my infant head are, in some measure, fulfilled; nor would I exchange the benefits which I have derived from my parents for the inheritance of any monarch* in the universe."

The Scheme of Redemption Glorious.

"I did not intend to say another word about my feelings; but I must, or else cease writing. I am so happy that I cannot possibly think nor write of any thing else. Such a glorious, beautiful, consistent scheme for the redemption of such miserable wretches! such infinite love and goodness, joined with such wisdom! I would, if possible, raise my voice so that the whole universe, to its remotest bounds, might hear me, if any language could be found worthy of such a subject. How transporting, and yet how humiliating, are the displays of divine goodness which, at some favored moments, we feel! what happiness in humbling ourselves in the dust, and confessing our sins and unworthiness!"

---

* The admirers of Cowper—between whom and the subject of this Memoir there are several strong points of resemblance—will be reminded at once of those beautiful lines—

"My boast is not that I deduce my birth
From loins enthroned, and rulers of the earth;
But higher far my proud pretensions rise—
The son of parents passed into the skies."

A Motive for Choosing Religious Companions.

"*Dec.* 2, 1805. There is no worldly blessing that is not heightened by religion, but none more so than friendship, whether it be between relatives by consanguinity, or those who are joined in marriage, or other friends. The idea of parting must embitter the pleasure of the man of the world; but the Christian, if he has chosen his friends aright, may hope to enjoy their society with more pleasure hereafter than he can now. For this reason I never should choose a partner for life whom I could not hope to meet beyond the tomb."

Our Old Friend Bunyan.

"I have of late taken some pleasure in recollecting the pilgrimages of our old friend Bunyan, and see a striking propriety in many parts of them which I did not formerly rightly understand. For some time past I have been with Tender Conscience in the caves of Good Resolution and Contemplation, and, like him, fell into the clutches of Spiritual Pride. It is astonishing, and what nothing but sad experience could make us believe, that Satan and a corrupt heart should have the art of extracting the most dangerous poison from those things which apparently would, and certainly ought, to have the most beneficial effects. If I do not, after all, fall into the hands of Old Carnal Security, I shall have reason to be thankful. There is such a fascination in the magic circle of worldly pleasures and pursuits as can hardly be conceived without experience; and I am astonished and vexed to find its influence continually thwarting and hindering me.

And so many plausible excuses are perpetually suggesting themselves that compliance can hardly be avoided."

Spiritual Pride.

"It seems to me one of the worst of the hellish offspring of fallen nature, that it should have such a tendency to pride, and above all, Spiritual Pride. How many artifices does it contrive to hide itself! If, at any time, I am favored with clearer discoveries of my natural and acquired depravity and hatefulness in the sight of God, and am enabled to mourn over it, in comes Spiritual Pride, with 'Ay, this is something like! this is holy mourning for sin; this is true humility.' If I happen to detect and spurn at these thoughts, immediately he changes his battery, and begins: 'Another person would have indulged those feelings, and imagined he was really humble, but you know better; you can detect and banish pride at once, as you ought to do.' Thus this hateful enemy continually harasses me. What proof that the heart is the native soil of pride, when it thus contrives to gather strength from those very exercises which one would think must destroy it utterly!"

The Town in an Uproar.

"I preached last Sabbath on man's depravity, and attempted to show that by nature man is, in stupidity and insensibility, a block; in sensuality and sottishness, a beast; and in pride, malice, cruelty, and treachery, a devil. This set the whole town in an uproar, and never was such a racket made about any poor sermon; it is perfectly inconceivable to any who have not seen it. But I cannot help hoping that amid all this smoke there may be some latent sparks which will burst out into a blaze."

Both Sides of the Question.

"Mr. R. has a unanimous call at Gorham; but he feels afraid to settle, because he is not qualified. I tell him to settle by all means; for, if he waits a little longer, he never will feel qualified to settle at all. If I had waited till this time, I surely should never have been a minister. I should give up now, but, whenever I think of it, something seems to say, 'What are you going to give up for? Suppose you are a poor, miserable, blind, weak, stupid worm of the dust, with mountains of opposition before you—is that any reason for discouragement? Have you yet to learn, that God has chosen the weak things of the world to confound the mighty, and that if you had the talents of an angel you could do nothing without his assistance? Has he not already helped you beyond all you dared ask or think; and has not he promised to help you in future? What, then, would you, poor, weak, stupid, cowardly fool, have more? What do you keep murmuring about all the time? Why don't you glory in your infirmities, that the power of Christ may rest upon you?' To all this I can answer nothing, and so I keep dragging on, because I dare not leave off without a discharge."

The Ministers of Christ in a Trying Situation.

"My friends, how trying is the situation of the ministers of Christ, if they have any love for their people or regard for their souls. They are like a man placed on the brink of a precipice to warn travelers that, if they proceed, they will inevitably be dashed in pieces. The travelers arrive, listen to the warning, and then, with a few exceptions, hold on their course, and perish before the eyes of him who labored in vain to save them."

Primeval Harmony.

"Of this universal concert man was appointed the terrestrial leader, and was furnished with natural and moral powers admirably fitted for this blessed and glorious employment. His body, exempt from dissolution, disease, and decay, was like a perfect and well-strung instrument, which never gave forth a false or uncertain sound, but always answered, with exact precision, the wishes of his nobler part, the soul. His heart did not then belie his tongue, when he sung the praises of his Creator; but all the emotions felt by the one were expressed by the other, from the high notes of ecstatic admiration, thankfulness, and joy, down to the deep tones of the most profound veneration and humility. In a word, his heart was the throne of celestial love and harmony, and his tongue at once the organ of their will, and the scepter of their power.

"We are told, in ancient story, of a statue formed with such wonderful art that whenever it was visited by the rays of the rising sun, it gave forth, in honor of that luminary, the most melodious and ravishing sounds. In like manner, man was originally so constituted by skill divine, that, whenever he contemplated the rays of wisdom, power, and goodness, emanating from the great Sun of the moral system, the ardent emotions of his soul spontaneously burst forth in the most pure and exalted strains of adoration and praise. Such was the world, such was man, at the creation. Even in the eye of the Creator all was good ; for, wherever he turned, he saw only his own image and heard nothing but his own praises. Love beamed from every countenance : harmony reigned in every breast, and flowed mellifluous from every tongue ; and the grand chorus of praise, begun by raptured seraphs round the throne and heard from heaven to earth, was re-echoed back from earth to heaven ; and this blissful sound, loud as the archangel's trump and sweet as the melody of his golden harp, rapidly spread, and was received from world to world, and floated, in gently undulating waves, even to the farthest bounds of creation."

The Discord and Jargon of Sin.

"To this primeval harmony man exhibits the lamentable contrast which followed, when sin 'untuned the tongues of angels, and changed their blissful songs of praise into the groans of wretchedness, the execrations of malignity, the blasphemies of impiety, and the ravings of despair.' Storms and tempests, earthquakes and convulsions, fire from above, and deluges from beneath, which destroyed the order of the natural world, proved that its baleful influence had reached our earth, and afforded a faint emblem of the jars and disorders which sin had introduced into the moral system. Man's corporeal part, that lyre of a thousand strings tuned by the finger of God himself, destined to last as long as the soul, and to be her instrument in offering up eternal praise, was, at one blow, shattered, unstrung, and almost irreparably ruined. His soul, all whose powers and faculties, like the chords of an Æolian harp, once harmoniously vibrated to every breath of the divine Spirit, and ever returned a sympathizing sound to the tones of kindness and love from a fellow-being, now became silent and insensible to melody, or produced only the jarring and discordant notes of envy, malice, hatred, and revenge. The mouth, filled with cursing and bitterness, was set against the heavens; the tongue was inflamed with the fire of hell. Every voice, instead of uniting in the song of 'Glory to God in the highest,' was now at variance with the voices around it, and in barbarous and dissonant strains sung praise to itself, or was employed in muttering sullen murmurs against the Most High—in venting slanders against fellow-creatures—in celebrating and deifying some worthless idol, or in singing the triumphs of intemperance, dissipation, and excess. The noise of violence and cruelty was heard mingling with the boasting of the oppressor, the cry of the oppressed, and the complaints of the wretched; while the shouts of embattled hosts, the crash of arms, the brazen clangor of trumpets, the shrieks of the wounded, the groans of the dying, and all the horrid din of war, together with the wailings of those whom it had rendered widows and orphans, overwhelmed and drowned every sound of benevolence, praise, and love. Such is the jargon which sin has introduced—such is the discord which, from every quarter of our globe, has long ascended up into the ears of the Lord of hosts."

Confidence in God under Trial.

"Confidence in the wisdom and goodness of divine providence usually reconciles the Christian to trials, and sustains him under the occurrence of events, which, at the time, are wholly inexplicable. He rests on the kind assurance of his Redeemer, 'What thou knowest not now, thou shalt know hereafter.' And, though this promise refers him to a period beyond the confines of mortality, when the light of heaven shall beam on the intricacies of Providence, and put to flight the darkness which envelopes them; yet, even in the present world, he is often surprised with discoveries of the design and tendency of such dispensations, which render him grateful for them, and cause him to bless God, who made them a part of his paternal discipline. In retracing his path through life he sees his most dreaded calamities connected with his choicest mercies, his lowest depression with his highest elevation—and so connected, that, without the former, the latter would not have been. That which threatened the destruction of his ability to do good he finds to be his highest qualification for usefulness."

A Minister a Burden-Bearer.

"I am borne down with heavy burdens; pressed out of strength above measure, so as, at times, to despair even of life. All this is necessary, absolutely necessary, and I desire to consider it as a mercy; but it is hard, very hard to bear. If any one asks to be made a successful minister, he knows not what he asks; and it becomes him to consider, whether he can drink deeply of Christ's bitter cup, and be baptized with his baptism. If we could learn, indeed, to give all the glory to God, and keep only the sin and imperfections to ourselves, we might be spared these trials. And one would think this easy enough. One would think, that Jonah could hardly be proud of his success among the Ninevites; and we have, if possible, less reason to be proud than he. But pride will live and thrive without reason, and in despite of every reason to the contrary."

"Jesus, Jesus is All!"

"The world—O what a bubble, what a trifle it is! Friends are nothing, fame is nothing, health is nothing, life is nothing; Jesus, Jesus is ALL! O what will it be to spend an eternity in seeing and praising Jesus! to see him as he is, to be satisfied with his likeness! O, I long, I pant, I faint with desire to be singing, 'Worthy is the Lamb!'—to be extolling the riches of sovereign grace—to be casting the crown at the feet of Christ! And why may we not do all this on earth?"

Ardent Desires to Glorify Christ.

"I have sometimes heard of spells and charms to excite love, and have wished for them, when a boy, that I might cause others to love me. But how much more do I now wish for some charm which should lead men to love the Saviour! What would I not give for the power to make sinners love him, for the faculty of describing his beauties and glories in such a manner as to excite warmer affections toward him in the hearts of Christians! Could I paint a true likeness of him, methinks I should rejoice to hold it up to the view and admiration of all creation, and be hid behind it forever. It would be heaven enough to hear him praised and adored, though no one should know or care about insignificant me."

A Brand Plucked Out of the Fire.

"'Is not this a brand plucked out of the fire?' What a just and striking description of every redeemed sinner! and what a glorious idea does it afford us of the work of redemption! To snatch a smoking brand from eternal burnings, and plant it among the stars in the firmament of heaven, there to shine like the sun forever—O, what a glorious work is this! a work worthy of God! a work which none but God could perform! Such a brand am I—a brand yet smoking with the half-extinguished fires of sin; a brand, scorched and blackened by the flames of hell. What then do I owe to Him who entered the furnace of divine wrath that he might bring me out! who spread himself over me as a shield from that fiery storm, which would have set me forth an example, like Sodom, suffering the vengeance of eternal fire."

"*If I could Borrow the Archangel's Trump.*"

"I have no heart to speak or write about any thing but Jesus; and yet I have little patience to write about him in our miserably defective language. O for a language suitable to speak his praises, and describe his glory and beauty! But they cannot be described—they cannot be conceived; for 'no man knoweth the Son, but the Father.' What a wonderful idea does that text give us of the Son! Saints in heaven do not know him perfectly; even the angels do not. None but the Father is able to comprehend all his excellence. Yet various, great, unsearchable, infinite, as are his excellences, they are all ours; our Saviour, our Head, 'our flesh and our bone.' O, wonder!—how passing wonder—is this! Methinks if I could borrow, for a moment, the archangel's trump, and make heaven, earth, and hell resound with 'Worthy is the Lamb that was slain,' I could contentedly drop into nothing! But no, I should wish to live, and make them resound with his name through eternity. What a transporting thought—to spend an eternity in exalting God and the Lamb; in beholding their glory, and hearing them extolled by all creatures!—this is heaven indeed. To be swallowed up and lost in God; to have our spirits embraced, wrapped up in his all-infolding Spirit; to forget ourselves, and think only of him; to lose, in a manner, our own separate existence, and exist only in him; to have his glory all in all to us; this is, indeed, a far more exceeding and eternal weight of glory."

A Half-Sleeping, Half-Waking Dream.

"I now find why my gracious Master has suffered me to be so grievously tormented in times past. How miserably qualified should I otherwise have been to speak a word in season to them that are weary! Still I, I, I! nothing but I's—seven in half a page. Well, I don't care—I am writing to my mother, and I know she loves to hear about I; so I will proceed, and tell her about a half-sleeping, half-waking dream I had the other morning. If it does her as much good as it did me, it wont be paper lost.

"After a curious kind of frame in sleep, I waked myself up with exclaiming, 'Lord, why is it that thou art never weary of heaping favors on ungrateful, perverse, stubborn wretches, who render thee only evil for good?' In a moment he seemed to reply as powerfully as if he had spoken with an audible voice, 'Because I am never weary of gratifying my dear Son, and showing the greatness of my love to him. Till I am weary of him, and cease to love him, I shall never be weary of heaping favors on his friends, however unworthy.' These words, it is true, contain nothing more than an obvious truth; but they conveyed more to my mind than all the books I ever read."

Getting a Wife without Loss of Time.

"*Exeter, Wednesday Eve.* MY DEAREST MOTHER: As I know the deep interest you take in every thing which concerns your son, I will go no farther before I inform you of the result of the business on which we conversed while I was at home. I cannot, indeed, go into particulars; but it may be some gratification to you to know that the business is concluded on, and nothing remains but to fix the wedding day. On this point alone we differed. . . .

"And now, my dearest mother, you must permit me to exult over you a little. When I used to talk of getting a wife without losing any time about it, you laughed at the idea, and thought it preposterous, impracticable, and absurd. But you see, that without going a mile purposely out of my way, or losing a single hour, I have found and courted, or rather Providence has found for me, a person who bids fairer to render me happy than any other woman I have seen."

Public Prayer a Kind of Devout Poetry.

"That public prayer may produce its proper and designed effects upon their hearts, it should be, if I may so express it, a kind of devout poetry. As in poetry, so in prayer, the whole subject-matter should be furnished by the heart; and the understanding should be allowed only to shape and arrange the effusions of the heart in the manner best adapted to answer the end designed. From the fullness of a heart overflowing with holy affections, as from a copious fountain, we should pour forth a torrent of pious, humble, and ardently affectionate feelings; while our understandings only shape the channel, and teach the gushing streams of devotion where to flow and when to stop. In such a prayer every pious heart among our hearers will join. They will hear a voice and utterance given to their feelings. They will hear their desires and emotions expressed more fully and perspicuously than they could express them themselves. Their hearts will spring forward to meet and unite with the heart of the speaker. The well of water which our Saviour assures us is in all who drink of his Spirit, will rise, and burst its way through the rubbish of worldly cares and affections which too often choke it; and the stream of devotion from many hearts will unite, and flow on, in one broad tide, to the throne of Jehovah; while, with one mind and one mouth, minister and people glorify God. Such was the prayer of Ezra, and such its effects: 'And Ezra blessed the Lord, the great God. And all the people answered, Amen, amen, with lifting up of their hands; and they bowed their heads and worshiped the Lord with their faces toward the ground.'"

A Fault in Public Prayer.

"A fault in public prayer consists in uttering the different parts in the same tone. When our prayers are the language of the understanding only, this will always be done; but not so when they flow from the heart. No person need be informed that in our intercourse with each other a different modification of the voice is employed to express every different emotion of the heart. No one would expect to hear a condemned malefactor plead for his life and return thanks for a pardon in the same tone. And why is it not equally unnatural for sinful beings, condemned to eternal death, to plead for pardon and return thanks for its bestowal in the same tone? Yet how often is this done! How often do we hear prayers flow on, from the commencement to the close, in the same uniform tone, with scarcely a perceptible inflection of the voice! Yet no two things can differ more widely than the feelings which are expressed in different parts of the same prayer. Surely, then, a corresponding difference ought to be perceived in the modifications of the voice."

How a True Embassador of Christ Delivers his Message.

"In delivering his message as an embassador of Christ, he would show that he felt deeply penetrated with a conviction of its truth and infinite importance. He would speak like one whose whole soul was filled with his subject. He would speak of Christ and his salvation as a grateful, admiring people would speak of a great and generous deliverer, who had devoted his life for the welfare of his country. He would describe religion as a traveler describes a country through which he has leisurely passed, or as an aged man describes the scenes of his former life. He would portray the Christian warfare as a veteran portrays a battle in which he has just been contending for liberty and life. He would speak of eternity as one whose eye had been wearied in attempting to penetrate its unfathomable recesses, and describe its awful realities like a man who stood on the verge of time, and had lifted the vail which conceals them from the view of mortals. 'Thoughts that glow and words that burn' would compose his public addresses; and while a sense of the dignity of his official character, and the infinite importance of his subject, would lead him to speak as one having authority, with indescribable solemnity, weight, and energy, a full recollection that he was by nature a child of wrath, and that he was addressing fellow-men, fellow-sinners, mingled with compassion for their wretched state and an ardent desire for their salvation, would spread an air of tenderness over his discourses, and invest him with that affectionate, melting, persuasive correctness of manner, which is best calculated to affect and penetrate the heart. To say all in a word, he would speak like an embassador of Him who spake as never man spake, and who could say, We speak what we do know, and testify what we have seen."

Three Things Make a Divine.

"If we would do much for God we must ask much of God; we must be men of prayer; we must, almost literally, pray without ceasing. You have doubtless met with Luther's remark, 'Three things make a divine—prayer, meditation, and temptation.' My dear brother, I cannot insist on this too much. Prayer is the first thing, the second thing, and the third thing necessary for a minister, especially in seasons of revival. The longer you live in the ministry, the more deeply, I am persuaded, you will be convinced of this. Pray then, my dear brother, pray, pray, pray. Read the account of Solomon's choice, 1 Kings iii, 5-15. If, like him, you choose wisdom, and pray for it, it will be yours."

Extempore Preaching.

"Since the failure of my health, I preach but three sermons in a week—two on the Sabbath, and one on Thursday evening. On that evening and Sabbath morning I preach without notes, but generally from a skeleton of my sermon. I should like to write more, but my health will not permit; and I find that when any good is done, it is my extempore sermons which do it. I am afraid of producing a faith which stands not in the power of God but in the wisdom of men, and therefore make as little use as possible of human arguments, but confine myself to a plain, simple exhibition of divine truth. The sword of the Spirit will not wound if it has a scabbard on it. I also aim to preach the truths of the Gospel in a practical and experimental, rather than in a dry and speculative manner. In preaching to professing Christians, I endeavor to rouse and humble rather than to comfort them; for if they can be kept humble, comfort will follow of course. Besides, I do not suppose that Christians need as much consolation now as they did in the primitive ages, when exposed to persecution."

Satan's Cunning.

"I wish, with all my heart, that Satan would fight against the peace of some of our Church more than he does; but he is too cunning to do that. He sees that they are slumbering, and he will take care not to wake them. You can scarcely form an idea how soporific the air of a seaport is, nor of the irresistible force with which the world assails Christians in such a place as this. The moment they step out-of-doors it rushes in at their eyes and ears in ten thousand shapes, so that unless their hearts are preoccupied with better things, they are filled with it in a moment. By turns I expostulate, and plead, and warn, and threaten, and weep, and pray, and sometimes almost scold, but all in vain. The world drags away its victims, and laughs my feeble efforts to scorn."

Meditations on the Priesthood of Christ.

"I have lately had some delightful meditations on the priesthood of Christ. I was led to them by thinking how a penitent Israelite must have regarded his high priest. We may consider such a man as saying, "I am a miserable, polluted sinner. I cannot enter the holy place where God dwells, but am kept at a distance. I cannot burn incense acceptably, cannot be permitted even to offer my own sacrifice. But I have a high priest, appointed and consecrated by God, who is permitted to approach him on my behalf. He carries my name, or the name of my tribe, on his breastplate. He offers sacrifice for me;

he burns incense for me; he enters the most holy place, and sprinkles atoning blood for me. In him I am accepted, and in him will I glory. Take away my high priest, and you take away my all; but, while I have him, while he is accepted in my behalf, I will exult and rejoice.' And with how much more reason may the Christian triumph and glory in his great High Priest, and rejoice that he is 'accepted in the Beloved.' I do not mention these thoughts as any thing new, but as thoughts which have been peculiarly sweet and precious to me of late. Yet, alas! I am continually seeking to be my own high priest, to find something in myself for the sake of which I may be accepted, at least in part."

Professors in Concentric Circles around Christ.

"Suppose professors of religion to be ranged in different concentric circles around Christ, as their common center. Some value the presence of their Saviour so highly that they cannot bear to be at any remove from him. Even their work they will bring up and do it in the light of his countenance; and, while engaged in it, will be seen constantly raising their eyes to him, as if fearful of losing one beam of his light. Others, who, to be sure, would not be content to live out of his presence, are yet less wholly absorbed by it than these, and may be seen a little further off, engaged here and there in their various callings, their eyes generally upon their work, but often looking up for the light which they love. A third class, beyond these, but yet within the life-giving rays, includes a doubtful multitude, many of whom are so much engaged in their worldly schemes that they may be seen standing sideways to Christ, looking mostly the other way, and only now and then turning their faces toward the light. And yet further out, among the last scattered rays, so distant that it is often doubtful whether they come at all within their influence, is a mixed assemblage of busy ones, some with their backs wholly turned upon the sun, and most of them so careful and troubled about their many things, as to spare but little time for their Saviour.

"The reason why the men of the world think so little of Christ, is, that they do not look at him. Their backs being turned to the sun, they can see only their own shadows, and are, therefore, wholly taken up with themselves; while the true disciple, looking only upward, sees nothing but his Saviour, and learns to forget himself."

Growth of Grace in the Heart Illustrated.

"The growth of grace in the heart may be compared to the process of polishing metals. First, you have a dark, opaque substance, neither possessing nor reflecting light. Presently, as the polisher plies his work, you will see here and there a spark darting out; then a strong light; till, by and by, it sends back a perfect image of the sun which shines upon it. So the work of grace, if begun in our hearts, must be gradually and continually going on; and it will not be completed till the image of God can be seen perfectly reflected in us."

The Thirsty Sinner by the Riverside.

"Suppose a number of persons standing by a river's side. They are invited to drink of its waters, but they are not thirsty, and, therefore, do not desire them. At length their thirst is excited, and they look round for a vessel with which to take up some water. But their vessels are all filled with some worthless thing, which they are as yet unwilling to part with. But as their thirst increases they become willing to relinquish what they had thought of so much value, and, finally, emptying their vessels of this rubbish, and receiving the water, they quench their thirst. Thus it is with sinners: Jesus Christ invites them to come to him, the Fountain of living waters. But they decline his invitations—their hearts being filled with the treasures of earth. They do not thirst for Christ till God takes away the love of this world and its vanities, and the Holy Spirit fills them with desire to come to him. Then they hunger and thirst after righteousness, and are prepared to receive Christ."

Love for the Absent One.

"Suppose two persons equally desirous to gain your affections: one far distant, and not expecting to see you for a long time; the other always present with you, and at liberty to use all means to win your love, able to flatter and gratify you in a thousand ways. Still you prefer the absent one; and, that you may keep him in remembrance, you often retire by yourself to think of his love to you, and view again and again the mementoes of his affection, to read his letters, and pour out your heart in return. Such is now your case; the world is always before you, to flatter, promise, and please. But if you really prefer to love God you will fix your thoughts on him, often retire for meditation and prayer, and recount the pleasant gifts of his providence, and especially his infinite mercy to your soul; you will read frequently his holy Word, which is the letter he has sent you, as really as if it were directed to you by name."

Pardon Impossible without Repentance.

"It is morally impossible for God to pardon sinners without repentance. The moment he should do it, he would cease to be a perfectly holy being; of course, all the songs of heaven would stop, and all the happiness of the universe be dried up. In his conduct he is governed by a regard to the good of the whole. If a sovereign, out of false pity to criminals, should pardon them indiscriminately, he would thus destroy the happiness of all his faithful subjects, and introduce misery and confusion into his kingdom. But infinitely worse consequences would ensue if God should neglect to punish those who continue willfully to transgress his law. His vast dominions would become one universal scene of anarchy and confusion; happiness would be banished forever; and misery, in its most aggravated forms, would prevail throughout the universe. Yet all this the sinner would think ought to be endured, rather than that he should be obliged to repent of his sins."

The Criminality of Sin.

"To assist you in estimating the criminality of sin, suppose that you had committed the first sin—that before you were born such a thing had never been heard or thought of, but that all beings had united in loving and serving God, till all at once you started up and began to disobey his commands. What a commotion would be excited! Instantly the news would spread through heaven and earth, with inconceivable rapidity, and all ranks and orders of beings would join in exclaiming, 'It cannot be! Where is the wretch who would dare to disobey Jehovah?' Suppose, then, that you were obliged to come forward and stand in the view of the assembled universe of myriads of sinless beings, who all regarded you with feelings of astonishment, horror, and detestation, too strong for utterance. How inexpressibly dreadful would sin appear in this point of view! And yet it is, in reality, just as dreadful and as criminal to sin now, as if no sin had ever been committed by another."

The Absurdity of Sinners' Excuses.

"When sinners have been awakened to see their guilt and danger, and are invited to come to Christ and be saved, they frequently make such excuses as these: 'I cannot believe that the invitations of the Gospel were intended for such sinners as I am; I am afraid I do not feel right, and that Christ will not receive me.' Suppose a table set in the street, and loaded with all kinds of food; and that a herald is sent to make proclamation that all who wish may come and partake freely. A poor man comes, and stands looking very wishfully at the table; and, when he is asked why he does not eat, replies, 'O, I am afraid the invitation is not meant for me; I am not fit.' Again he is assured that the invitation is intended for all those who are hungry, and that no other qualification is necessary. Still he objects, 'But I am afraid I am not hungry enough.' In the same way do sinners deprive themselves, by their own folly, of those blessings which are freely offered them by their Creator."

A Mediator Rejected.

"Suppose the rebellious subjects of a very wise and good king condemned to death. The king has a son, who, from compassion to these poor wretches, offers to make satisfaction to his father for their crimes if he will pardon them. The king consents on one condition. He places his son at the door of his palace and makes proclamation that every one who comes to him for pardon, and is led in by his son, shall be forgiven for his sake. One of the culprits comes, and, rejecting the proffered hand of the prince, rushes to the throne himself. Can this man expect mercy? Thus God has provided a Mediator, and commanded all to approach in his name; and none should expect to be received who do not come to God in this appointed way."

A Newspaper, an Almanac, and the Bible.

"A wayfaring man stops at a tavern, and to beguile the time of his stay there, looks round for some book. He sees, perhaps, a newspaper, an almanac, and the Bible; but chooses to pore over either of the former, in preference to the Word of God, thinking it hardly possible to be amused or interested in that. Even a Christian will sometimes do thus. This is as if a man should be introduced into an apartment, in one division of which were Jesus Christ and the apostles, and in the other the most dissolute and frivolous company; and on being invited by the Saviour to sit with them and enjoy their company, should refuse, and seat himself with the others. Would not this be a most gross insult to the Saviour? and do you not equally undervalue and refuse his company when you thus neglect and despise his holy Word—through which he converses with you, and invites you near to himself—and choose some foolish production instead of it?"

God's Image Reflected by his Saints.

"In explanation of the command to glorify God: It may seem strange and presumptuous to speak of such poor, sinful, worthless beings as we are as glorifying, or as capable of glorifying, God. But the perfect Christian may be compared to a perfect mirror, which, though dark and opaque of itself, being placed before the sun reflects his whole image, and may be said to increase his glory, by increasing and scattering his light. In this view we may regard heaven, where God is perfectly glorified in his saints, as the firmament studded with ten thousand times ten thousand and thousands of thousands of mirrors, every one of them reflecting a perfect image of God, the Sun in the center, and filling the universe with the blaze of his glory."

Good Impressions—Illustration.

"Whenever you feel any thing within you, my dear young friends, urging you to attend to religion, it is the Spirit of God; and if you refuse to comply, you will grieve him away. Suppose God should let down from heaven a number of very fine cords, and if any person should take hold of one, it would continue to grow larger and stronger, till at length he is drawn by it into heaven. Great care would be necessary, especially at first, not to break it; for if once broken it might never be renewed. How careful should we expect the person to be to whom one of these cords was extended not to break it, to avoid all violence, and follow wherever it led him! Just so anxiously ought you to cherish those good impressions which are produced on your minds by the Spirit of God; for if you once grieve him he may never return."

The High and Low Seat.

"Suppose a man builds a temple, with one seat in it very high and much ornamented, and another very far below it. You ask him for whom those seats are designed, and he replies: 'Why, the most elevated one is for me, and the one below it is for God.' Now in this case you can all see the horrible absurdity and impiety of such conduct; and yet each of you, who continues impenitent, is doing this. You have given yourselves the first place in your affections; you have thought more of yourselves than of God, and have done more to please yourselves than to please God; in short, you have, in every thing, preferred yourselves before him."

A Proper Course of Reading for Christians.

"It may be proper, and perhaps advantageous, for a Christian to read, sparingly, works of taste. Some knowledge of the philosophy of the mind is desirable, and may be obtained without very great expense of time. Church history, and a knowledge of ancient eastern customs, will be very useful. Every kind of knowledge which expands, strengthens, and adorns the mind may be properly sought by the Christian, and ought to be sought by every Christian who has leisure and opportunity for reading. Our aim in seeking it should be to qualify ourselves to serve and glorify God more effectually, and to increase our power of being useful to our fellow-creatures. It is an old remark that 'knowledge is power.' To increase our knowledge, then, is to increase our power of doing good. Highly as I prize such writers as Fénélon, à Kempis, etc., I am convinced we may study them, not, perhaps, too much, but too exclusively. We may study them to the exclusion of other writers whose works demand our attention; and we may be so intent upon watching our feelings as to forget to watch our words and actions. As some are content with a religion which is all body, so others may aim at a religion which is all soul; but religion has a body as well as a soul. If some think it sufficient to cleanse the outside of the cup, others may be so much occupied in cleansing it within as to forget that it has an outside. Both deserve attention."

The Son Comforts the Mother.

"My dear mother, break away; O that God would enable you to break away from all your cares and sorrows, and fly, rise, soar up to the New Jerusalem! See its diamond walls, its golden streets, its pearly gates, its shining inhabitants, all in a blaze with reflected light and glory, the light of God, the glory of the Lamb! Say with David, 'Toward this city I will go in the strength of the Lord God; I will make mention of thy righteousness, even of thine only.' My mother, what a righteousness is this! The righteousness of God! A righteousness as much better than that of Adam, nay, than that of angels, as God is better than his creatures. Since, then, my dear mother, you have such a heaven before you, such a righteousness to entitle you to heaven, and such blessed chambers to hide in during the little moment which separates you from heaven, dry up your tears, banish your anxieties, leave sorrow and sighing to those who have no such blessings in store or reversion, and sing, sing, as Noah sat secure in the ark, and sang 'the grace that steered him through.'"

Closet Duties—Satan's Devices.

"On maintaining the daily performance of closet duties, the fate of the whole battle will turn. This your great adversary well knows. He knows that if he can beat you out of the closet he shall have you in his own power. You will be in the situation of an army cut off from supplies and reinforcements, and will be obliged either to capitulate or to surrender at discretion. He will, therefore, leave no means untried to drive or draw you from the closet. And it will be hard work to maintain that post against him and your own heart. Sometimes he will probably assail you with more violence, when you attempt to read or pray, than at any other time, and thus try to persuade you that prayer is rather injurious than beneficial. At other times he will withdraw, and be quiet, lest, if he should distress you with his temptation, you might be driven to the throne of grace for help. If he can prevail upon us to be careless and stupid, he will rarely distress us. He will not disturb a false peace, because it is a peace of which he is the author. But if he cannot succeed in lulling us asleep, he will do all in his power to distress us. And when he is permitted to do this, and the Holy Spirit withdraws his sensible aid and consolations; when, though we cry and shout, God seems to shut out our prayers, it is by no means easy to be constant in secret duties. Indeed, it is always most difficult to attend to them when they are most necessary."

Weighty Words to a Christian Minister.

"Some time since I took up a little work purporting to be the lives of sundry characters as related by themselves. Two of those characters agreed in remarking that they were never happy until they ceased striving to be great men. This remark struck me, as you know the most simple remarks will strike us when Heaven pleases. It occurred to me at once, that most of my sins and sufferings were occasioned by an unwillingness to be the nothing which I am, and by consequent struggles to be something. I saw that if I would but cease struggling, and consent to be any thing or nothing just as God pleases, I might be happy. You will think it strange that I mention this as a new discovery. In one sense it was not new; I had known it for years. But I now saw it in a new light. My heart saw it, and consented to it; and I am comparatively happy. My dear brother, if you can give up all desire to be great, and feel heartily willing to be nothing, you will be happy too. You must not even wish to be a great

Christian; that is, you must not wish to make great attainments in religion for the sake of knowing that you have made them, or for the sake of having others think that you have made them. Very true, very good, you will say, though somewhat trite; but how am I to bring myself to such a state? Let me ask, in reply, Why are you not troubled when you see one man receive military, and another masonic honors? Why are you not unhappy because you cannot be a colonel, a general, or a most worshipful grand high priest? Because, you answer, I have no desire for these titles or distinctions. And why do you not desire them? Simply because you are not running a race in competition with those who obtain them. You stand aside, and say, Let those who wish for these things have them. Now if you can, in a similar manner, give up all competition with respect to other objects; if you can stand aside from the race which too many other ministers are running, and say, from your heart, 'Let those who choose to engage in such a race divide the prize; let one minister run away with the money, and another with the esteem, and a third with the applause, etc.; I have something else to do, a different race to run; be God's approbation the only prize for which I run; let me obtain that, and it is enough:' I say, if you can, from the heart, adopt this language, you will find most of your difficulties and sufferings vanish. But it is hard to say this. It is almost impossible to persuade any man to renounce the race without cutting off his feet, or, at least, fettering him. This God has done for me; this he has been doing for you. And you will, one day, if you do not now, bless him for all your sufferings, as I do for mine. I have not suffered one pang too much. God was never more kind than when I thought him most unkind; never more faithful than when I was ready to say, His faithfulness has failed. Let him fetter you, then, if he pleases. Consent that he should cut off your feet, if he pleases. Any thing is a blessing which prevents us from running the fatal race, which we are so prone to run; which first convinces us that we are nothing, and then makes us willing to be so."

A Proof of Faith in Prayer.

"The command, 'Be careful for nothing,' is unlimited; and so is the expression 'casting all your care upon him.' If we cast our burdens upon another, can they continue to press upon us? If we bring them away with us from the throne of grace, it is evident we do not leave them there. With respect to myself, I have made this one test of my prayers. If, after committing any thing to God, I can, like Hannah, come away, and have my countenance no more sad, my heart no more pained, or anxious, I look upon it as one proof that I prayed in faith; but if I bring away my burden, I conclude that faith was not in exercise."

"*Satan has Jumped on to the Saddle.*"

"MY DEAR BROTHER: I am sorry to learn that your health is not better, but rather worse, than when I was at R. Should it not have improved before you receive this, I beg you will attend to it without delay; attend to it, as your first and chief duty; for such, be assured, it is. 'A merciful man is merciful to his beast;' and you must be merciful to your beast, or, as Mr. M. would say, to your 'animal.' Remember that it is your Master's property; and he will no more thank you for driving it to death, than an earthly master would thank a servant for riding a valuable horse to death, under pretense of zeal for his interest. The truth is, I am afraid Satan has jumped on to the saddle, and when he is there, in the guise of an angel of light, he whips and spurs at a most unmerciful rate, as every joint in my poor broken-winded animal can testify, from woeful experience. He has temptations for the conscience, as Mr. Newton well observes; and when other temptations fail, he makes great use of them. Many a poor creature has he ridden to death, by using his conscience as a spur; and you must not be ignorant, nor act as if you were ignorant of his devices. Remember Mr. Brainerd's remark, that diversions, rightly managed, increased rather than diminished his spirituality. I now feel that I am never serving our Master more acceptably than when, for his sake, I am using means to preserve my health, and lengthen my life; and you must feel in a similar manner, if you mean to do him much service in the world."

Exalted Views of God.

"O what a Master do I serve! I have known nothing, felt nothing, all my days even, in comparison with what I now see in him. Never was preaching such sweet work as it is now. Never did the world seem such a nothing. Never did heaven appear so near, so sweet, so overwhelmingly glorious. . . . God's promises appear so strong, so solid, so real, so substantial—more so than the rocks and everlasting hills; and his perfections—what shall I say of them? When I think of one, I wish to dwell upon it forever; but another, and another, equally glorious, claims a share of admiration; and, when I begin to praise, I wish never to cease, but have it the commencement of that song which will never end. Very often have I felt as if I could that moment throw off the body without staying to 'first go and bid them farewell that are at home in my house.' Let who will be rich, or admired, or prosperous; it is enough for me that there is such a God as Jehovah, such a Saviour as Jesus, and that they are infinitely and unchangeably glorious and happy."

Satan's Questions Answered.

"I rejoice the more in this work, because it enables me to stop the mouth of my old adversary, and to prove to his face that he is a liar. I could not doubt that I had been enabled to pray for a revival these many years. Nor could I persuade myself that Christ had not promised it to me. The essence of a promise consists in voluntarily exciting expectation of some benefit. In this sense, a revival had often been promised to me. And when it was not granted; when, one time after another, promising appearances died away; and especially when I was left to such exercises as rendered it impossible that I should ever be favored with a revival—Satan had a fine opportunity to work upon my unbelief, and to ask, Where is your God? what do you get by praying to him? and where is the revival which he has been so long encouraging you to expect, and to pray for? Now I can answer these questions triumphantly, and put the lying tongue to silence. But the work is all God's; and I stand and look on to see him work; and this is favor enough, and infinitely more than I deserve."

Inscriptions on Immortal Minds.

"What if God should place in your hand a diamond, and tell you to inscribe on it a sentence which should be read at the last day, and shown there as an index of your own thoughts and feelings? What care, what caution would you exercise in the selection! Now, this is what God has done. He has placed before you immortal minds, more imperishable than the diamond, on which you are about to inscribe, every day and every hour, by your instructions, by your spirit, or by your example, something which will remain, and be exhibited for or against you at the judgment day."

The Dying Christian on the Last Summit of Life.

"Dr. Clarke, in his travels, speaking of the companies that were traveling from the East to Jerusalem, represents the procession as very long; and, after climbing over the extended and heavy ranges of hills that bounded the way, some of the foremost at length reached the top of the last hill, and, stretching up their hands in gestures of joy, cried out, 'The Holy City! the Holy City!' and fell down and worshiped; while those who were behind pressed forward to see. So the dying Christian, when he gets on the last summit of life, and stretches his vision to catch a glimpse of the heavenly city, may cry out of its glories, and incite those who are behind to press forward to the sight."

Happiness in a Surrender of the Will.

"Since I have lost my will I have found happiness. There can be no such thing as disappointment to me, for I have no desires but that God's will may be accomplished.

"I have been all my life like a child whose father wishes to fix his undivided attention. At first, the child runs about the room, but his father ties up his feet; he then plays with his hands, until they likewise are tied. Thus he continues to do, till he is completely tied up; then, when he can do nothing else, he will attend to his father. Just so God has been dealing with me, to induce me to place my happiness with him alone. But I blindly continued to look for it here. And God has kept cutting off one source of enjoyment after another, till I find that I can do without them all, and yet enjoy more happiness than ever in my life before."

The Happy Cripple.

"Christians might avoid much trouble and inconvenience if they would only believe what they profess—that God is able to make them happy without any thing else. They imagine that if such a dear friend were to die, or such and such blessings to be removed, they should be miserable; whereas God can make them a thousand times happier without them. To mention my own case—God has been depriving me of one blessing after another; but as every one was removed, he has come in and filled up its place; and now, when I am a cripple, and not able to move, I am happier than ever I was in my life before, or ever expected to be, and, if I had believed this twenty years ago, I might have been spared much anxiety.

"If God had told me some time ago that he was about to make me as happy as I could be in this world, and then had told me that he should begin by crippling me in all my limbs, and removing me from all my usual sources of enjoyment, I should have thought it a very strange mode of accomplishing his purpose. And yet, how is his wisdom manifest even in this! for if you should see a man shut up in a close room, idolizing a set of lamps, and rejoicing in their light, and you wished to make him truly happy, you would begin by blowing out all his lamps, and then throw open the shutters, to let in the light of heaven."

An Assemblage of Motives to Holiness.

"What an assemblage of motives to holiness does the Gospel present! I am a Christian—what then? Why, I am a redeemed sinner—a pardoned rebel—all through grace, and by the most wonderful means which infinite wisdom could devise. I am a Christian—what then? Why, I am a temple of God, and surely I ought to be pure and holy. I am a Christian—what then? I am a child of God, and ought to be filled with filial love, reverence, joy, and gratitude. I am a Christian—what then? Why, I am a disciple of Christ, and must imitate Him who was meek and lowly in heart, and pleased not himself. I am a Christian—what then? Why, I am an heir of heaven, and hastening on to the abodes of the blessed, to join the full choir of glorified ones, in singing the song of Moses and the Lamb; and surely I ought to learn that song on earth."

An Overflowing Fountain.

"Look back to the time when God existed independent and alone; when there was nothing but God; no heavens, no earth, no angels, no men. How wretched should we be, how wretched would any creature be, in such a situation! But Jehovah was then infinitely happy—happy beyond all possibility of increase. He is an overflowing fountain, a bottomless and shoreless ocean, of being, perfection, and happiness; and when this infinite ocean overflows, suns and worlds, angels and men, start into existence."

"I Am that I Am."

"I would ask you to pause and contemplate, for a moment, this wonderful Being. But where shall we stand to take a view of him? When we wish to contemplate the ocean, we take our stand upon its shore. But this infinite ocean of being and perfection has no shore. There is no place where we can stand to look at him, for he is in us, around us, above us, below us. Yet, in another sense, there is no place where we may not look at him, for he is every-where. We see nothing which he has not made, no motion which he does not cause; for he is all, and above all, God over all, blessed forever. Even he himself cannot tell us fully what he is, for our minds cannot take it in. He can only say to us, I Am that I Am. I am JEHOVAH."

Eternity of God.

"Try, for a moment, to conceive of a Being without a beginning; a Being who does not become older as ages roll away. Fly back, in imagination, millions of millions of millions of years, till reason is confounded, and fancy wearied in the flight. God then existed, and, what may at first appear paradoxical, he had then existed as long as he has now; you would then be no nearer the beginning of his existence than you are now, for it has no beginning, and you cannot approach to that which does not exist. Nor will this being ever come to an end. Add together ages of ages; multiply them by the leaves on the trees, the sand on the sea-shore, and the dust of the earth, still you will be no nearer the termination of Jehovah's existence than when you first began your calculation. And let us remember that the duration of his existence is the only measure of our own. As it respects futurity, we are all as immortal as Jehovah himself."

Love of God.

"In the words, 'God is love,' we have a perfect portrait of the eternal and incomprehensible Jehovah, drawn by his own unerring hand. The mode of expression here adopted differs materially from that usually employed by the inspired writers in speaking of the divine perfections. They say, God is merciful, God is just, God is holy; but never do they say, God is mercy, God is justice, God is holiness. In this instance, on the contrary, the apostle, instead of saying, God is loving, or good, or kind, says God is love, love itself. By this expression we must understand that

God is all pure, unmixed love, and that the other moral perfections of his character are only so many modifications of this love. Thus his justice, his mercy, his truth, his faithfulness, are but so many different names of his love or goodness. As the light which proceeds from the sun may easily be separated into many different colors, so the holy love of God, which is the light and glory of his nature, may be separated into a variety of moral attributes and perfections. But, though separated, they are still love. His whole nature and essence are love; his will, his works, and his words, are love; he is nothing, can do nothing, but love."

Folly and Absurdity!

"Would you not consider a person foolish and absurd who should extravagantly love and prize a drop of stagnant water, and yet view the ocean with indifference or disgust? or who should constantly grovel in the dust to admire a shining grain of sand, yet neglect to admire the sun which caused it to shine? Of what folly and absurdity, then, are we guilty when we love the imperfectly amiable qualities of our fellow-worms, or admire the sublimity and beauty of the works of nature, and yet exercise no love to Him to whom they are indebted for all; Him whose glory gilds the heavens, and from whom angels derive every thing that can excite admiration or love."

A Rebellious Will—Illustration.

"Suppose that the members of our bodies, instead of being controlled by the will of the head, had each a separate, independent will of its own: would they not, in this case, become useless, and even mischievous? Something like this, you are sensible, occasionally takes place. In certain diseases, the members seem to escape from the control of the will, and act as if they were governed by a separate will of their own. When this is the case, terrible consequences often ensue. The teeth shut suddenly and violently, and lacerate the tongue; the elevated hands beat the face and other parts of the body; the feet refuse to support it, and it rolls in the dust a melancholy and frightful spectacle. Such effects we call convulsions. There are convulsions in the moral as well as in the natural world, and they take place when the will of man refuses to be controlled by the will of God. Did all men submit cordially to his will, they would live together in love and harmony, and, like members of a healthy body, would all promote each other's welfare, and that of the whole system. But they have refused to obey his will, and have set up their own wills in opposition to it; and what has been the consequence? Convulsions, most terrible convulsions, which have, in ten thousand thousand instances, led one member of this great body to injure another; and not only disturbed, but almost destroyed the peace of society. What are wars, insurrections, revolutions? What are robberies, piracies, murders, but convulsions in the moral world? convulsions which would never have occurred, had not the will of man refused to submit to the will of God. And never will these convulsions cease, never will universal love, and peace, and happiness prevail, until the rebellious will of man shall again submit to the controlling will of God, and his will shall be done on earth as it is in heaven."

An Angel Visitor Astonished.

"Should an angel who knew nothing of our characters, but who had heard of the blessings which God has bestowed on us, visit this world, would he not expect to find every part of it resounding with the praises of God and his love? Would he not expect to hear old and young, parents and children, all blessing God for the glad tidings of the Gospel, and crying, Hosanna to the Son of David? How, then, would he be grieved and disappointed! How astonished to find that Being whom he had ever heard praised in the most rapturous strains by all the bright armies of heaven, slighted, disobeyed, and dishonored, by his creatures on earth! Would you not be ashamed, would you not blush to look such a visitor in the face? to tell him how little you have done for God, tell him that you are not one of his servants? O, then, let us strive to wipe away this foul stain, this disgrace to our race and our world. Let not this world be the only place, except hell, where God is not praised. Let us not be the only creatures, except devils, who refuse to praise him."

The World the Diana of its Inhabitants.

"The world is, in some form or other, the great Diana, the grand idol of all its inhabitants, so long as they continue in their natural sinful state. They bow down to it; they worship it; they spend and are spent for it; they educate their children in its service; their hearts, their minds, their memories, their imaginations, are full of it; their tongues speak of it; their hands grasp it; their feet pursue it. In a word, it is all in all to them, while they give scarcely a word, a look, or a thought to Him who made and preserves them, and who is really all in all. Thus men rob God of their bodies and spirits, which are his, and practically say, We are our own; who is Lord over us?"

Our Treatment of the Word of God a Test.

"From the manner in which we habitually treat the Bible, we may learn what are our feelings and dispositions toward God; for as we treat the word of God, so should we treat God himself were he to come and reside among us, in a human form, as he once dwelt on earth in the form of his Son. The contents of Scripture are a perfect transcript of the divine mind. If, then, God should come to dwell among us, he would teach the same things that the Scriptures teach, and pronounce upon us the same sentence that they pronounce. We should therefore feel toward him as we now feel toward them. If we reverence, and love, and obey the Scriptures, then we should reverence, love, and obey God. But if we dislike or disbelieve the Scriptures, if we seldom study them, or read them only with indifference or neglect, we should treat God in the same manner. Never would he be a welcome guest in a family where his word is neglected."

Neglect of Prayer—Its Practical Import.

"The man who refuses, or neglects to pray, who regards prayer not as a privilege, but as a wearisome and needless task, practically says, in the most unequivocal manner, I am not dependent on God; I want nothing that he can give; and therefore I will not come to him, nor ask any favor at his hands. I will not ask him to crown my exertions with success, for I am able and determined to be the architect of my own fortune. I will not ask him to instruct or guide me, for I am fully competent to be my own instructor and guide. I will not ask him to strengthen and support me, for I am strong in the vigor and resources of my own mind. I will not request his protection, for I am able to protect myself. I will not implore his pardoning mercy nor his sanctifying grace, for I need, I desire, neither the one nor the other. .I will not ask his presence and aid in the hour of death, for I can meet and grapple, unsupported, with the king of terrors, and enter, undaunted and alone, any unknown world into which he may usher me. Such is the language of all who neglect prayer."

The Sinner's Wish.

"My friends, God offers you the water of life, without money and without price. Every one may come and take it if he will; and is not this sufficient? Would you have the water of life forced upon you? What is it that you wish? My friends, I will tell you what you wish. You wish to live as you please here, to disobey your Creator, to neglect your Saviour, to fulfill the desires of the flesh and of the mind, and at death to be admitted into a kind of sensual paradise, where you may taste again the same pleasures which you enjoyed on earth. You wish that God should break his word, stain his justice, purity, and truth, and sacrifice the honor of his law, his own rightful authority, and the best interests of the universe, to the gratification of your sinful propensities."

Christian Experience against Infidel Objections.

"Suppose that, while you are dying of a fatal disease, a medicine of great reputed efficacy is offered you, on making trial of which, you find yourself restored to health and activity. Full of joy and gratitude, you propose the remedy to others afflicted with the same disease. One of these persons replies to you, 'I am surprised that you place so much faith in the virtues of this medicine. How do you know it was really discovered by the person whose name it bears? Or, even if it were, it is so many years ago, and the medicine has passed through so many hands since, that it is probably corrupted, or perhaps some other has been substituted in the place of the genuine medicine.' Says another, 'It may not be suited to the constitutions of men in this age, though it was undoubtedly useful to those who first used it.' 'The disease and the cure are both equally imaginary,' says a third. 'There are many other remedies of equal or superior efficacy,' objects a fourth. 'None of the most celebrated physicians recommend it,' replies a fifth; while a sixth attempts to silence you by objecting to the vials in which it is put up, and repeating that boxes would have been more suitable. What weight would all these objections have with you? Would they induce you to throw away the healing balm, whose effects you even then felt, sending life, and health, and vigor through your whole frame? Even thus may infidels and cavilers urge objections against the Gospel; but the Christian heeds them not, for he has felt in his own soul its life-giving power."

Christianity as a Delusion.

"Surely, if Christianity be a delusion, it is a blessed delusion indeed; and he who attempts to destroy it is an enemy to mankind. It is a delusion which teaches us to do justly, love mercy, and walk humbly with our God; a delusion which teaches us to love our Maker supremely, and our neighbor as ourselves; a delusion which bids us love, forgive, and pray for our enemies, render good for evil, and promote the glory of God and the happiness of our fellow-creatures by every means in our power; a delusion which, wherever it is received, produces a humble, meek, charitable, and peaceful temper, and which, did it universally prevail, would banish wars, vice, and misery from the world. It is a delusion which not only supports and comforts its believers in their wearisome progress through this vale of tears, but attends them in death, when all other consolations fail, and enables them to triumph over sorrows, sickness, anguish, and the grave. If delusion can do this, in delusion let me live and die; for what could the most blessed reality do more?"

Insufficiency of Human Reason.

"Viewed through any other medium than that of revelation, man is a riddle which man cannot expound; a being composed of inconsistencies and contradictions which unassisted reason must forever seek in vain to reconcile. In vain does she endeavor to ascertain the origin, object, and end of his existence. In vain does she inquire in what his duty and happiness consist. In vain does she ask what is his present concern, and what his future destination. Wherever she turns for information, she is soon lost in a labyrinth of doubts and perplexities, and finds the progress of her researches interrupted by a cloud of obscurity which the rays of her feeble lamp are insufficient to penetrate.

"Suppose you should see a man carrying a little glimmering taper in his hand at noonday, with his back turned to the sun, and foolishly endeavoring to persuade himself and others that he had no need of the sun, and that his taper gave more light than that glorious luminary: how amazingly great would be his folly! Yet this illustration very feebly represents the folly of those who walk in the sparks of their own kindling, while they disregard the glorious Sun of righteousness."

Natural Religion a Failure.

"I know that those who hate and despise the religion of Jesus, because it condemns their evil deeds, have endeavored to deprive him of the honor of communicating to mankind the glad tidings of life and immortality. I know that they have dragged the moldering carcass of paganism from the grave, animated her lifeless form with a spark stolen from the sacred altar, arrayed her in the spoils of Christianity, re-enlightened her extinguished taper at the torch of revelation, dignified her with the name of Natural Religion, and exalted her in the temple of reason, as a goddess able, without divine assistance, to guide mankind to truth and happiness. But we also know that all her boasted pretensions are vain—the offspring of ignorance, wickedness, and pride. We know that she is indebted to that revelation which she presumes to ridicule and condemn for every semblance of truth or energy which she displays. We know that the most she can do is to find men blind and leave them so; and to lead them still further astray, in a labyrinth of vice, delusion, and wretchedness. This is incontrovertibly evident, both from past and present experience; and we may defy her most eloquent advocates to produce a single instance in which she has enlightened or reformed mankind. If, as is often asserted, she is able to guide us in the path of truth and happiness, why has she ever suffered her votaries to remain a prey to vice and ignorance? Why did she not teach the learned Egyptians to abstain from worshiping their leeks and onions? Why not instruct the polished Greeks to renounce their sixty thousand gods? Why not persuade the enlightened Romans to abstain from adoring their deified murderers? Why not prevail on the wealthy Phœnicians to refrain from sacrificing their infants to Saturn? Or, if it was a task beyond her power to enlighten the ignorant multitude, reform their barbarous and abominable superstitions, and teach them that they were immortal beings, why did she not, at least, instruct their philosophers in the great doctrine of the immortality of the soul, which they earnestly labored in vain to discover? They enjoyed the light of reason and natural religion in its fullest extent; yet so far were they from ascertaining the nature of our future and eternal existence, that they could not determine whether we could exist at all beyond the grave; nor could all their advantages preserve them from the grossest errors and most unnatural crimes."

The Height of Folly and Madness.

"What would you say of a man who should throw away his compass because he could not tell why it points to the north? or reject an accurate chart because it did not include a delineation of coasts which he never expected to visit, and with which he had no concern? What would you say of a man who should reject all the best astronomical treatises because they do not describe the inhabitants of the moon and of the planets; or who should treat with contempt every book which does not answer all the questions that may be asked respecting the subject of which it treats? Or, to come still nearer to the point, what would you say of a man who, when sick of a mortal disease, should refuse an infallible remedy unless the physician would first tell him how he took the disease, how such diseases first entered the world, why they were permitted to enter it, and by what secret laws or virtues the offered remedy would effect his cure? Would you not say a man so unreasonable deserves to die? He must be left to suffer for his folly. Now this is precisely the case of those who neglect the Bible, because it does not reveal those secret things which belong to God. Your souls are assailed by fatal diseases, by diseases which have destroyed millions of your fellow-creatures, which already occasion you much suffering, and which, you are assured, will terminate in death unless removed. An infallible Physician is revealed to you in the Bible, who has, at a great expense, provided a certain remedy; and this remedy he offers you freely, without money and without price. But you refuse to take this remedy because he does not think it necessary to answer every question which can be asked respecting the origin of your disease, the introduction of such diseases into the world, and the reasons why they were ever permitted to enter it. Tell me, you exclaim, how I became sick, or I will not consent to be well. If this be not the height of folly and madness, what is it?

"We have not the smallest reason to suppose that, if God had revealed all those secret things which belong to him, it would have made it more easy than it is now to know and perform our duty. Suppose, for instance, that God should answer all the questions which may be asked respecting the origin of moral evil and its introduction into the world; would this knowledge at all assist us in banishing evil from the world, or from our own bosoms? As well might we pretend that a knowledge of the precise manner in which a man was killed would enable us to restore him to life. Or, should God inform us of the manner in which divinity and humanity are united in the person of Jesus Christ, would this knowledge assist us in performing any one of the duties we owe the Saviour? As well might we pretend that a knowledge of the manner in which our souls are united to our bodies would assist us in performing any of the common actions of life."

Two Sets of Armor.

"The armor with which Satan furnishes his followers is directly the reverse of that Christian armor described by the Apostle Paul. Instead of a girdle of truth, he girds the sinner with the girdle of error and deceit. Instead of the breastplate of Christ's righteousness, he furnishes him with a breastplate of his own fancied righteousness. Instead of the shield of faith, the sinner has the shield of unbelief; and with this he defends himself against the curses of the law and the arrows of conviction. Instead of the sword of the Spirit, which is the word of God, he teaches him to yield the sword of a tongue set on fire of hell, and furnishes him with a magazine of cavils, excuses, and objections, with which to attack religion and defend himself. He also builds him many refuges of lies, in which, as in a strong castle, he proudly hopes to shelter himself from the wrath of God."

God Meets the Sinner's Excuses.

"Numerous as are the excuses which sinners make when urged to embrace the Gospel, they may all be reduced to three. The first is, that they have no time to attend to religion; the second is, that they do not know how to become religious; and the third, that they are not able to become so. Want of time, want of knowledge, or want of power, is pleaded by all. Foreseeing that they would make these excuses, God determined that they should have no reason to make them. By giving them the Sabbath, he has allowed them time for religion; by giving them his word, and messengers to explain it, he has taken away the excuse of ignorance; and by offering them the assistance of his Holy Spirit, he has deprived them of the pretense that they are unable to obey him. Thus he has obviated all their excuses; and therefore, at the last day, every mouth will be stopped, and the whole impenitent world will stand guilty and self-condemned before God."

A Change of Position—Results.

"When a man stands with his back to the sun, his own shadow and the shadows of surrounding objects are before him. But when he turns toward the sun, all these shadows are behind him. It is the same in spiritual things. God is the great Sun of the universe. Compared with him, creatures are but shadows. But while men stand with their backs to God, all these shadows are before them, and engross their affections, desires, and exertions. On the contrary, when they are converted, and turn to God, all these shadows are thrown behind them, and God becomes all in all, so that they can say from the heart, Whom have we in heaven but thee? and there is none upon earth that we desire besides thee."

Christ a Magnet.

"Suppose you wished to separate a quantity of brass and steel filings, mixed together in one vessel, how would you effect this separation? Apply a loadstone, and immediately every particle of iron will attach itself to it, while the brass remains behind. Thus if we see a company of true and false professors of religion, we may not be able to distinguish between them; but let Christ come among them, and all his sincere followers will be attracted toward him, as the steel is drawn to the magnet, while those who have none of his spirit will remain at a distance."

Adam our Federal Head.

"It is sometimes asked how it can be right that we should suffer in consequence of the sins of our first parents. In the first place, it is right because we imitate their example, and thus justify their conduct. We break the covenant, and disobey the law of God, as well as they. Another answer may be given by considering the subject in a different light. The angels who kept not their first estate had no covenant head, or representative, but each one stood for himself. Yet they fell. God was therefore pleased, when he made man, to adopt a different constitution of things; and since it had appeared that holy beings, endowed with every possible advantage for obeying God's law, would disobey it and ruin themselves, he thought proper, instead of leaving us, like the angels, to stand for ourselves, to appoint a covenant head or representative to stand for us, and to enter into covenant with him. Now let us suppose, for a moment, that we and all the human race had been brought into existence at once, and that God had proposed to us that we should choose one of our number to be our representative, and to enter into covenant with him on our behalf. Should we not, with one voice, have chosen our first parent for this responsible office? Should we not have said, 'He is a perfect man, and bears the image and likeness of God; if any one must stand or fall for us, let him be the man?' Now since the angels, who stood for themselves, fell, why should we wish to stand for ourselves? And if we must have a representative to stand for us, why should we complain, when God has chosen the same person for this office that we should have chosen had we been in existence and capable of choosing for ourselves?"

The Attributes of God Harmonized in Redemption.

"In the plan of redemption God appears to be, at once, a just God and a Saviour; thus he can be just and yet the justifier of him that believeth in Jesus; and justice and truth, as well as mercy and peace, will welcome to heaven every redeemed sinner who is brought there through the merits of Christ. Thus we see that these divine attributes, which were set at variance by the fall of the first Adam, are re-united and satisfied by the atonement of the second. Mercy may now say, I am satisfied, for my petitions in behalf of wretched man have been answered, and countless millions of that ruined race will sing the praises of boundless mercy for ever and ever. Truth may say, I am satisfied, for God's veracity and faithfulness remain inviolate, notwithstanding the salvation of sinners; and not one word that he has ever spoken has failed of its full accomplishment. Justice may say, I am satisfied, for the honor of the law over which I watch has been secured; sin has met with deserved punishment; the Prince of life has died to satisfy my claims; and God has shown the whole universe that he loves me, even better than he loves his only Son; for when that Son cried, in agony, Father, spare me, and I demanded that he should not be spared, God listened to my demands rather than to his cries. Finally, Peace may say, I am satisfied, for I have been permitted to proclaim peace on earth, and have seen God reconciling a rebellious world to himself. Come, then, my sister attributes, Mercy, Truth, and Righteousness, let us once more be united in perfect harmony, and join to admire the plan which thus reconciles us to each other."

A New Lesson for Angels.

"In this work creatures may see, if I may so express it, the very heart of God. From this work angels themselves have probably learned more of God's moral character than they had ever been able to learn before. They knew before that God was wise and powerful; for they had seen him create a world. They knew that he was good; for he had made them perfectly holy and happy. They knew that he was just; for they had seen him cast down their own rebellious brethren from heaven to hell for their sins. But until they saw him give repentance and remission of sins through Christ, they did not know that he was merciful; they did not know that he could pardon a sinner. And O! what an hour was that in heaven when this great truth was first made known—when the first penitent was pardoned! Then a new song was put into the mouths of angels; and while, with unutterable emotions of wonder, love, and praise, they began to sing it, their voices swelled to a higher pitch, and they experienced joys unfelt before. O how did the joyful sounds, His mercy endureth forever! spread from choir to choir, echo through the high arches of heaven, and thrill through every enraptured angelic breast; and how did they cry, with one voice, Glory to God in the highest, on earth peace, good-will toward man!"

The Glory that Shines in the Gospel.

"On no page less ample than that of the eternal, all-infolding Mind which devised the Gospel plan of salvation can its glories be displayed; nor by any inferior mind can they be fully comprehended. Suffice it to say, that here the moral character of Jehovah shines full-orbed and complete. Here all the fullness of the Godhead, all the insufferable splendors of Deity, burst at once upon our aching sight. Here the manifold perfections of God, holiness and goodness, justice and mercy, truth and grace, majesty and condescension, hatred of sin and compassion for sinners, are harmoniously blended, like the parti-colored rays of solar light, in one pure blaze of dazzling whiteness. Here, rather than on any other of his works, he founds his claims to the highest admiration, gratitude, and love of his creatures. Here is the work which ever has called forth, and which through eternity will continue to call forth, the most rapturous praises of the celestial choirs, and feed the ever-glowing fires of devotion in their breasts; for the glory which shines in the Gospel is the glory which illuminates heaven, and the Lamb that was slain is the light thereof."

"*Glad Tidings! Glad Tidings!*"

"Do any doubt whether the Gospel is indeed glad tidings of great joy? Come with me to the Garden of Eden. Look back to the hour which succeeded man's apostasy. See the golden chain which bound man to God and God to man sundered, apparently forever, and this wretched world, groaning under the weight of human guilt and its Maker's curse, sinking down, far down, into a bottomless abyss of misery and despair. See that tremendous Being who is a consuming fire encircling it on every side, and wrapping it, as it were, in an atmosphere of flame. Hear from his lips the tremendous sentence, Man has sinned, and man must die! See the king of terrors advancing with gigantic strides to execute the awful sentence, the grave expanding her marble jaws to receive whatever might fall before his wide-wasting scythe, and hell beneath, yawning dreadfully, to engulf forever its guilty, helpless, despairing victims. Such was the situation of our ruined race after the apostasy. Endeavor, if you can, to realize its horrors. Endeavor to forget, for a moment, that you ever heard of Christ or his Gospel. View yourselves as immortal beings hastening to eternity, with the curse of God's broken law, like a flaming sword, pursuing you; death, with his dart dipped in mortal poison, awaiting you; a dark cloud, fraught with the lightnings of divine vengeance, rolling over your heads; your feet standing in slippery places, in darkness, and the bottomless pit beneath expecting your fall. Then, when not only all hope, but all possibility of escape, seemed taken away, suppose the flaming sword suddenly quenched; the sting extracted; the Sun of Righteousness bursting forth and painting a rainbow on the before threatening cloud; a golden ladder let down from the opening gates of heaven, while a choir of angels, swiftly descending, exclaim, 'Behold, we bring you glad tidings of great joy, for unto you is born a Saviour who is Christ the Lord.' Would you, could you, while contemplating such a scene, and listening to the angelic message, doubt whether it communicated glad tidings? Would you not rather unite with them in exclaiming, 'Glad tidings! Glad tidings! Glory to God in the highest, that there is peace on earth, and good-will toward men.'"

Christ an Unrivaled Friend.

"Does not our Friend as far excel all other friends as heaven exceeds earth, as eternity exceeds time, as the Creator surpasses his creatures? If you doubt this, bring together all the glory, pomp, and beauty of the world; nay, assemble every thing that is great and excellent in all the worlds that ever were created; collect all the creatures which the breath of Omnipotence ever summoned into being—and we, on our parts, will place beside them our Saviour and Friend, that you may see whether they will bear a comparison with him. Look, then, first at your idols; behold the vast assemblage which you have collected, and then turn and contemplate our Beloved. See all the fullness of the Godhead dwelling in One who is meek and lowly as a child. See his countenance beaming with ineffable glories, full of mingled majesty, condescension, and love, and hear the soul-reviving invitations which proceed from his lips. See that hand in which dwells everlasting strength, swaying the scepter of universal empire over all creatures and all worlds; see his arms expanded to receive and embrace returning sinners; while his heart, a bottomless, shoreless ocean of benevolence, overflows with tenderness, compassion, and love. In a word, see in him all natural and moral excellence, personified and embodied in a resplendent form, compared with whose effulgent, dazzling glories the splendors of the meridian sun are dark. He speaks, and a world emerges from nothing. He frowns, and it sinks to nothing again. He waves his hand, and all the creatures which you have collected to rival him sink and disappear. Such, O sinner, is our Beloved, and such is our Friend. Will you not then embrace him as your Friend? If you can be persuaded to do this, you will find that the one half, nay, that the thousandth part, has not been told you."

The Sage and the Pupil.

"A celebrated philosopher of antiquity, who was accustomed to receive large sums from his pupils in return for his instructions, was one day accosted by an indigent youth who requested admission into the number of his disciples. 'And what,' said the sage, 'will you give me in return?' 'I will give you myself,' was the reply. 'I accept the gift,' answered the sage, 'and engage to restore you to yourself, at some future period, much more valuable than you are at present.' In similar language does our great Teacher address those who apply to him for instruction, conscious that they are unable to purchase his instructions, and offering to give him themselves. He will readily accept the gift; he will educate them for heaven, and will, at length, restore them to themselves, incomparably more wise, more happy, and more valuable, than when he received them."

The Three Occasions of Christ's Anger.

"We read of Christ being angry but three times during the whole period of his residence on earth, and in each of those instances his anger was excited, not by insults and injuries offered to himself, but by conduct which tended to interrupt or frustrate his benevolent exertions in doing good. When he was reviled as a man gluttonous, intemperate, and possessed by a devil, he was not angry; when he was buffeted, spit upon, and crowned with thorns, he was not angry; when nailed to the cross, and loaded with insults in his last agonies, he was not angry. But when his disciples forbade parents to bring their infant children to receive his blessing; when Peter endeavored to dissuade him from dying for sinners; and when sinners, by their hardness of heart, rendered his intended death of no service to themselves; then he was angry and much displeased."

The Sufferings of Christ Real.

"It has been supposed by many that the sufferings of Christ were rather apparent than real; or at least that his abundant consolations, and his knowledge of the happy consequences which would result from his death, rendered his sorrows comparatively light, and almost converted them to joys. But never was supposition more erroneous. Jesus Christ was as truly a man as either of us; and, as man, he was as really susceptible of grief, as keenly alive to pain and reproach, and as much averse from pain and suffering, as any of the descendants of Adam. And though a knowledge of the happy consequences which would result from his sufferings rendered him willing to endure them, it did not in the smallest degree take off their edge, or render him insensible to pain. No, his sufferings, instead of being less, were incomparably greater than they appeared to be. No finite mind can conceive of their extent; nor was any of the human race ever so well entitled to the appellation of the Man of Sorrows as the man Jesus Christ.

"As Christ died for all, so he felt and wept for the sufferings of all. The temporal and eternal calamities of the whole human race, and of every individual among them all, seemed to be collected and laid upon him. He saw, at one view, the whole mighty aggregate of human guilt and human wretchedness, and his boundless benevolence and compassion made it, by sympathy, all his own. It has been said by philosphers, that if any man could see all the misery which is daily felt in the world he would never smile again. We need not wonder, then, that Christ, who saw it all, never smiled, though he often wept."

The Power of Love.

"How infinite, how inconceivable, must have been that love which brought down the Son of God from the celestial world to redeem our ruined race! which led him to exchange the bosom of his Father for a vail of flesh; the adoration of angels for the scoffs and insults of sinners; and the enjoyment of eternal life for an accursed, painful, and ignominious death! Nothing but love could have done this. Not all the powers of heaven, earth, and hell combined could have dragged him from his celestial throne, and wrested the scepter of the universe from his hands. No, it was love alone—divine, omnipotent love—which drew him down; it was in the bands of love that he was but a willing captive, through all the trials and sufferings of a laborious life; and it was these bands which bound him at the bar of Pilate, which fettered his arm of everlasting strength, and prevented his blasting his murderers."

Christ's Self-Denial.

"The life of Christ was one of self-denial. He denied himself, for thirty years, all the glories and felicity of the heavenly world, and exposed himself to all the pains and sorrows of a life on earth. He denied himself the praises and adorations of saints and angels, and exposed himself to the blasphemies and reproaches of men. He denied himself the presence and enjoyment of God, and exposed himself to the society of publicans and sinners. He denied himself every thing that nature desires; he exposed himself to every thing she dreads and abhors—to poverty, contempt, pain, and death.

When he entered on his glorious and godlike design, he renounced all regard to his own comfort and convenience, and took up the cross—a cross infinitely heavier and more painful than any of his disciples had been called to bear—and continued to carry it through a rough and thorny road, till his human nature, exhausted, sunk under the weight. In short, he considers himself, his time, his talents, his reputation, his happiness, his very existence, as not his own but another's; and he even employed them accordingly. He lived not for himself, he died not for himself; but for others he lived, and for others he died."

Christ Satisfied.

"If we love, and prize, and rejoice in any object in proportion to the labor, pain, and expense which it has cost us to obtain it, how greatly must Christ love, and prize, and rejoice in every penitent sinner! His love and joy must be unutterable, inconceivable, infinite. For once I rejoice that our Saviour's toils and sufferings were so great, since the greater they were the greater must be his love for us and his joy in our conversion. And if he thus rejoiceth over one sinner that repenteth, what must be his joy when all his people are collected, out of every tongue and nation, and presented spotless before his Father's throne! What a full tide of felicity will pour in upon him, and how will his benevolent heart expand with unutterable delight, when, contemplating the countless myriads of the redeemed, he says, Were it not for my sufferings, all these immortal beings would have been, throughout eternity, as miserable, and now they will be as happy, as God can make them! It is enough. I see of the travail of my soul, and am satisfied."

Christ's Reception of Penitent Sinners.

"The meanest beggar, the vilest wretch, the most loathsome, depraved, abandoned sinner, is perfectly welcome to the arms and the heart of the Saviour, if he comes with the temper of the penitent prodigal. To all who come with this temper he ever lends a gracious ear; he listens to catch the first penitential sigh; he watches their first feeble step toward the path of duty; he prevents them with his grace, hastens to meet them, and, while they are ready to sink at his feet with mingled shame, confusion, and grief, he puts underneath them his everlasting arms, embraces, cheers, supports, and comforts them; wipes away their tears, washes away their stains, clothes them with his righteousness, unites them to himself forever, and feeds them with the bread and water of life. Thus he binds up the broken reed, enkindles the smoking flax, and, like a most tender, compassionate shepherd, gathers the helpless lambs in his arms and carries them in his bosom. Thus, by the condescending grace of our Immanuel, heaven is brought down to earth; the awful majesty and inaccessible glories of Jehovah are shrouded in a vail of flesh; a new and living way is opened for our return to God; and sinful, guilty worms of the dust may talk with their Maker face to face, as a man talketh with his friend."

Going On to Perfection.

"The professed disciple of Christ who desponds and trembles when he hears his Master calling him to go on to perfection may derive courage and support from looking at the promises of Christ, and at their Author. Among the blessings promised, you will find every thing which any man can need to assist him in arriving at perfection. There are promises of light and direction to find the path which leads to it; promises of assistance to walk in that path; promises of strength to resist and overcome all opposition; promises of remedies to heal us when wounded, of cordials to invigorate us when faint, and of most glorious rewards to crown the end of our course. You will hear Jehovah saying, 'Fear not, for I am with thee; be not dismayed, for I am thy God: I will strengthen thee; yea, I will help thee; yea, I will uphold thee with the right hand of my righteousness.' 'Though thou art in thyself but a worm, thou shalt thresh the mountains, and beat them small as the dust.' Look next at Him who gives these promises. It is one who is almighty, and who therefore can fulfill them. It is one who cannot lie, and therefore will fulfill them. It is one who possesses all power in heaven and on earth; one whose treasures of grace are unsearchable and inexhaustible; one in whom dwells all the fullness of the Godhead bodily. With all this fullness faith indissolubly unites us. Say, then, ye who despond and tremble when you contemplate the almost immeasurable distance between your own moral characters and that of Christ, what, except faith in these promises and in their Author, is necessary to support, encourage, and animate you in going on to perfection? If Christ himself is perfect; if faith makes you members of this perfect Head; if it causes his fullness to flow into your souls; then it is most evident that he can and will enable all who exercise faith in him to imitate his example, and finally to become perfect as he is perfect.

"Let not the Christian listen to the suggestions of indolence, despondency, and unbelief; but let him listen rather to the calls and promises of Christ. See what he has already done for those of our race who relied on his grace. Look at Enoch, who walked with God; at Abraham, the friend of God; at Moses, the confidential servant of God; at Daniel, the man greatly beloved of God; at Stephen, full of faith and the Holy Ghost; at St. Paul, glowing with an ardor like that of 'the rapt seraph, who adores and burns;' and at the many other worthies with whom the historian and biographer have made us acquainted.

See to what heights they soared, how nearly they approached to perfection. And who enabled them to make these approaches, to soar to these heights? He, I answer, who now calls upon you to follow them; he who now offers you the same assistance which he afforded them. Rely, then, with full confidence on his perfections and promises, and recommence with new vigor your Christian warfare. Do you still hesitate and linger? O thou of little faith, wherefore dost thou doubt? Why cast round a trembling, desponding glance upon the roaring wind and stormy waves which oppose thy progress? Look rather at him who calls thee onward; at the omnipotent arm which is to be thy strength and support. Look till you feel faith, and hope, and courage reviving in your breast. Then say to your Lord, I come. I will follow where thou leadest the way. I will once more aim, with renovated strength, at the perfection which I have long deemed unattainable."

Advantages of Possessing Christ.

"How great are the privileges which result from an ability to say, Christ is mine! If Christ is yours, then all that he possesses is yours. His power is yours, to defend you; his wisdom and knowledge are yours, to guide you; his righteousness is yours, to justify you; his Spirit and grace are yours, to sanctify you; his heaven is yours, to receive you. He is as much yours as you are his, and as he requires all that you have to be given to him, so he gives all that he has to you. Come to him, then, with holy boldness, and take what is your own. Remember you have already received what is most difficult for him to give—his body, his blood, his life. And surely he who has given these will not refuse you smaller blessings. You will never live happily or usefully, you will never highly enjoy or greatly adorn religion, until you can feel that Christ, and all that he possesses, are yours, and learn to come and take them as your own."

The Bible Entirely Practical.

"We may challenge any man to point out a single passage in the Bible which does not either teach some duty, or inculcate its performance, or show the grounds on which it rests, or exhibit reasons why we should perform it. For instance: all the preceptive parts of Scripture prescribe our duty; all the invitations invite us to perform it; all the promises and threatenings are motives to its performance; all the cautions and admonitions warn us not to neglect it; the historical parts inform us what have been the consequences of neglecting and of performing it; the prophetical parts show us what these consequences will be hereafter; and the doctrinal parts show us on what grounds the whole superstructure of duty or of practical religion rests."

Earnestness in Prayer a Test.

"We may judge of the state of our hearts by the earnestness of our prayers. You cannot make a rich man beg like a poor man; you cannot make a man that is full cry for food like one who is hungry: no more will a man who has a good opinion of himself cry for mercy like one who feels that he is poor and needy."

Symptoms of Spiritual Decline.

"The symptoms of spiritual decline are like those which attend the decay of bodily health. It generally commences with loss of appetite, and a disrelish for spiritual food, prayer, reading the Scriptures and devotional books. Whenever you perceive these symptoms be alarmed, for your spiritual health is in danger; apply immediately to the great Physician for a cure.

"The best means of keeping near to God is the closet. Here the battle is won or lost."

Impatience at not Receiving Answers to Prayer.

"If a man begins to be impatient because his prayers for any blessings are not answered, it is a certain proof that a self-righteous dependence on his own merits prevails in his heart to a great extent; for the language of impatience is, I deserve the blessing; I had a right to expect that it would be bestowed, and it ought to have been bestowed ere this. It is evident that a man who feels that he deserves nothing will never be impatient because he receives nothing; but will say, I have nothing to complain of; I receive as much as I deserve. Again, when a man wonders, or thinks it strange, that he does not receive a blessing for which he has prayed, it shows that he relies on his own merits. The language of such feelings is, It is very strange that I, who have prayed so well and so long, and had so much reason to expect a blessing, do not receive it. Persons who feel truly humble, on the contrary, are surprised, not when blessings are withheld, but when they are bestowed.

It appears very strange and wonderful to them that God should bestow any favors on creatures so unworthy as themselves, or pay any regard to prayers so polluted as their own. This is the temper to which every person must be brought before God will answer his prayers."

Praise Procures the Divine Blessing.

"No one needs to be told that the surest method to obtain new favors from an earthly benefactor is, to be thankful for those which he has already bestowed. It is the same with respect to our heavenly benefactor. Praise and thanksgiving are even more prevalent than sacrifices or prayers. I have somewhere met with an account of a Christian who was shipwrecked upon a desolate island, while all his companions perished in the waves. In this situation he spent many days in fasting and prayer that God would open a way for his deliverance; but his prayers received no answer. At length, musing on the goodness of God in preserving him from the dangers of the sea, he resolved to spend a day in thanksgiving and praise for this and other favors. Before the conclusion of the day a vessel arrived, and restored him in safety to his country and friends. Another instance, equally in point, we find in the history of Solomon. At the dedication of the temple many prayers were made, and many sacrifices offered, without any token of the divine acceptance. But when singers and players on instruments began, as one, to make one sound, to be heard in praising and thanking the Lord, saying, 'For he is good, for his mercy endureth forever'—then the glory of the Lord descended and filled the temple. The reason why praise and thanksgiving are thus prevalent with God is, that they, above all other duties, glorify him. 'Whoso offereth praise,' says he, 'glorifieth me.' And those who do thus honor him he will honor."

The Communion a Funeral Scene.

"At the communion-table we are in fact assembled to attend our Saviour's funeral, to look at his dead body as we look at the countenance of a deceased friend before the coffin is closed. And if every wrong, every worldly feeling, should die away while we are contemplating the corpse of a friend, how much more ought this to be the case, when this friend is Christ! It may be profitable some times to shut ourselves up, in imagination, in our Saviour's tomb, and feel as if he were there buried with us."

Sympathy with Christ as a Man of Sorrows.

"Was Christ a man of sorrows and acquainted with grief? Then, Christians, we need not be surprised or offended if we are often called to drink of the cup of sorrows; if we find this world a vale of tears. This is one of the ways in which we must be conformed to our glorious Head. Indeed, his example has sanctified grief, and almost rendered it pleasant to mourn. One would think that Christians could scarcely wish to go rejoicing through a world which their Master passed through mourning. The paths in which we follow him are bedewed with his tears, and stained with his blood. It is true, that from the ground thus watered and fertilized many rich flowers and fruits of paradise spring up to refresh us, in which we may and ought to rejoice. But still our joy should be softened and sanctified by godly sorrow. When we are partaking of the feast which his love has spread for us, we should never forget how dearly it was purchased.

> "'There's not a gift his hand bestows
> But cost his heart a groan.'

The joy, the honor, the glory, through eternity, shall be ours; but the sorrows, the sufferings, the agonies which purchased it, were all his own."

The Grand Law of Nature.

"'Not for ourselves, but others'—is the grand law of nature, inscribed by the hand of God on every part of creation. Not for itself, but others, does the sun dispense its beams; not for themselves, but others, do the clouds distill their showers; not for herself, but others, does the earth unlock her treasures; not for themselves, but others, do the trees produce their fruits, or the flowers diffuse their fragrance and display their various hues. So, not for himself, but others, are the blessings of heaven bestowed on man; and whenever, instead of diffusing them around, he devotes them exclusively to his own gratification, and shuts himself up in the dark and flinty caverns of selfishness, he transgresses the great law of creation; he cuts himself off from the created universe and its Author; he sacrilegiously converts to his own use the favors which were given him for the relief of others, and must be considered not only as an unprofitable, but as a fraudulent servant, who has worse than wasted his Lord's money. He who thus lives only to himself, and consumes the bounty of heaven upon his lusts, or consecrates it to the demon of avarice, is a barren rock in a fertile plain; he is a thorny bramble in a fruitful vineyard; he is the grave of God's blessings; he is the very Arabia Deserta of the moral world. And if he is highly exalted in wealth or power, he stands, inaccessible and strong, like an insulated towering cliff, which exhibits only a cold and cheerless prospect, intercepts the genial beams of the sun, chills the vales below with its gloomy shade, adds fresh keenness to the freezing blast, and tempts down the lightnings of angry heaven. How different this from the gently-rising hill, clothed to its summit with fruits and flowers, which attracts and receives the dews of heaven, and, retaining only sufficient to supply its numerous offspring, sends the remainder in a thousand streams to bless the vales which lie at its feet!"

Man can do what God Requires.

"What God calls a man to do he will carry him through. I would undertake to govern half a dozen worlds if God called me to do it; but I would not undertake to govern half a dozen sheep unless God called me to it."

Covetousness a Pit without a Bottom.

"Suppose you had to pass over a pit which had no bottom, would you endeavor to fill it up, or bridge it over?"

A Little Court within the Breast.

"Every thing we do or say should be immediately tried by a little court within our own breasts. Our motives should be examined, and a decision made on the spot."

Contemplation of Eternity.

"As the eye which has gazed at the sun cannot immediately discern any other object—as the man who has been accustomed to behold the ocean, turns with contempt from a stagnant pool—so the mind which has contemplated eternity overlooks and despises the things of time."

Death the Porter of Paradise.

"The power of death, the last enemy, is destroyed, as it respects all who believe in Christ. Instead of being the jailer of hell and the grave, he is now, as it respects Christ's people, the porter of paradise. All he can now do is to cause them to sleep in Jesus, release their immortal spirits from the fetters which bind them to earth, and deposit their weary bodies in the tomb, as a place of rest, till Christ comes at the last day, to raise them, incorruptible, glorious, and immortal, and reunite them to their souls in a state of perfect, never-ending felicity.

Honor and Danger of the Gospel Ministry.

"Every benevolent person is gratified by being made the bearer of pleasing intelligence. The messenger who is commissioned to open the prison doors of an insolvent debtor or pardoned criminal, and restore him to the embraces of his family; the officer who is sent by his commander-in-chief to carry home tidings of an important victory; and still more the embassador who is appointed to proclaim pardon and peace, in his sovereign's name, to conquered rebels; thinks himself, and is thought by others, to have received no common favor. Should God put into your hands the wonder-working rod of Moses; should he commission and enable you to work miracles of beneficence, to enrich the poor, to comfort the miserable, to restore sight to the blind, hearing to the deaf, health to the diseased, and life to the dead, you would esteem it a favor and honor incomparably greater than earthly monarchs can bestow. But in committing the Gospel to your care, God has conferred on you honors and favors compared with which even the power of working miracles is a trifle. He has put into your hands the cross of Christ, an instrument of far greater efficacy than the rod of Moses. He has sent you to proclaim the most joyful tidings that heaven can desire, or that earth can hear. He has sent you to preach deliverance to captives, the recovery of sight to the blind, the balm of Gilead and the great Physician to the spiritually wounded and diseased, salvation to the self-destroyed, and everlasting life to the dead. In a word, he commissions and enables them to work miracles, not upon the bodies, but upon the souls of men; miracles not merely of power, but of grace and mercy; miracles, to perform which an angel would think himself highly honored in being sent down from heaven; miracles, from the performance of which it is difficult to say whether greater glory redounds to God or greater happiness to man. Well, then, may every minister of Christ exclaim with Paul, 'I thank my God for that he counted me faithful, putting me into the ministry.'

"Though, in committing the Gospel to their trust, God has conferred on ministers the greatest honor and favor which can be given to mortals, yet, like all other favors, it brings with it a great increase of responsibility. Remember that the more highly any one is exalted, in this respect, the more difficult it becomes to stand, and the more dangerous it is to fall. He who falls from a pulpit seldom stops short of the lowest abyss in hell."

A Thousand Years as One Day in Heaven.

"You have, doubtless, often observed that when your minds have been intently and pleasingly occupied, you have become almost unconscious of the flight of time; minutes and hours have flown away with, apparently, unusual swiftness, and the setting or rising sun has surprised you long before you expected its approach. But in heaven the saints will be entirely lost and swallowed up in God; and their minds will be so completely absorbed in the contemplation of his ineffable, infinite, uncreated glories, that they will be totally unconscious how time, or, rather, how eternity passes; and not only years, but millions of ages, such as we call ages, will be flown ere they are aware. Thus a thousand years will seem but as one day, and so great, so ecstatic will be their happiness, that one day will be as a thousand years. And as there will be nothing to interrupt them, no bodily wants to call off their attention, no weariness to compel them to rest, no vicissitude of seasons or of day and night to disturb their contemplations, it is more than possible that innumerable ages may pass away before they think of asking how long they have been in heaven, or even before they are conscious that a single hour has elapsed."

"O What Must it Be to be There!"

"How often, Christians, have your hearts been made to burn with love, and gratitude, and admiration, and joy, while Christ has opened to you the Scriptures, and caused you to know a little of that love which passeth knowledge! How often has one transient glimpse of the light of God's countenance turned your night into day, banished your sorrows, supported you under heavy afflictions, and caused you to rejoice with joy unspeakable and full of glory! O, then, what must it be to escape forever from error, and ignorance, and darkness, and sin, into the region of bright, unclouded, eternal day; to see your God and Redeemer face to face; continually to contemplate, with immortal strength, glories so dazzlingly bright that one moment's view of them would now, like a stream of lightning, turn your frail bodies into dust; to see the eternal volume of the divine counsels, the mighty map of the divine mind, unfolded to your eager, piercing gaze; to explore the heights and depths, the lengths and breadths of the Redeemer's love, and still to see new wonders, glories, and beauties pouring upon your minds in constant, endless succession, calling forth new songs of praise;—songs in which you will unite, not, as now, with mortal companions and mortal voices, but with the innumerable choir of angels, with the countless myriads of the redeemed, all shouting with a voice like the voice of many waters, Alleluia, for the Lord God omnipotent reigneth!"

The Bereaved Mother Comforted.

" Suppose, now, some one was making a beautiful crown for you to wear; and you knew it was for you, and that you were to receive it and wear it as soon as it should be done. Now, if the maker of it were to come, and, in order to make the crown more beautiful and splendid, were to take some of your jewels to put into it,—should you be sorrowful and unhappy because they were taken away for a little while, when you knew they were gone to make up your crown?"

Doubts Arising from Infirmities Removed.

"Suppose you were to see a little sick child lying in its mother's lap, with its faculties impaired by its sufferings, so that it was, generally, in a troubled sleep; but now and then it just opens its eyes a little, and gets a glimpse of its mother's face, so as to be recalled to the recollection that it is in its mother's arms; and suppose that always, at such a time, it should smile faintly with evident pleasure to find where it was,—should you doubt whether that child loved its mother or not?"

"*One Broken Wing.*"

"Madam, I think your husband is looking upward—making some effort to rise above the world toward God and heaven. You must not let him try alone. Whenever I see the husband struggling alone in such efforts it makes me think of a dove endeavoring to fly upward while it has one broken wing. It leaps and flutters, and perhaps raises itself a little way, and then it becomes wearied, and drops back again to the ground. If both wings co-operate then it mounts easily."

How Rich the Poorest Christian.

"A pious man once visited a friend who had recently come into possession of a very large landed property. His friend, after some conversation, led him to the top of his house, which commanded an extensive prospect, and directing his attention successively to a great number of valuable objects, added, after the mention of each particular, 'That is mine.' After he had finished the long catalogue of his possessions, his guest asked, 'Do you see yonder cottage on the waste? There lives a poor widow who can say more than you can; she can say, Christ is mine.' My friends, did the rich man or the poor widow possess the more valuable property? But the very question is dishonorable to Christ. Could the rich man have pointed to the sun and moon, the planets, and the fixed stars, and said with truth, 'All these are mine;' still his possessions, weighed against the poor widow's treasure, would have been lighter than vanity.

"The Creator must be worth infinitely more than the whole creation. He can do that for those who possess him which the whole creation cannot do. He can wash away their sins, he can sanctify their natures, he can support them under afflictions, he can prepare them for death, he can fill their souls with happiness, and he can make that happiness eternal; neither of which the whole creation could do for its possessor. O how rich, then, how incalculably rich is the poorest Christian! He is the only being who is not now able and who never will be able to calculate the worth of his possessions. In possessing Christ he possesses all things, for he possesses Him who created and who disposes of all things. He is a joint heir with Him who is heir of all things. Well, then, might the apostle say to Christians, All things are yours. Well may Christ say to his poorest disciple, I know thy poverty, but thou art rich. And well may every Christian, contemplating his portion, cry, Thanks be unto God for his unspeakable gift!"

And the Lamb is the Light Thereof.

"The unfathomable flood of light and glory which unceasingly flows from the Father is collected and concentrated in the person of his Son, for he is the brightness of the Father's glory and the express image of his person. Heaven is therefore illuminated not only with God's glory, but with the brightest and most dazzling effulgence of divine, uncreated light—a light which enlightens and cheers the soul as well as the body. Of the nature and degree of this light, who but the happy beings that enjoy it can form any conception. There are, indeed, several passages in Scripture which seem intended to give us some idea of it, but they serve little more than to convince us that it is altogether inconceivable.

"For instance, St. John informs us that he saw, in vision, a mighty angel come down from heaven, and that the earth was lightened with his glory. But if the glory of a single angel was sufficient to lighten the earth, what must be the glory of the Lord of angels; and how overpowering the light of heaven, where millions of angels continually reside, and God and the Lamb display their brightest glories!

"Again: when Christ appeared to the same apostle, his eyes were as a flame of fire, and his feet as brass glowing in a furnace, and his countenance as the sun shining in his strength; so that, unable to support the sight, St. John fell at his feet as dead. But if his glories were thus overpowering when, in condescension to the weakness of his servant, he drew a vail over them, what must they be in the regions above, where they are seen in all their brightness, without any interposing vail?

"Once more: when Moses came down from the mount, after a short interview with God, his face shone with a luster so dazzling, that even his brother and the elders of Israel were unable to gaze upon it. But if a transient view of the glory of God, seen as it were through a glass darkly, could impart such a luster to a piece of animated clay, what insufferable splendor must the constant presence of Jehovah give to the diamond walls, the pearly gates, and the golden streets of the New Jerusalem? How must they glow and shine, as in a furnace, when the Sun of Righteousness pours upon them his effulgent beams in a full tide of glory! and how must the spiritual bodies of their inhabitants, which resemble the glorified body of their Redeemer, eclipse all that is called brilliant and dazzling on earth? We are indeed assured that all the righteous shall shine forth as the sun in the kingdom of their Father, and as the brightness of the firmament for ever and ever. Say then, my friends, does the New Jerusalem need any created luminaries to shine in it, or do its inhabitants need the light of the sun, when every individual among them is himself a sun? Not only the moon, but the sun itself, would be invisible amid these celestial glories; or if visible, it would appear only as a cloud, or a dark spot on the face of the celestial sky. Then, says the prophet, shall the moon be confounded and the sun ashamed, when the Lord of Hosts shall reign in Mount Zion, and in Jerusalem, and before his ancients gloriously."

No Night in Heaven.

"Do the rays of light grow weary in their flight from the sun? or does the thunderbolt need to pause and seek refreshment in the midst of its career? As little do the inhabitants of heaven become weary in praising and enjoying God. As little do they need refreshment or repose; for their spiritual bodies will be far more active and refined than the purest light, and their labor itself will be the sweetest rest. Hence heaven is styled the *rest* which remains for God's people, and they are represented as serving him unceasingly in his temple above. They will not, therefore, lose a third part of eternity in sleep. No night will be necessary to refresh them; the pulse of immortality will beat strong in every vein; the golden harp will never drop from their hands; their tongues will never grow weary of extolling their God and Redeemer, but will through eternity pour forth songs of praise as unceasing as the displays of those glories which excite them."

The New Jerusalem and its Inhabitants.

"Behold a city, built with the most perfect regularity, extending in every direction farther than the eye can reach, surrounded by a wall of jasper, of immeasurable height, and entirely composed of gold, pearls, diamonds, and precious stones. See its golden streets thronged with inhabitants, whose bodies, composed of light seven times refined, are far more dazzlingly bright and glorious than all the sparkling gems which surround them. See among them the patriarchs, the prophets, the apostles, and martyrs, distinguished from their fellow-saints by their superior brightness. See the gates guarded, and the streets filled by thousands of thousands, and ten thousand times ten thousand of angels and archangels, thrones and dominions, principalities and powers, each one of whom seems sufficiently glorious to be himself a god. See the golden streets, the diamond walls, and pearly gates of this celestial city, reflecting from every part streams of light and glory, which flow in a full tide from all directions, not from the sun, but from a throne, more dazzlingly bright than ten thousand suns, raised high in the midst. See the innumerable stirring throngs of saints and angels, enveloped in the boundless flood of light and glory, all falling prostrate before the throne, and with one voice praising Him who liveth for ever and ever. Hear their united voices, as the voice of many waters, and as the voice of mighty thunderings, exclaiming, 'Alleluia! for the Lord God Omnipotent reigneth. Blessing, and glory, and honor, and power, be unto Him that sitteth on the throne and to the Lamb for ever and ever.' Then raise your eyes to contemplate the object of this worship, Him who fills this throne. See the Ancient of days, the great I Am, the Being of beings, the Being who is, the Being who was, the

Being who shall be forever. See at his right hand a man, the friend, the brother, the Redeemer of man, clothed with the brightness of his Father's glory, the express image of his person. See him with a countenance of mingled majesty, meekness, condescension, and love, surveying the countless myriads of his people around him, and his eye successively meeting their eyes in turn, and pouring into their souls such ineffable happiness as is almost too much for mortals to bear."

The Sailor Spoken on his Life Voyage.

" Ho, there! creature of God, immortal spirit, voyager to Eternity! whither art thou bound? Heard I the answer aright? Was it, 'I don't know?' Not know where you are bound? Heard you ever such an answer to this question before? Should you hear such an answer from a spoken vessel, would you not conclude its crew to be either drunk or mad? and would you not soon expect to hear of its loss? Not know where you are bound? And have you, then, for so many years, been beating about in the fogs of ignorance and uncertainty, with no port in view, the sport of storms and currents; driven hither and thither as the winds change, without any hope of ever making a harbor, and liable, every moment, to strike upon a lee shore? Not know where you are bound? Alas, then, I fear you are bound to the Gulf of Perdition, and that you will be driven on the rocks of Despair, which are now right ahead of you, and which, sooner or later, bring up all who know not where they are bound, and who care not what course they steer. If I have taken my observation correctly, you are in the Lee Current, which sets directly into a gulf where you will find no bottom with a thousand fathoms of line. Not know where you are bound? You must then be in distress. You have either unshipped your rudder, or you have no compass, chart, or quadrant on board; nor any pilot who can carry you into the port of Heaven."

The Bible a Compass, Chart, and Quadrant.

"For a compass, chart, and quadrant, God has given us the Bible; and most completely does it answer the purpose of all three. By this book, as a compass, you may shape your course correctly; for it will always traverse freely, and it has no variation. By this book, as a quadrant, you may at any time, by night or by day, take an observation, and find out exactly where you are. And in this book, as on a chart, not only the port of Heaven, but your whole course, with every rock, shoal, and breaker on which you can possibly strike, is most accurately laid down. If, then, you make a proper use of this book, mind your helm, keep a good lookout, and carefully observe your pilot's directions, you will without fail make a prosperous voyage, and reach the port of Heaven in safety. It may not, however, be amiss to give a few hints respecting the first part of your course:

Drunkard's Rock.

"If you examine your chart you will find put down, not far from the latitude in which you now are, a most dangerous rock, called the Rock of Intemperance, or Drunkard's Rock. This rock, on which there is a high beacon, is almost white with the bones of poor sailors who have been cast away upon it. You must be careful to give this rock a good berth, for there is a very strong current setting toward it. If you once get into that current you will find it very difficult getting out again, and will be almost sure to strike and go to pieces. You will often find a parcel of wreckers round this rock, who will try to persuade you that it is not dangerous, and that there is no current. But take care how you believe them. Their only object is plunder.

A Dangerous Whirlpool.

"Not far from this terrible rock you will find marked a whirlpool, almost equally dangerous, called the Whirlpool of Bad Company. Indeed this whirlpool often throws vessels upon Drunkard's Rock, as it hurries them round. It lies just outside the Gulf of Perdition, and every thing which it swallows up is thrown into that gulf. It is surrounded by several little eddies, which often draw mariners into it before they know where they are. Keep a good lookout, then, for these eddies, and steer wide of this whirlpool; for it has swallowed up more sailors than ever the sea did. In fact, it is a complete Hell Gate.

The Straits of Repentance.

"Besides this whirlpool and rock, there are several shoals laid down in your chart which I cannot now stay to describe. Indeed these seas are full of them, which makes sailing here extremely dangerous. If you would be sure to shun them all and to keep clear of the terrible gulf already mentioned, you must immediately go about, make a signal for a pilot, and steer for the Straits of Repentance, which you will see right ahead. These straits, which are very narrow, form the only passage out of the dangerous seas you have been navigating into the great Pacific Ocean, sometimes called the Safe Sea, or Sea of Salvation, on the further shore of which lies your port. It is not very pleasant passing these straits; and therefore many navigators have tried hard to find another passage. Indeed, some who pretend to be pilots will tell you there is another; but they are wrong; for the great Master Pilot himself has declared that every one who does not pass the Straits of Repentance will certainly be lost.

The Bay of Faith.

"As you pass these straits, the spacious Bay of Faith will begin to open, on the right-hand side of which you will see a high hill, called Mount Calvary. On the top of this hill stands a Light-House, in the form of a cross, which, by night, is completely illumined from top to bottom, and by day, sends up a pillar of smoke, like a white cloud. It stands so high, that, unless you deviate from the course laid down in your chart, you will never lose sight of it in any succeeding part of your voyage. At the foot of this Light-House you will find the Pilot I have so often mentioned waiting for you. You must by all means receive him on board; for without Him, neither your own exertions nor all the charts and pilots in the world can preserve you from fatal shipwreck.

The Highlands of Hope.

"As you enter the Bay of Faith you will see, far ahead, like a white cloud in the horizon, the Highlands of Hope, which lie hard by your port. These lands are so high that when the air is clear you will have them continually in sight during the remainder of your voyage, and while they are in sight you may be sure of always finding good anchoring ground, and of safely riding out every storm."

The Sailor at his Evening Watch.

"Whenever you are keeping your evening watch on deck look up, and see the God of whom you have now heard—the God whose name, I fear, some of you 'take in vain,'—throned in awful silence, and darkness, and majesty, on the sky, crowned with a diadem of ten thousand stars, holding the winds and thunderbolts in his hand, and setting one foot on the sea and the other on the land, while both land and sea obey his word, and tremble at his nod."

The Destruction of the World.

"Yes, prepare, ye accountable creature, prepare to meet your God; for he has said, Behold I come, I come near to judgment! And hath he said it, and shall he not do it? Hath he spoken, and shall he not make it good? Yes, when his appointed hour shall arrive, a mighty angel will lift his hand to heaven, and swear by Him who liveth for ever and ever, that there shall be time no longer. Then our world, impetuously driven by the last tempest, will strike, and be dashed in pieces on the shores of eternity. Hark! what a crash was there! One groan of unutterable anguish, one loud shriek of consternation and despair is heard, and all is still. Not a fragment of the wreck remains to which the struggling wretches might cling for support; but down, down, down they sink, whelmed deep beneath the billows of almighty wrath. But see! something appears at a distance mounting above the waves, and nearing the shore. It is the ark of salvation! It is the life-boat of heaven! It has weathered the last storm; it enters the harbor triumphantly; heaven resounds with the acclamations of its grateful, happy crew."

Sir William Jones' Estimate of the Bible.

"From the almost innumerable testimonies of this nature, which might easily be adduced, we shall select only that of Sir William Jones, a judge of the supreme court of judicature in Bengal—a man, says his learned biographer, who, by the exertion of rare intellectual talents, acquired a knowledge of arts, sciences, and languages which has seldom been equaled, and scarcely, if ever, surpassed. 'I have carefully and regularly perused the Scriptures,' says this truly great man, 'and am of opinion that this volume, independent of its divine origin, contains more sublimity, purer morality, more important history, and finer strains of eloquence, than can be collected from all other books, in whatever language they may have been written."

Historic Information of the Bible.

"If any imagine that Sir William Jones has estimated too highly the historical information which this volume contains, we would only request them to peruse it with attention, and particularly to consider the assistance which it affords in accounting for many otherwise inexplicable phenomena in the natural, political, and moral world. A person who has never attended to the subject will, on recollection, be surprised to find for how large a proportion of his knowledge he is indebted to this neglected book.* It is the only book which satisfactorily accounts, or even professes to account, for the introduction of natural and moral evil into the world, and for the consequent present situation of mankind. To this book we are also indebted for all our knowledge of the progenitors of our race, and of the early ages of the world; for our acquaintance with the manners and customs of those ages; for the origin and explanation of many remarkable traditions which have extensively prevailed; and for almost every thing which is known of many once flourishing nations, especially of the Jews, the most singular and interesting people, perhaps, that ever existed. It is the Bible alone, which, by informing us of the deluge, enables us to account satisfactorily for many surprising appearances in the internal structure of the earth, as well as for the existence of marine exuviæ on the summits of mountains, and in other places far distant from the sea. By the same volume we are assisted in accounting for the multiplicity of languages which exist in the world; for the origin and universal prevalence of sacrifices; and many other facts of an equally interesting nature. We shall only add, that while the Scriptures throw light on the facts here alluded to, the existence of these facts powerfully

---

* It will be recollected that we here refer to such information only as uninspired men might communicate.

tends, on the other hand, to establish the truth and authenticity of the Scriptures."

Antiquity of the Holy Scriptures.

"In addition to these intrinsic excellences of the Bible, which give it, considered merely as a human production, powerful claims to the attention of persons of taste and learning, there are various circumstances, of an adventitious nature, which render it peculiarly interesting to a reflecting mind. Among these circumstances we may, perhaps not improperly, mention its great antiquity. Whatever may be said of its inspiration, some of the books which compose it are unquestionably the most ancient literary compositions extant, and perhaps the most ancient that ever were written; nor is it very improbable that letters were first employed in recording some part of them, and that they were written in the language first spoken by man. It is also not only the most ancient book, but the most ancient monument of human exertion, the eldest offspring of human intellect, now in existence. Unlike the other works of man, it inherits not his frailty. All the contemporaries of its infancy have long since perished and are forgotten. Yet this wonderful volume still survives. Like the fabled pillars of Seth, which are said to have bid defiance to the deluge, it has stood for ages unmoved in the midst of that flood which sweeps away men, with their labors, into oblivion. That these circumstances render it an interesting object of contemplation, it is needless to remark. Were there now in existence a tree which was planted, an edifice which was erected, or any monument of human ingenuity which was formed at that early period in which some parts of the Bible were written, would it not be contemplated with the keenest interest, carefully preserved as a precious relic, and considered as something little less than sacred? With what emotions, then, will a thoughtful mind often open the Bible; and what a train of interesting reflections is it, in this view, calculated to excite! While we contemplate its antiquity, exceeding that of every object around us except the works of God, and view it, in anticipation, as continuing to exist unaltered until the end of time, must we not feel almost irresistibly impelled to venerate it, as proceeding originally from Him who is yesterday, to-day, and forever the same, and whose works, like his years, fail not?"

Unsuccessful Opposition to the Word of God.

"The interest which this volume excites by its antiquity will be greatly increased if we consider the violent and persevering opposition it has encountered, and the almost innumerable enemies it has resisted and overcome. We contemplate, with no ordinary degree of interest, a rock which has braved for centuries the ocean's rage, practically saying, 'Hitherto shalt thou come, but no farther; and here shall thy proud waves be stayed.' With still greater interest, though of a somewhat different kind, should we contemplate a fortress which, during thousands of years, had been constantly assaulted by successive generations of enemies, around whose walls millions had perished, and to overthrow which the utmost efforts of human force and ingenuity had been excited in vain. Such a rock, such a fortress, we contemplate in the Bible. For thousands of years this volume has withstood, not only the iron tooth of time, which devours men and their works together, but all the physical and intellectual strength of man. Pretended friends have endeavored to corrupt and betray it; kings and princes have perseveringly sought to banish it from the world; the civil and military powers of the greatest empires have been leagued for its destruction; the fires of persecution have often been lighted to consume it and its friends together; and at many seasons death, in some horrid form, has been the almost certain consequence of affording it an asylum from the fury of its enemies. It has also been almost incessantly assailed by weapons of a different kind, which, to any other book, would be far more dangerous than fire or sword. In these assaults wit and ridicule have wasted all their shafts; misguided reason has been compelled, though reluctantly, to lend her aid, and after repeated defeats has again been dragged to the field; the arsenals of learning have been emptied to arm her for the contest; and in search of means to prosecute it with success, recourse has been had, not only to remote ages and distant lands, but even to the bowels of the earth, and the region of the stars. Yet still the object of all these attacks remains uninjured, while one army of its assailants after another has melted away. Though it has been ridiculed more bitterly, misrepresented more grossly, opposed more rancorously, and burnt more frequently, than any other book, and perhaps than all other books united, it is so far from sinking under the efforts of its enemies that the probability of its surviving until the final consummation of all things is now evidently much greater than ever. The rain has descended; the floods have come; the storm has arisen and beat upon it; but it falls not, for it is founded upon a rock. Like the burning bush, it has ever been in the flames, yet is still unconsumed; a sufficient proof, were there no other, that He who dwelt in the bush preserves the Bible."

Benefits of the Bible to Our Race.

"Nor have its effects been confined to individuals. Nations have participated largely in its benefits. Armed with this volume, which is at once sword and shield, the first heralds of Christianity went forth conquering and to conquer. No less powerful than the wonder-working rod of Moses, its touch crumbled into dust the temples of paganism, and overthrew, as in a moment, the immense fabric of superstition and idolatry which had been for ages erecting. To this volume alone it is owing that we are not now assembled in the temple of an idol; that stocks and stones are not our deities; that cruelty, intemperance, and impurity do not constitute our religion; and that our children are not burnt as sacrifices at the shrine of Moloch. To this volume we are also indebted for the Reformation in the days of Luther; for the consequent revival and progress of learning, and for our present freedom from papal tyranny. Nor are these benefits, great as they are, all which it has been the means of conferring on man. Wherever it comes, blessings follow in its train. Like the stream which diffuses itself, and is apparently lost, among the herbage, it betrays its course by its effects. Wherever its influence is felt, temperance, industry, and contentment prevail; natural and moral evils are banished or mitigated; and churches, hospitals, and asylums for almost every species of wretchedness arise to adorn the landscape and cheer the eye of benevolence. Such are the temporal benefits which even infidelity itself, if it would for once be candid, must acknowledge that the Bible has bestowed on man. Almost coeval with the sun, its fittest emblem, it has, like that luminary, from the commencement of its existence, shed an unceasing flood of light on a benighted and wretched world. Who, then, can doubt that He who formed the sun, gave the Bible to be 'a light to our feet, and a lamp to our path?' Who that contemplates this fountain, still full and overflowing, notwithstanding the millions who have drank of its waters, can doubt that it has a real though invisible connection with that river of life which flows forever at the right hand of God."

Divine Origin of the Bible.

"The ancient Greeks had one sentence which they believed, though without foundation, to have descended from heaven; and to evince their gratitude and veneration for this gift, they caused it to be engraved, in letters of gold, on the front of their most sacred and magnificent temple. We, more favored, have not a sentence only but a volume, which really descended from heaven; and which, whether we consider its contents or its Author, ought to be indelibly engraven on the heart of every child of Adam. Its Author is the author of our being; and its contents afford us information of the most satisfactory and important kind on subjects of infinite consequence, respecting which all other books are either silent, or speak only doubtfully and unauthoritatively. It informs us, with the greatest clearness and precision, of every thing necessary either to our present or future happiness; of every thing, in fact, which its Author knows, the knowledge of which would be really useful to us; and thus confers those benefits which the tempter falsely pretended would result from eating the forbidden fruit—making us as gods, knowing good and evil."

The Bible a Mirror.

"In the fabulous records of pagan antiquity we read of a mirror endowed with properties so rare that, by looking into it, its possessor could discover any object which he wished to see, however remote; and discern, with equal ease, persons and things above, below, behind, and before him. Such a mirror, but infinitely more valuable than this fictitious glass, do we really possess in the Bible. By employing this mirror in a proper manner, we may discern objects and events, past, present, and to come. Here we may contemplate the all-infolding circle of the Eternal Mind, and behold a most perfect portrait of Him whom no mortal eye hath seen, drawn by his own unerring hand. Piercing into the deepest recesses of eternity, we may behold him existing independent and alone, previous to the first exertion of his creating energy. We may see heaven, the habitation of his holiness and glory, 'dark with the excessive brightness' of his presence; and hell, the prison of his justice, with no other light than that which the fiery billows of his wrath cast, 'pale and dreadful,' serving only to render 'darkness visible.' Here, too, we may witness the birth of the world which we inhabit; stand as it were by its cradle, and see it grow up from infancy to manhood, under the forming hand of its Creator. We may see light at his summons starting into existence, and discovering a world of waters without a shore. Controlled by his word, the waters subside, and islands and continents appear, not, as now, clothed with verdure and fertility, but sterile and naked as the sands of Arabia. Again he speaks, and a landscape appears, uniting the various beauties of spring, summer, and autumn, and extending further than the eye can reach. Still all is silent; not even the hum of insects is heard, and the stillness of death pervades creation; till, in an instant, songs burst from every grove, and the startled spectator, raising his eyes from the carpet at his feet, sees the air, the earth, and the sea filled with life and activity in a thousand various forms. Here, too, we may contemplate the origin and infancy of our race; trace from its source to its termination that mighty river of which we compose a part, and see it separating into two great branches, one of which flows back in a circle, and loses itself in the fountain whence it arose, while the other rushes on impetuously in an opposite direction, and precipitates itself into a gulf which has no bottom. In this glass we may also discover the fountain whence flow those torrents of vice and wretchedness which deluge the earth; trace the glorious plan of divine providence running, like a stream of lightning, through the dark and stormy cloud of sublunary events, and see light and order breaking in upon the mighty chaos of crimes, revolutions, wars, and convulsions which have ever distracted the world, and which, to a person unacquainted with the Scriptures, must ever appear to produce no beneficial effect, but to succeed each other without order, and to happen without design. Here, too, we may contemplate ourselves in every conceivable situation and point of view; see our hearts laid open, and all their secret recesses displayed; trace, as on a map, the paths which lead to heaven and to hell; ascertain in which we are walking, and learn what we have been, what we are, and what we shall be hereafter. Above all, we may here see displayed to view that wonderful scheme for the redemption of self-destroyed man into which 'angels desire to look,' and without which the knowledge of God and of ourselves would serve only to plunge us in the depths of despair. We may behold Him, whom we had previously seen creating the world, lying as a helpless infant in a manger, expiring in agonies on the cross, and imprisoned in the tomb. We may see him rising, ascending to heaven, sitting down 'at the right hand of the throne of the Majesty on high,' and there swaying the scepter of universal empire, and ever living to make intercession for his people. Finally, we may see him coming in the clouds of heaven, with power and great glory, to judge the world. We may see the dead, at his command, rising from their graves; standing in awful silence and suspense before his tribunal, and successively advancing, to receive from his lips the sentence which will confer on each of them an eternal weight of glory or consign them forever to the mansions of despair. Such are the scenes and objects which the Scriptures place before us; such the information which they afford. Who will deny that this information is important, or that it is such as we might naturally expect to find in a revelation from God?"

Scripture Precepts—Their Importance.

"Equally important to the present and future happiness of man are the precepts which the Scriptures inculcate. With the greatest clearness and precision, and with an authority to which no other book can pretend, they teach us our duty to God, to our fellow-creatures, and to ourselves. That spiritual kingdom whose laws they promulgate consists in 'righteousness, and peace, and joy in the Holy Ghost;' and were these laws universally obeyed, nothing but righteousness, peace, and holy joy would be found on earth. Should any one deny this, after perusing them attentively, it would prove nothing but the weakness of his understanding or the depravity of his heart. They require us to regard God with filial, and our fellow-creatures with fraternal, affection. They require rulers to 'be just, ruling in the fear of God,' and subjects to 'lead quiet and peaceable lives, in all godliness and honesty.' They require the husband to 'love the wife even as himself,' and the wife 'to reverence her husband.' They require parents to educate their children 'in the nurture and admonition of the Lord;' and children to 'love, honor, and obey' their parents. They require masters to treat their servants with kindness, and servants to be submissive, diligent, and faithful. They require of all, temperance, contentment, and industry;

and stigmatize, as worse than an infidel, him who neglects to provide for the necessities of his family. They provide for the speedy termination of animosities and dissensions, by requiring us to forgive and pray for our enemies whenever we pray for ourselves; and to make reparation to all whom we may have injured, before we presume to appear with our offerings in the presence of God. In a word, they teach us that 'denying ungodliness, and worldly lusts, we should live soberly, righteously, and godly in this present world; looking for that blessed hope, and the glorious appearing of the great God and our Saviour, Jesus Christ.' These duties they require us to perform with constancy and perseverance, on penalty of incurring the everlasting displeasure of our Creator, and its dreadful consequences."

Instructive Examples.

"In addition to these instructions and precepts the Scriptures furnish us with the most instructive examples—examples which most plainly and convincingly teach us both what we must shun and what we are to pursue. On every rock where immortal souls have been wrecked, at the entrance of every path which leads to danger, they show us some self-destroyed wretch, standing like a pillar of salt, to warn succeeding travelers not to approach it; while at the gate and in the path of life they place many divinely instructed and infallible guides, who lead the way, beckon us to follow, and point to the happy mansions in which it ends. Knowing how powerfully we are influenced by the example of those with whom we associate, they introduce us to the society of the most amiable and excellent of our species; make us perfectly acquainted with their characters and pursuits; admit us into not only their closets, but their hearts; unvail to us all their secret springs of action, and show us the hidden source whence they derived wisdom and strength to subdue their sinful propensities and overcome the world. By opening this volume, we may at any time walk in the garden of Eden with Adam; sit in the ark with Noah; share the hospitality, or witness the faith, of Abraham; ascend the mount of God with Moses; unite in the secret devotions of David, or listen to the eloquent and impassioned addresses of St. Paul. Nay more, we may here converse with Him who spake as never man spake; participate with the spirits of the just made perfect in the employment and happiness of heaven, and enjoy sweet communion with the Father of our spirits, through his Son, Jesus Christ. Such is the society to which the Scriptures introduce us;—such the examples which they present to our imitation; requiring us to follow them, 'who through faith and patience inherit the promises;' to walk in the steps of our divine Redeemer; and to be 'followers of God, as dear children.'"

The Bible a Vehicle of Consolation and Hope.

"Nor does this precious volume contain nothing but instructions, precepts, examples, and threatenings. No, it contains also 'strong consolation;' consolation suited to every possible variety and complication of human wretchedness, and of sufficient efficacy to render the soul not only resigned, but joyful, in the lowest depths of adversity;—not only tranquil, but triumphant, in the very jaws of death. It is the appointed vehicle by which the Spirit of God, the promised Comforter, communicates not only his instructions, but his consolations, to the soul. It is, if I may so express it, the body which he assumed in order to converse with men; and he lives and speaks in every line. Hence it is said to 'be quick,' or living, 'and powerful.' Hence its words 'are spirit, and they are life;'—the living, life-giving words of the living God. The consolation which it imparts, and the blessings which it offers, are such as nothing but omnipotent goodness can bestow. It finds us guilty, and freely offers us pardon. It finds us polluted with innumerable defilements, and offers us moral purity. It finds us weak and enslaved, and offers us liberty. It finds us wretched, and offers happiness. It finds us dead, and offers everlasting life. It finds us 'having no hope, and without God in the world,' with nothing before us, 'but a certain fearful looking for of judgment and fiery indignation,' and places glory, and honor, and immortality full in our view; and while it urges us to pursue them, by the exercise of faith in the Redeemer, and 'patient continuance in well doing,' it encourages and animates us in the pursuit by the most condescending offers of assistance, and 'exceedingly great and precious promises;' promises signed by the immutable God, and sealed with the blood of his eternal Son; promises which, one would think, are sufficient to render indolence active and timidity bold. Unfailing pleasures; durable riches; immortal honors; imperishable mansions; an unfading crown; an immovable throne; an everlasting kingdom; an eternal weight of glory; perfect, uninterrupted, never-ending, perpetually-increasing felicity, in the full fruition of God, are the rewards, which these promises assure to all penitent believers. But in vain do we attempt to describe these rewards; for 'eye hath not seen, nor ear heard, neither have entered into the heart of man the things which God hath prepared for them that love him.'"

Consequences Resulting from the Loss of the Bible.

"In proportion to the importance of its contents are the evils which would result from its absence or loss. Destroy this volume, as the enemies of human happiness vainly endeavored to do, and you render us profoundly ignorant of our Creator; of the formation of the world which we inhabit; of the origin and progenitors of our race; of our present duty and future destination; and consign us, through life, to the dominion of fancy, doubt, and conjecture. Destroy this volume, and you rob us of the consolatory expectation, excited by its predictions, that the stormy cloud which has so long hung over a suffering world will at length be scattered, and a brighter day succeed;—you forbid us to hope that the hour is approaching when nation shall no more lift up sword against nation, and righteousness, peace, and holy joy shall universally prevail, and allow us to anticipate nothing but a constant succession of wars, revolutions, crimes, and miseries, terminating only with the end of time. Destroy this volume, and you deprive us, at a single blow, of religion, with all the animating consolations, hopes, and prospects which it affords; and leave us nothing but the liberty of choosing—

miserable alternative!—between the cheerless gloom of infidelity and the monstrous shadows of paganism. Destroy this volume, and you unpeople heaven, bar forever its doors against the wretched posterity of Adam, restore to the king of terrors his fatal sting, bury hope in the same grave which receives our bodies, consign all who have died before us to eternal sleep or endless misery, and allow us to expect nothing at death but a similar fate. In a word, destroy this volume, and you take from us, at once, every thing which prevents existence from becoming of all curses the greatest. You blot out the sun, dry up the ocean, take away the atmosphere of the moral world, and degrade man to a situation from which he may look up with envy to 'the brutes that perish.'"

God's Boundless Empire.

"Think of the innumerable armies of heaven; the perhaps scarcely less numerous hosts of hell; the multitudes of the human race, who have existed, who now exist, and will hereafter exist on earth before the end of time. Then raise your eyes to the numerous suns and worlds around us. Borrow the telescope of the astronomer, and penetrating far into unfathomable recesses of the etherial regions, see new suns, new worlds, still rising into view. Consider that all we can discover is perhaps but a speck, a single sand on the shore, in comparison with what remains undiscovered; that all these innumerable worlds are probably inhabited by immortal beings, and that God's plan of government for this boundless empire must embrace eternity;—consider these things, and then say whether God's purposes, thoughts, and ways must not necessarily be high above ours as the heavens are above the earth, or as his sphere of action exceeds ours. Must not the thoughts and ways of a powerful earthly monarch be far above those of one of his subjects who is employed in manufacturing a pin, or cultivating a few acres of ground? Can such a subject be competent to judge of his sovereign's designs, or even to comprehend them? How far, then, must the thoughts and ways of the eternal Monarch of heaven, the King of kings and Lord of lords, exceed ours; and how little able are we to judge of them, further than the revelation which he has been pleased to give enables us."

The Infinite Contrast.

"God is perfectly benevolent and holy, but we are entirely selfish and sinful. We love sin, that abominable thing which his soul hates. We care for nothing but our own private interest, while his concern is for the interest of the universe. Hence his thoughts, his affections, his maxims and pursuits, must be entirely different from ours. Do not the thoughts and ways of angels differ from those of devils? Do not even the thoughts and ways of good men differ widely from those of the wicked? How infinitely, then, must a perfectly holy God differ from us, polluted worms, who are dead in trespasses and sins! If man at his best estate, and even angels themselves, are incompetent to comprehend God's thoughts and ways, because he is infinitely superior to them in wisdom, and knowledge, and power, how unable must we be, since sin has blinded our understanding, hardened our hearts, defiled the whole man, debased all our faculties, and exposed us to innumerable temptations, prejudices, and mistakes, which lead us to hate and shun the pure light of divine truth, to delude and deceive ourselves, and to form erroneous opinions respecting almost every thing around us; to call evil good, and good evil; to put sweet for bitter, and bitter for sweet; shadows for realities, and realities for shadows; darkness for light, and light for darkness. The pleasures, ways, and pursuits of an oyster, inclosed in its shell, at the bottom of the sea, do not by any means differ so widely from those of the eagle that soars to the clouds and basks in the beams of the sun, as do the thoughts and ways of sinners from those of the infinitely benevolent and holy Monarch of the universe."

The Plan of Redemption above Human Conception.

"In devising a way of salvation, and in providing a Saviour, God's thoughts and ways are very different from ours, and far, very far, above them. We should have thought, that if God intended to save sinners, he would bring them to repentance and save them at once; or, at least, after suffering them to endure for a season the bitter consequences of their own folly and disobedience. We never should have thought of providing for them a Redeemer; still less should we have thought of proposing that God's only Son, the Creator and Preserver of all things, should undertake this office; and least of all should we have expected that he would, for this purpose, think it necessary to become man. If we had been informed that this was necessary, and it had been left for us to fix the time and manner of his appearing, we should have concluded that he ought to come soon after the fall; to be born of illustrious parents; to make his appearance on earth in all the splendor, pomp, and glory imaginable; to overcome all opposition by a display of irresistible power; to ride through the world in triumph, conquering and to conquer. Such were the expectations of the Jews; and such, most probably, would have been ours. But never should we have thought of his being born of a virgin in abject circumstances; born in a stable, cradled in a manger, living for many years as a humble artificer; wandering, despised, and rejected of men, without a place to lay his head, and finally arraigned, tried, condemned, and crucified, as a vile malefactor, that he might thus expiate our sins, and by his death give life to the world. Had we been forewarned of these things we should have considered them as too foolish, incredible, and absurd to obtain the smallest credit; and instead of thinking them cunningly devised, should have thought them very clumsily-contrived fables, unworthy of the least notice or regard. And thus in fact they have appeared, and do still appear, to the wise men of this world; 'For,' says the apostle, 'the cross of Christ is foolishness to them that perish.'"

The Folly of Judging of God by Our Limited Knowledge of Him.

"An ancient writer tells us of a man who, having a house for sale, carried a brick to market to exhibit as a specimen. You may perhaps smile at his folly in supposing that any purchaser would or could judge of a whole house, which he never saw, by so small a part of it. But are we not guilty of much greater folly in attempting to form an opinion of God's conduct from that little part of it which we are able to discover? In order to form a correct opinion of it we ought to have a correct view of the whole; we ought to see the whole extent and duration of God's kingdom; to be equal to him in wisdom, knowledge, power, and goodness; in one word, we ought to be God ourselves."

The Reasonableness of Faith.

"The very essence of faith consists in a humble, docile, childlike temper, which disposes us to embrace, without objecting or disputing, every thing which God reveals; and to believe that all his words and dispensations are, even though we cannot see how, perfectly right. Christians are often ridiculed for exercising this implicit faith in God, and believing what they cannot fully comprehend. But we appeal to every one present whether in so doing they do not act reasonably. If God's ways and thoughts are high above ours, ought we not implicitly to believe all his declarations; to believe that all he says and does is perfectly right? Is it not reasonable for children thus to believe their parents? for a sick man to trust in a skillful physician? for a passenger unacquainted with navigation to trust to the master of the vessel? for a blind man to follow his guide? If so, then it is much more reasonable for such ignorant, short-sighted, fallible creatures as we are to submit and trust implicitly to an infinitely wise, good, and infallible Being; and when any of his words or works appear wrong, to ascribe it to our own ignorance, blindness, or prejudice, rather than to suppose that there is any thing wrong in him."

The World Created for Christ.

"This world was created for Christ. It was created, in the first place, for the display of his natural perfections; for the display of creative wisdom and power to angelic minds. Accordingly we are told, that when he laid the foundation of the earth these sons of God sung his praises together and shouted for joy. It was created, in the second place, to serve as a stage on which he might display to all intelligent creatures his moral perfections, and especially on which he might display the glories of an incarnate God, and act the wonders of the great scheme of redemption. It was also created to be a province of his dominions, the place where his mediatorial kingdom should be set up, and where his chosen people should be prepared by his grace for admission into his kingdom above. When it shall have served for all these purposes, when Christ shall have done with it, the end of its creation will of course be accomplished, and then the earth will of course be destroyed. Then the visible heavens, being on fire, will be dissolved, and the elements shall melt with fervent heat, and earth, with the works thereof, shall be burned up, and its destruction, no less than its creation, will display the perfection of its Creator."

The Human Race Created for Christ.

"The human race was created that Christ might display his infinite condescension in assuming their nature. In order to display this condescension in the most clear and striking manner, it was necessary that he should assume the nature of the lowest class of rational beings—a nature subject to many evils and infirmities—a nature in which he might become visible, and act and speak in a visible manner. Had he taken the nature of angels into union with his own, it would have been a less wonderful act of condescension, nor could the act have been made equally apparent; for angels are spiritual beings, and the divine nature of Christ is spiritual, and the union of two beings purely spiritual could not be made to appear so evidently as the union of a spiritual being with our nature, which is partly material. We can conceive of God manifest in the flesh, much more clearly than of God manifest in an angel. We may further observe, that a part of the designed display of Christ's condescension consisted in his becoming subject to hunger, thirst, weariness, and pain, and in his dying in the nature which he assumed. He was to appear in the likeness of frail, sinful flesh. But angels are subject to none of these infirmities. They can neither hunger, nor thirst, nor be weary, nor die. Christ could not therefore appear in the nature of a sinful angel as he could in the likeness of sinful flesh. Hence, in order to the full display of his condescension, it was necessary that rational beings should be created inferior to angels, or in other words, such beings as those who compose the human race.

"The human race was created that Christ might display all his perfections which men or angels have ever seen. The glory of God appears most resplendent and full-orbed in the face of Jesus Christ. Power, wisdom, goodness, justice, truth, love, mercy, grace, and faithfulness here shine with united luster in full brilliancy, nor can we determine which appears most glorious or lovely. In God's other works, some drops of that overflowing fountain, some rays from the infinite sun, are seen; but in the work of redemption, in the glorious Gospel of the blessed God, the whole Deity, the whole fullness of the Godhead, flows out in one boundless tide; a tide which will forever fill to the brim every holy mind, and in which all holy beings will bathe with rapturous delight through eternity."

A Proof of Christ's Divinity.

"The assertion that all things were created by Christ, is sufficient to prove his divinity; for he who built all things must be God. But when, in addition to this, we are assured that all things were created *for* him, we have a proof of his divinity which is, if possible, still more convincing; for, supposing for a moment that God could and would employ a creature to perform the work of creation, can we suppose that he would permit that creature to create all things for himself, for his own pleasure and glory? Surely not. God has said, I am Jehovah, that is my name, and my glory I will not give to another. The glory of creating all things, of upholding all things, of governing all things, of redeeming and judging the world, is all given to Christ. Nay more, all things were created on purpose that the glory resulting from all might be given to Christ. If, then, Christ be not Jehovah, Jehovah's glory is all given to another, and nothing remains to himself. But view Christ as God manifest in the flesh, and the difficulty vanishes.

Then in honoring the Son, we honor the Father. Then we shall understand why all the inhabitants of heaven are represented as ascribing joint glories to Him that sitteth on the throne, and to the Lamb. By him that sitteth on the throne, is meant the divine, and by the Lamb slain, the human nature of Christ. Both are inseparably united, and Christ's human nature is the temple in which he will be worshiped by saints and angels through eternity."

The Cross the Central Object of Creation.

"From this subject we may learn, that, if we would view every object in its true light, and rightly estimate its nature and design, we must consider it with reference to Christ and his cross. To the cross of Christ all eternity has looked forward; to the cross of Christ all eternity will look back. The cross of Christ was, if I may so express it, the first object which existed in the divine mind; and with reference to this great object all other objects were created. With reference to the same object they are still preserved. With reference to the same object every event that takes place in heaven, earth, and hell is directed and overruled. Surely, then, this object ought to engage our undivided attention. We ought to regard this world merely as a stage on which the cross of Christ was to be erected, and the great drama of the crucifixion acted. We ought to regard the celestial luminaries merely as lamps, by the light of which this stupendous spectacle may be beheld. We ought to view angels, men, and devils as subordinate actors on the stage, and all the commotions and revolutions of the world as subservient to this one grand design. Separate any part of this creation, or any event that has ever taken place, from its relation to Christ, and it dwindles into insignificancy. No sufficient reason can be assigned for its existence, and it appears to have been formed in vain. But when viewed as connected with him, every thing becomes important; every thing then appears to be a part of one grand, systematic, harmonious whole; a whole worthy of Him that formed it. It was such a view of things which led the apostle to exclaim, 'God forbid that I should glory, save in the cross of our Lord Jesus Christ.'"

Introduction of Sin into the World.

"The introduction of sin is thus described by the inspired historian: 'And when the woman saw that the tree was good for food, and that it was pleasant to the eyes, and a tree to be desired to make one wise, she took of the fruit thereof, and did eat, and gave also unto her husband with her; and he did eat.'

"In this account of the conduct of the first sinner we see, in the first place, *selfishness*, or a preference of herself to God; for had she loved him supremely, she would have chosen to obey his commands rather than to gratify herself. This must ever be the first sin; for so long as any creature prefers God to himself, he will choose to please God rather than to gratify himself; of course, he will avoid every sin, and no temptation will induce him to offend his Maker, while he loves him with all his heart. But so soon as any creature begins to prefer himself to God, he will choose to gratify himself rather than please his Maker; and will of course commit any sin which promises him self-gratification or self-aggrandizement.

"The second thing to be noticed in the conduct of the first sinner is *pride*. She saw that it was a tree to be desired to make one wise; that is, she fancied, as the tempter had asserted, that it would cause her to become as a god, knowing good and evil. Now this wish was the effect of pride, and it was accompanied by the inseparable attendant of pride, discontent—discontent with the situation in which God had placed her. This sin is the natural consequence of selfishness; for as soon as we begin to prefer ourselves to God, we shall wish to put ourselves in the place of God, and to rise above the sphere of action which he has assigned us, and to grasp at those things which he has not thought proper to bestow.

"The third thing in her conduct, the third step in the way of sin, was *sensuality*, or a disposition to be governed and guided by her senses, and to seek their gratification in an unlawful manner. She saw that the fruit of the tree was good for food, and pleasant to the eyes. Here was something to gratify two of the senses, those of tasting and seeing; and this gratification, though forbidden, she was determined to enjoy. The influence of sin, which had hitherto existed only in the passions of the mind, began to extend itself to the appetites of the body, and by this influence they were inflamed to such a degree that they prompted her to disregard the dictates of reason and conscience, and the commands of God.

"The next step in the fatal way was *unbelief;* a distrust of God's word, and a consequent belief of the tempter's suggestions. God had said, 'In the day thou eatest, thou shalt surely die.' This threatening she now disbelieved. The tempter said, 'God doth know that ye shall not surely die; but in the day that ye eat of it your eyes shall be opened, and ye shall be as gods, knowing good and evil.' This falsehood she did believe. This disbelief of God's word, and belief of Satan's suggestions, was the natural consequence of sins already mentioned; for when the passions and appetites are inflamed by the influence of sin, they immediately blind the understanding in such a manner that it can no longer discover the evidence which attends divine truth, nor the force of those arguments and motives which should induce us to obey it. Every thing which is urged against a compliance with our sinful inclinations then appears weak and groundless, while those sophistical reasonings which favor their gratification seem powerful and conclusive. In this state, therefore, the mind is completely prepared to disbelieve the God of truth, whose word opposes and forbids its sinful inclinations, and to believe the father of lies, who urges us to gratify them. And this, in fact, is the source of all the unbelief which prevails in the world; for the evidence attending God's word is so convincing that men never would, never could, disbelieve, did they not first wish to disbelieve it.

"But to proceed: God's threatenings being thus disbelieved, and the lies of the tempter embraced as truth, every barrier which opposed Eve's progress was removed, and the sinful propensities that have been mentioned broke out in open, actual disobedience. She took of the fruit of the tree and did eat.

Thus she made a full entrance into that way, which wicked men have ever since trodden. The first step was selfishness; the second, pride; the third, sensuality; the fourth, unbelief; and the last, actual, open, willful disobedience."

The Broad and Narrow Way.

" All along the path He has set up way-marks with the inscription, *This road conducts to hell;* while a hand, pointing to a narrow path, which opens to the right, has written over it, *This path leads to heaven.* Lest you should be so occupied by the cares and business of the world as to pass these way-marks without noticing them, he has placed at each of them a watchman to warn thoughtless travelers, and to call their attention to these inscriptions; and lest any should rush on without stopping to hear their warnings, he has placed the Sabbath, like a gate, across their path to compel them to stop till it be opened, and to hear the warning voice. To one of these gates, my impenitent hearers, you have now come. It has compelled you to pause, a few moments, in your sinful career; and to pass away the time till the Sabbath is gone you have come to the house of prayer. Here is a watchman appointed by your Creator. I stand to call your attention to the inscriptions which he has recorded; to the marks which he has drawn of the various paths in which men walk. Sinner, stop! I have a message to thee from God. See it written with his own finger, *This broad road leads to destruction!* Look at the map which he has drawn. See here a way opening out of the gates of paradise, leading on, broad and crooked, through the mazes of the world, and terminating at the iron gate of the bottomless abyss. See written on its margin, *Destruction and misery are in this path; it leads down to the chambers of eternal death.* This is the path of the openly irreligious. See close by its side another path, opened by the first murderer. See written on it, *There is a way which seemeth right unto a man, but the end thereof is death.* This is the path of the self-righteous, the formalist, the hypocrite, and, like the other, leads to death. Sinners, you have seen this path; it is yours; it is the path in which you are now walking. You have also seen its end. Let it be yours then no longer. This day, this hour, forsake it, and enter that path which opens to the right hand. Here you may see it; and the strait gate which leads into it opens to every one who knocks. Close by its side stands a cross; rays of light darting from it illuminate and mark out the path. Just within the gate stands an invisible guide with extended hand, offering to lead, to assist, to support you; while at the termination are the wide-open gates of heaven, from which issue a flood of glory, which you will discover more and more clearly as you approach them. O then, enter this path! Strive, strive to enter in at the strait gate!"

How to See our Sins as God Sees Them.

"'Thou hast set our iniquities before thee, our secret sins in the light of thy countenance.' That is, our iniquities or open transgressions, and our secret sins, the sins of our hearts, are placed, as it were, full before God's face, immediately under his eye; and he sees them in the pure, clear, all-disclosing light of his own holiness and glory. Now if we would see our sins as they appear to him—that is, as they really are—if we would see their number, blackness, and criminality, and the malignity and desert of every sin, we must place ourselves and our sins in the center of that circle which is irradiated by the light of his countenance; where all his infinite perfections are clearly displayed; where his concentrated glories blaze, and burn, and dazzle with insufferable brightness. And in order to this, we must, in thought, leave our dark and sinful world, where God is unseen and almost forgotten, and where, consequently, the evil of sinning against him cannot be fully perceived, and mount up to heaven, the peculiar habitation of his holiness and glory, where he does not, as here, conceal himself behind the vail of his works and of second causes, but shines forth the unvailed God, and is seen as he is.

"Let us then, my hearers, attempt this adventurous flight. Let us follow the path by which our blessed Saviour ascended to heaven, and soar upward to the great capital of the universe, to the palace and the throne of its greater King. As we rise, the earth fades from our view; now we leave worlds, and suns, and systems behind us. Now we reach the utmost limits of creation; now the last star disappears, and no ray of created light is seen. But a new light now begins to dawn and brighten upon us. It is the light of heaven, which pours in a flood of glory from its wide-open gates, spreading continual meridian day far and wide through the regions of etherial space. Passing swiftly onward through this flood of day, the songs of heaven begin to burst upon your ears, and voices of celestial sweetness, yet loud as the sound of many waters and of mighty thunderings, are heard, exclaiming, 'Alleluia! for the Lord God omnipotent reigneth. Blessing, and glory, and honor, and power, be unto Him that sitteth on the throne, and to the Lamb, forever.' A moment more, and you have passed the gates; you are in the midst of the city, you are in the immediate presence of God, and all his glories are blazing around you like a consuming fire! Flesh and blood cannot support it; your bodies dissolve into their original dust, but your immortal souls remain, and stand naked spirits before the great Father of Spirits. Nor in losing their tenements of clay have they lost the powers of perception. No; they are now all eye, all ear; nor can you close the eyelids of the soul, to shut out for a moment the dazzling, overpowering splendors which surround you, and which appear like light condensed, like glory which may be felt. You see, indeed, no form or shape; and yet your whole souls perceive, with intuitive clearness and certainty, the immediate, awe-inspiring presence of Jehovah. You see no countenance; and yet you feel as if a countenance of awful majesty, in which all the perfections of divinity shone forth, were beaming upon you wherever you turn. You see no eye; and yet a piercing, heart-searching eye, an eye of omniscient purity, every glance of which goes through your souls like a flash of lightning, seems to look upon you from every point of surrounding space. You feel as if enveloped in an atmosphere, or plunged in an ocean, of existence, intelligence, perfection, and glory; an ocean, of which your laboring minds can take in only a drop; an ocean, the depth of which you cannot fathom, and the breadth of which you can never fully explore. But while you feel utterly unable to comprehend this infinite Being, your views of him, so far as they extend, are perfectly clear and distinct. You have the most vivid perceptions, the most deeply graven impressions, of an infinite, eternal, spotless mind, in which the images of all things, past, present, and to come, are most harmoniously seen, arranged in the most perfect order, and defined with the nicest accuracy;—of a mind, which wills with infinite ease, but whose volitions are attended by a power omnipotent and irresistible, and which sows worlds, suns, and systems through the fields of space with far more facility than the husbandman scatters his seed upon the earth;—of a mind, whence have flowed all the streams which ever watered any part of the universe with life, intelligence, holiness, or happiness, and which is still full, overflowing, and inexhaustible. You perceive also, with equal clearness and certainty, that this infinite, eternal, omnipotent, omniscient, all-wise, all-creating mind is perfectly and essentially holy, a pure flame of holiness, and that, as such, he regards sin with unutterable, irreconcilable detestation and abhorrence. With a voice which reverberates through the wide expanse of his dominions you hear him saying, as the Sovereign and Legislator of the universe, Be ye holy; for I, the Lord your God, am holy. And you see his throne surrounded, you see heaven filled, by those only who perfectly obey this command. You see thousands of thousands, and ten thousand times ten thousand of angels and archangels, pure, exalted, glorious intelligences, who reflect his perfect image, burn like flames of fire with zeal for his glory, and seem to be so many concentrations of wisdom, knowledge, holiness, and love; a fit retinue for the thrice holy Lord of hosts, whose holiness and all-filling glory they unceasingly proclaim.

"And now, my hearers, if you are willing to see your sins in their true colors—if you would rightly estimate their number, magnitude, and criminality—bring them into the hallowed place where nothing is seen but the whiteness of unsullied purity, and the splendors of uncreated glory; where the sun itself would appear only as a dark spot; and there, in the midst of this circle of seraphic intelligences, with the infinite God pouring all the light of his countenance round you, review your lives, contemplate your offenses, and see how they appear. Recollect that the God in whose presence you are is the Being who forbids sin, the Being of whose eternal law sin is the transgression, and against whom every sin is committed."

The Righteousness of Christ—How Obtained.

"How may an interest in the righteousness of Christ be obtained? I answer, It cannot be purchased, for it is infinitely above all price, nor will he sell his favors. It cannot be merited; for the best merit nothing but destruction. It must come as a free gift. But to whom will it be given? I answer, It is freely and unconditionally offered to all who will accept it by faith. None, however, will ever accept it but those who see that they have no righteousness of their own to plead. Hence our Saviour informs us that publicans and harlots, the very refuse of society, will sooner enter the kingdom of heaven than those who, like the Pharisees, trust in themselves that they are righteous. Hence, also, we find that the promises of the Gospel are ever made to the poor in spirit, to the self-condemned sinner, to the mourners for sin, and to the penitent and contrite heart. Such characters see and feel that they have nothing of their own to plead; nothing which they dare place in the balance. They see, as did the apostle, that in them there dwells no good thing; they see that they are wholly unworthy of God's favor, and deserve nothing but death at his hands; they see that if they ever are saved, they must be saved by free, sovereign grace. Hence they are willing to throw themselves at Christ's feet, and resign themselves entirely to his disposal. They are willing to receive him by faith, as he is freely offered in the Gospel, and to depend on his righteousness and intercession alone for salvation. But never will the self-righteous sinner do this; never will he submit to be saved in this humbling way. He may, indeed, be willing that Christ should supply the deficiencies of his own imaginary righteousness, and atone for the few trifling sins which he has committed; but he is resolved to have at least part of the glory of his salvation; he will not depend on Christ alone, and therefore in reality does not depend upon him at all, nor will he receive any benefit from him; for our Saviour will have no partners in this work. He will have all the glory, or we never shall join in the song of the redeemed."

Thoughts are Words in the Ear of God.

"We must leave every one to reflect, as he pleases, on the atheistical thoughts, the impious and profane thoughts, the impure, covetous, vain, foolish, and absurd thoughts, which have passed through his mind and been entertained there. And while you reflect on this, remember that thoughts are the language of disembodied spirits; that thoughts are words, in the ear of God; and that our guilt, in his sight, is no less great than if we had actually given utterance to every thought which has lodged in our minds. Agreeably, we find our Saviour answering the *thoughts* of those around him, just as he would if they had expressed them in words; and in many passages, God charges sinners with saying what, it appears, they only thought. In the ear of Jehovah, then, our thoughts have a tongue; and what he hears them say we may learn from the inspired declaration. Every imagination of the thoughts of man's heart is evil continually."

Sin an Infinite Evil.

"Every sin is an infinite evil, because it tends to produce infinite mischief. Let us trace this tendency. Suppose all the universe to be holy and happy. A thought or feeling tending to produce sin rises in the breast of some one creature. This thought or feeling is indulged. It gains strength by indulgence; gradually it extends its influence over the faculties of the mind, enslaves the whole man, and prompts him to disobey God. Now did it proceed no further, it would still be an infinite evil, for it has depraved and ruined an immortal being—a being who, but for sin, would have been eternally happy; but who must, in consequence of sin, be forever miserable. But it will not stop there. The being thus ruined by sin will become a tempter, and seduce his fellow-beings; and they, in turn, will tempt others; and, unless God prevent, the infection will spread through the created universe, transforming holy beings into devils, and all worlds into hell! Such, my hearers, is the tendency of sin. Do any deny it? We appeal to facts. The whole universe was once holy and happy. A thought or feeling tending to produce sin rose in the breast of Satan. He indulged it, and it ruined him. It transformed him from an archangel into a devil. He tempted other angels, and they became devils. He tempted our first parents; they complied, sinned, and became the parents of a sinful race. Thus all the sin and all the misery in the universe, all on earth and all in hell, may be traced back to one sinful thought or feeling entertained, at first, in a single breast; and this sin and misery would be far greater than they are, were it not for the restraining power and grace of God. Such, then, is the tendency of sin, of every sin; and such effects it would produce, did not God prevent. A sinful thought, or feeling, is like a spark of fire. It seems but a little thing, and is easily extinguished; but it has a tendency to consume and destroy; and let it have room and opportunity to exert itself, let it be fed by combustible materials, and fanned by the winds, and it would destroy every thing destructible in the universe. Similar is the tendency of sin; and who, then, will say that it is not an infinite evil?"

Everlasting Punishment—Argument.

"If our sins are infinite in number and criminality, then, of course, they deserve an infinite or everlasting punishment; such a punishment as God threatens in his word. There is scarcely any truth which men are more disposed to deny than this. They contend that it cannot be just for God to punish sins, committed during the short period of our residence on earth, with everlasting misery. But let us examine this objection. Do you not all acknowledge that a murderer may justly be put to death? Yet he might have been employed but a moment in committing that murder. The fact is, in other cases we never think of inquiring how much time was spent in the commission of any crime. We consider only the nature and magnitude of the crime, and its effects upon society. If the crime is great, and its effects highly pernicious, we conclude at once that it deserves a severe punishment. Now sin is an infinite evil; the effects which it tends to produce are infinitely mischievous. Of course, it deserves an infinite punishment. And permit me to add, that complaints of the severity of this punishment come with a very ill grace from impenitent sinners; for they will persist in sin notwithstanding this punishment. It seems, then, that instead of being too severe, it is not sufficiently severe to deter them from sin. If men will now violate God's laws, what would they do had he annexed to their violation only a temporary punishment?

"If sin deserves an infinite punishment, then it is perfectly right that God should inflict such a punishment upon sinners. It is no impeachment of his character, no reflection upon his goodness, to say that he will inflict it. This evidently follows as a necessary consequence from what has been said, for justice consists in treating every one as he deserves to be treated; and if sinners deserve an endless punishment, then it is perfectly just and right for God to inflict such a punishment upon them.

"If it is just that God should inflict such a punishment upon impenitent sinners then he must inflict it; he is bound by the strongest obligations to inflict it, for he must do what is just and right. And if it is just and right thus to punish impenitent sinners, then it cannot be just and right not to do it. To spare them would not be treating them as they deserve, and justice consists in treating them according to their deserts. In a word, it is as much an act of injustice to spare the guilty as it would be to condemn the innocent. This God himself teaches us in his word. He that justifieth the wicked, and he that condemneth the just, even they both are an abomination to the Lord. And will the just God do that which he declares to be an abomination in his sight? The Judge of all the earth must do right."

The Folly and Absurdity of Pride.

"How foolish, how absurd, how ruinous, how blindly destructive of its own object, does pride appear! By attempting to soar, it only plunges itself in the mire; and, while endeavoring to erect for itself a throne, it undermines the ground on which it stands and digs its own grave. It plunged Satan from heaven into hell; it banished our first parents from paradise; and it will, in a similar manner, ruin all who indulge it. It keeps us in ignorance of God, shuts us out from his favor, prevents us from resembling him, deprives us, in this world, of all the honor and happiness which communion with him would confer; and in the next, unless previously hated, repented of, and renounced, will bar forever against us the door of heaven, and close upon us the gates of hell. O, then, my friends, beware, above all things, beware of pride! Beware, lest you indulge it imperceptibly; for it is, perhaps, of all sins, the most secret, subtle, and insinuating. That you may detect it, remember that he only who seeks after God in his appointed way, is humble; and that all who neglect thus to seek him are most certainly proud in heart, and, consequently, an abomination unto the Lord."

Why the Remembrance of God is Painful.

"If we are condemned it will be painful to remember that God is our Creator and Benefactor, for the remembrance will be attended with a consciousness of base ingratitude. It will be painful to think of him as Lawgiver, for such thoughts will remind us that we have broken his law. It will be painful to think of his holiness; for if he is holy, he must hate our sins, and be angry with us as sinners: of his justice and truth; for these perfections make it necessary that he should fulfill his threatenings and punish us for our sins. It will be painful to think of his omniscience; for this perfection makes him acquainted with our most secret offenses, and renders it impossible to conceal them from his view: of his omnipresence; for the constant presence of an invisible witness must be disagreeable to those who wish to indulge their sinful propensities. It will be painful to think of his power; for it enables him to restrain or destroy, as he pleases: of his sovereignty; for sinners always hate to see themselves in the hands of a sovereign God: of his eternity and immutability; for from his possessing these perfections, it follows that he will never alter the threatenings which he has denounced against sinners, and that he will always live to execute them. It will be painful to think of him as Judge; for we shall feel that as sinners, we have no reason to expect a favorable sentence from his lips. It will even be painful to think of the perfect goodness and excellence of his character; for his goodness leaves us without excuse in rebelling against him, and makes our sins appear exceedingly sinful. Thus it is evident that the consciousness of sin committed and guilt contracted must render the government and all the perfections of God objects of terror and anxiety to the sinner, and, of course, the recollection of them to him must be painful."

The Eternity of Those who Forget God.

"No sooner do men leave the body than that holy, just, eternal Being, of whom every remembrance troubled them, bursts at once, in all his burning glories, upon their aching sight! And if merely to remember him were painful, what must the sight of him be? Think of a wretch deprived of his eyelids, and condemned to gaze unremittingly at a scorching sun, till the balls of sight were withered and dried up, and you will have some faint conception of the feelings of a sinful creature doomed to gaze, through eternity, at the, to him, heart-withering perfections of that God, who is a consuming fire to all the workers of iniquity."

Various Means Employed to Save Sinners.

"God has employed a great variety of means to persuade sinners to embrace the Gospel. He has sent judgments to subdue and mercies to melt them; arguments to convince and motives to persuade them; threatenings to terrify and invitations to allure them. In different parts of his word he has exhibited divine truth in every possible variety of form. In one place it is presented plainly to the mind in the form of doctrines; in another, it is couched under the vail of some instructive and striking parable; in a third, it is presented to us in a garb of types and shadows; in a fourth, it is illustrated by the most beautiful figures; and, in a fifth, exemplified in some well-drawn character or interesting portion of history. In a word, he addresses us, by turns, in language the most plain and simple, the most grand and commanding, the most pointed and energetic, the most sublime and beautiful, the most impressive and affecting, the most pathetic and melting. God and men, this world and the next, time and eternity, death and judgment, heaven and hell,—these rise successively to our view, portrayed in the most vivid colors, and exhibited in various forms, while the whole created universe is put in requisition to furnish images for the illustration of these awful realities; and the infinite wisdom of God himself is exerted, if I may so express it, to the utmost in devising and employing the most suitable means to impress them upon our minds, and cause them to affect our hearts. Thus he has addressed himself, by turns, to our eyes and to our ears, to our understandings and consciences, to our imaginations and to our affections, to our hopes and to our fears; and caused divine truth to seek admission to our minds by every avenue, to try every possible way of access."

Caprice of Sinners in Judging Christians.

"If professors of religion and its ministers live as they ought, 'soberly, righteously, and godly,' they are said to be too rigid, superstitious, righteous overmuch. If, on the contrary, they are of a more cheerful, social turn, the world immediately exclaims, These are your professors, your saints; but in what respect do they differ from others? If they are punctual in attending public and private meetings for religious worship, spend much time in prayer, and devote a considerable portion of their property to charitable and religious purposes, it is immediately said that religion makes men idle, and negligent of their families. If, on the other hand, they are industrious, frugal, and attentive to business, they are no less quickly accused of loving the world as well as their neighbors, who make no pretensions to religion. If a minister reasons with his hearers in a cool, dispassionate manner, and labors to convince their understandings, he is accused of being dry and formal in his preaching, or of not believing what he says. If another preaches in a more lively, animated strain, clearly proclaims the terrors of the Lord, and warns his hearers to fly from the wrath to come, he is charged with endeavoring to work on men's passions, and to frighten them into religion. If he insists much on the doctrines of Christianity, the necessity of faith, and the impossibility of being justified by our own works, he is accused of undervaluing morality, and representing the practice of good works as needless. If, on the other hand, he clearly exhibits the pure morality of the Gospel, inculcates holiness of heart and life, and states the dreadful consequences of neglecting it, he is charged with driving men to despair by unreasonable strictness and severity. Thus in almost innumerable ways men ascribe their neglect of the Gospel to the faults of its professors, or to something in the manner in which it is preached, and thus harden themselves and others in unbelief."

The Natural Affections Christianized.

"But while all will allow that a naturally bad temper needs to be sanctified, there are many who by no means suppose that tempers naturally amiable equally need sanctification. But if we take the Scriptures for our guide, a little reflection will convince us that this is actually the case. The Scriptures teach, that without holiness no man shall see the Lord. But there is nothing of the nature of holiness in a naturally amiable temper. Holiness consists in conformity to the law of God. But persons who possess the temper of which we are speaking naturally pay no more regard to the law of God than others do. They are not gentle, kind, and affectionate, because God requires them to be, or because they wish to please him; for they often live without God in the world. They do not naturally love prayer, or the

Bible, or the Saviour, or any part of religion; but it is as difficult to draw their attention and affections to these subjects as it would be if their tempers were unamiable. The young ruler who asked our Saviour what he should do to inherit eternal life, evidently possessed a naturally amiable disposition. Yet when Christ said to him, Take up thy cross and follow me, he was no more willing to obey than were the scribes and Pharisees. Hence we find that when our Saviour asserted the necessity of regeneration, repentance, and faith, he represented them as alike necessary to all, and made no exception in favor of amiable characters. It is therefore evident that, in his view, such characters need sanctification no less than other men. Their natural affections must be *Christianized*, if I may so express it, or baptized by the Holy Spirit, before they can possess any thing of the nature of true religion. Until this is done, they are no more Christians, merely for possessing such affections, than an animal of a mild and tractable disposition is a Christian."

An Important Distinction.

"Those who are sanctified and those who are not differ very widely, even in those respects in which they seem to be alike. For instance, both classes eat and drink; but he who is sanctified eats and drinks to the glory of God, while the unconverted sinner eats and drinks to gratify himself. Both classes love their children; but in unsanctified persons parental love is a merely animal affection, inordinate, wrongly directed, and not subordinate to the love of God; in those who are sanctified, on the contrary, it is a holy affection rightly directed, regulated by God's law, and in subordination to his love. Both classes may pity and relieve the distressed; but the former are led to do this by a blind animal instinct, which is capricious, irregular, and partial in its operations; while the compassion of the latter is elevated and ennobled by divine grace, and resembles that which glowed in the bosom of our Saviour. Both classes may possess amiable tempers and live correct moral lives; but the amiable tempers of the former, and the morality which they sometimes produce, do not spring from religion; they are not influenced by religion; nor have they any reference either to God and his law or to Christ and his Gospel. The temper and morals of the latter, on the contrary, spring from religion in the heart; they are the effects of God's law written in the heart; their love to men flows wholly from love to God; their morality is true Christian morality, and they are constrained by the love of Christ to imitate his example. In short, the governing motives, the main-springs of action, in the sanctified and unsanctified man, are totally different; and since God looks at motives—since, in his view, the character of every action is determined by its motive—it is evident that the same actions which are good when performed by a good man, may be altogether wrong when performed by a sinner. The sanctified and the unsanctified may apparently resemble each other in temper and conduct, and yet the latter may be justly punished, while the former are rewarded."

"He shall See of the Travail of his Soul and be Satisfied."

"This prediction has already been partially fulfilled. Already has our Redeemer seen much of the fruit of his sufferings. Our once barren world, watered by his tears and his blood, has already produced a large harvest of righteousness and salvation. His cross, like Aaron's rod, has budded and blossomed, and begun to bear precious, incorruptible fruit. From his cross sprang all the religious knowledge, all the real goodness, all the true happiness which have existed among mortals since the fall. On his cross, which, like the ladder seen by Jacob in vision, unites heaven and earth, myriads of immortal beings who were sinking into the bottomless abyss have ascended to the celestial mansions;—other myriads, now alive, are following them in the ascent. In the patriarchs, prophets, and pious Israelites; in the apostles and other primitive preachers of Christianity; in the numerous converts who, by their instrumentality, were turned from darkness to light; in all the truly pious individuals who have since existed among men; in all the real Christians who are now on earth, our Redeemer has seen the fruits of his sufferings. In every real Christian now present he sees one of these fruits; sees a soul which has been redeemed by his blood from endless wretchedness and despair, and made an heir of glory and honor and immortality. O then, how much, how very much, has he already seen effected in fulfillment of the promise before us! How many immortal souls have been plucked as brands from everlasting burnings! How many individuals have been instructed, sanctified, pardoned, comforted, and made more than conquerors through Him who loved them! How many pious families have rejoiced together in his goodness! How many Churches have been planted, watered, and made to flourish! How much happiness have the members of all these Churches enjoyed in life, in death, and in heaven! What an exceedingly great and almost innumerable multitude of happy spirits, redeemed from among men, are now surrounding the throne of God and the Lamb! And even while I speak, the number of these happy spirits, and the harvest which springs from a Saviour's sufferings, is increasing. Even while I speak, sinners in different parts of the world are flocking into the kingdom of God. Even while I speak, immortal souls, washed in a Saviour's blood, sanctified by his Spirit, and just made victorious over the last enemy, death, are entering heaven from the four quarters of the globe, and commencing their everlasting song, 'Now unto Him that loved us, and washed us from our sins in his own blood, be glory and dominion for ever and ever.'

"And while our thrice blessed Redeemer has thus seen, and still sees, the happiness of human beings increased by his sufferings, he has also seen, and still sees, the glory of God augmented in an equal degree. He has seen millions who were once enemies to his Father, transformed to friends; he has seen millions who once blindly worshiped false gods, and ascribed to them the glory of creating, preserving, and governing the world, turning from their worthless idols to worship the only living and true God, who made heaven and earth. He has seen his Father's law obeyed and honored by multitudes, who, but for him, would have continued to trample it under foot. He has seen ten thousand times ten thousand of prayers and ascriptions of praise ascending from a world which, but for his interposition, would never have offered one of these acceptable spiritual sacrifices to his Father. He has seen the eternal throne surrounded, and him who sits upon it adored, by almost countless multitudes who were once dishonoring God on earth, and preparing to blaspheme him in hell. In fine, he has seen his religion flying through the world as on angel's wings, scattering blessings wherever she comes, and loudly proclaiming peace on earth, good-will to men, and glory to God in the highest. Surely, then, the prediction before us has already been partially fulfilled."

The Happiness of Jesus Christ.

"Estimate as far as you are able the amount of happiness which a single individual will enjoy in heaven during a whole eternity. Proceed to multiply this amount of happiness by the almost countless number of the redeemed. Then recollect that Jesus Christ has said, 'It is more blessed to give than to receive;' that is, there is more blessedness, or happiness, in giving than in receiving. Now Jesus Christ gives, and saints and angels receive, all the happiness which creatures will ever enjoy in heaven. Of course, as the giver of this happiness is more blessed, more happy, than all the receivers, could we then concentrate in one bosom all the happiness which is enjoyed by all the saints and angels in heaven it would still be inferior, far inferior, to that which is enjoyed by

Jesus Christ alone. Christian, does not your heart exult to hear of the happiness which your Saviour enjoys? Does it not labor, and swell almost to bursting, while vainly attempting to fathom that bottomless tide of felicity which every moment pours, and through eternity will continue to pour, all its fullness into his infinite mind!"

The Battle and the Victory.

" Let no one say, 'Since God has promised that his Son shall see of the travail of his soul and be satisfied, we may safely sit still and leave him to fulfill this promise.' He will indeed fulfill it, but he will fulfill it by human agency. And before it can be fulfilled, before every enemy can be put under our Saviour's feet, many exertions must be made, much treasure expended, aud many battles fought. Satan, the prince and god of this world, will not resign his usurped dominion without a struggle. The more clearly he perceives that his time is short, the greater will be his wrath, and the more violent his efforts. During that portion of time which yet remains, the war which he has long waged with the Captain of our salvation will be carried on with unexampled fury. If you would survey the progress and result of this war, cast your eyes over the world, which is to be at once the field of battle and the prize of victory. See the earth filled with strongholds and high places, in which the prince of darkness has fortified and made himself strong against the Almighty. See all the hosts of hell, and a large proportion of the inhabitants, the power, the wealth, the talents, and influence of the world ranged under his infernal standard. See his whole artillery of falsehoods, sophistries, objections, temptations, and persecution brought into the field, to be employed against the cause of truth. See ten thousand pens, and ten times ten thousand tongues, hurling his poisoned darts among its friends. On the other hand, see the comparatively small band of our Saviour's faithful soldiers drawn up in opposing ranks, and advancing to the assault, clothed in panoply divine, the banner waving over their heads, while in their hands they wield unsheathed the sword of the Spirit, the word of God, the only weapon which they are allowed or wish to employ. The charge is sounded, the assault is made, the battle is joined,— far and wide its fury rages; over mountains and plains, over islands and continents, extends the long line of conflict; for a time, alternate victory and defeat wait on either side. Now, exulting acclamations from the Christian army proclaim the fall of some stronghold of Satan. Anon, infuriated shouts from the opposing ranks announce to the world that the cause of Christ is losing ground, or that some Christian standard-bearer has fallen. Meanwhile, far above the noise and tumult of the battle, the Captain of our salvation sits serene, issuing his commands, directing the motions of his followers, sending seasonable aid to such as are ready to faint, and occasionally causing to be seen the lighting down of his own glorious arm, before which whole squadrons fall, or fly, or yield themselves willing captives. Feeble, and yet more feeble still, gradually becomes the opposition of his foes. Loud, and yet louder still, rise the triumphant acclamations of his friends, till at length the cry of Victory! victory! resounds from earth to heaven;

and, Victory! victory! is echoed back from heaven to earth. The warfare ceases; the prize is won; all enemies are put under the conquering Saviour's feet; the whole earth, with joy, receives her king; and his kingdom, which consists in righteousness, and peace, and holy joy, becomes co-extensive with the world."

The Sword of the Spirit in the Hand of Omnipotence.

"Of what use is a sword, even though it be the sword of Goliath, while it lies still in its scabbard, or is grasped by the powerless hand of an infant? In those circumstances it can neither conquer nor defend, however well suited it might be to do both in the hand of a warrior. It is the same with the sword of the Spirit. While it lies in its scabbard, or is wielded only by the infantile hand of Christ's ministers, it is a powerless and useless weapon; a weapon at which the weakest sinner can laugh, and against which he can defend himself with the utmost ease. But not so when He, who is Most Mighty, girds it on. Then it becomes a weapon of tremendous power! a weapon resistless as the bolt of heaven! 'Is not my word like a fire, and a hammer, saith the Lord, which breaketh the rock in pieces?' It is indeed; for what can be more efficacious and irresistible than a weapon sharper than a two-edged sword, wielded by the arm of Omnipotence? What must His sword be whose glance is the lightning? Armed with this weapon, the Captain of our salvation cuts his way to the sinner with infinite ease, though surrounded by rocks and mountains; scatters his strongholds and refuges of lies; and with a mighty blow cleaves asunder his heart of adamant, and lays him prostrate and trembling at his feet. Since such are the effects of this weapon in the hand of Christ, it is with the utmost propriety that the Psalmist begins by requesting him to gird it on, and not suffer it to be inactive in its scabbard, or powerless in the feeble grasp of his ministers."

The Glory and Majesty of Christ.

"In what do the glory and majesty of Christ consist? I answer, Glory is the display, or manifestation, of excellency. Now Christ is possessed of excellences or perfections of various kinds; he has some excellences, which belong to him as God; some, which belong to him as man; and some, which are peculiar to him as God and man united in one person. Of course he has a threefold glory. This glory, as God, consists in a display of the infinite perfections and excellences of his nature. This glory he possessed with his Father before the world was. His glory as man consists in the perfect holiness of his heart and life. His glory as God and man united in one person, the Mediator, consists in his perfect suitableness to perform all those works which the office of mediator requires of him. This is the glory of which St. John speaks, 'We behold his glory, the glory as of the only begotten of the Father, full of grace and truth.' This is the glory in which Christ appears when he goes forth to subdue sinners to himself; and this, therefore, is the glory which is meant in our text. If it be asked in what this glory more particularly consists, I answer, It consists in a fullness or sufficiency of every excellence and perfection necessary to qualify him for the all-important office of mediator between God and man; every thing which is necessary either to satisfy the justice and honor of God, or to excite and justify the utmost love, admiration, and confidence of man. Now all this Christ possesses in perfection. He possesses every thing necessary to satisfy the justice and secure the honor of God; for he has once and again declared, by a voice from heaven, that in him, or with him, he is ever well pleased. He also possesses every thing necessary to excite, encourage, and justify the highest love, admiration, and confidence of sinful men; for in him all fullness dwells, even all the fullness of the Godhead. There is in him a fullness of truth to enlighten sinners, and lead them to believe in him; for in him are hidden all the treasures of divine wisdom and knowledge. He has also a fullness of grace, to pardon, sanctify, and save them; for the riches of his grace are unsearchable. Now the display or manifestation of this infinite fullness of grace and truth constitutes the glory in which the Psalmist wished Christ to appear. He wished him also to appear in his majesty. The difference between majesty and glory consists in this: glory is something which belongs either to the person or the character of a being, but majesty is more properly an attribute of office, especially of regal office. This office Christ sustains. He is exalted to be a Prince as well as a Saviour; he is King of kings and Lord of lords; and it is principally in his character of a king that he subdues his enemies, and dispenses pardon. The Psalmist, therefore, wished him to appear in this character, arrayed in his awful majesty, that while his glory excited admiration, and delight, and love, his majesty might produce reverential awe, and lead sinners to submission and obedience."

The Prophet's Vision.

"While beseeching the Redeemer to ride forth prosperously, and predicting his success, the prophet seems suddenly to have seen his prayers answered, and his predictions fulfilled. He saw his all-conquering Prince gird on his resistless sword; array himself in glory and majesty; ascend the chariot of his Gospel, display the banner of his cross, and ride forth, as on the wings of the wind, while the tremendous voice of a herald proclaimed before him, Prepare ye the way of the Lord; exalt the valleys and level the hills; make the crooked ways straight and the rough places plain; for, behold, the Lord God comes; he comes with a strong hand; his reward is with him, and his work before him. From the bright and fiery cloud which enveloped his chariot, and concealed it from mortal eyes, he saw sharp arrows of conviction, shot forth on every side, deeply wounding the obdurate hearts of sinners, and prostrating them in crowds around his path, while his extended right hand raised them again, and healed the wounds which his arrows had made, and his omnipotent voice spoke peace to their despairing souls, and bade them follow in his train, and witness and share in his triumph. From the same bright cloud he saw the vengeful lightnings flashing thick and dreadful, to blast and consume every thing that opposed his progress; he saw sin, and death, and hell with all its legions, baffled, defeated, and flying in trembling consternation before him; he saw them overtaken, bound, and chained to his triumphant chariot wheels; while enraptured voices were heard from heaven exclaiming, Now is come salvation, and strength, and the kingdom of God, and the power of his Christ. Such was the scene which seems to have burst upon the ravished sight of the entranced prophet. Transported with the view, he exclaims, Thine arrows are sharp in the hearts of thine enemies, whereby the people fall under thee."

A Revival Scene.

"And similar scenes, though on a smaller scale, are witnessed by the eye of faith in every place through which Christ now rides invisibly in the chariot of his salvation. Then the sword of the Spirit, the word of God, which, in the feeble hands of his ministers, had long seemed like a sword rusting in its scabbard, or grasped by an infant, becomes a weapon of resistless energy. Then the arrows of conviction, which had been vainly aimed and feebly sent, are guided between the joints of the harness, and sinners feel them quivering in their hearts. Then the obdurate and incorrigible enemies of Christ are either laid low by the stroke of death or blasted and seared by the lightnings of his vengeance, and left, like a withered oak on which the bolt of heaven has fallen, to stand naked and barren, till the appointed time for cutting them down and casting them into the fire! Then truth, and meekness, and righteousness, which had long seemed dead, revive, and ignorance, falsehood, and unrighteousness are compelled to fly. Then the bonds of sin are burst; Satan is unable to retain his captives; death and the grave lose their terrors; joyful acclamations are heard in heaven, celebrating the return of penitent sinners; and crowds of those whom Christ's arrows have wounded and his right hand healed again, are seen flocking around his chariot, shouting the praises and extolling the triumphs of their great Deliverer; while those who, like the Psalmist, have been praying and waiting for his appearance, join in the song, and exultingly cry, Thine arrows are sharp in the hearts of thine enemies, whereby the people fall under thee."

A Desperate and Fatal Game.

"You would pity and condemn the madness of a man who should stake his whole fortune on the turn of a die, without the smallest prospect of gain. But, my delaying hearers, you are playing a far more dreadful and desperate game than this. You are staking your souls, your salvation, on the continuance of life; on an event as uncertain as the turn of the die. You stake them without any equivalent; for if life should be spared you gain nothing; but should it be cut short you lose all—you are ruined for eternity. You run the risk of losing every thing dear, and of incurring everlasting misery—for what? For the sake of living a little longer without religion, of spending a few more days or years in disobeying and offending your Creator, of committing sins which you know must be repented of. And is it wise— rather, is it not madness—to incur such a risk? Let the following case furnish the reply. I will suppose that you intend to defer the commencement of a religious life for one year only. Select, then, the most healthy, vigorous person of your acquaintance; the man whose prospects are fairest for long life, and say, whether you would be willing to stake your soul on the chance of that man's life continuing for a year? Would you be willing to say, I consent to forfeit salvation, to be miserable forever, if that man dies before the expiration of a year? There is not, I presume, a single person present who would not shudder at the thought of entering into such an engagement if he supposed it would be binding. My delaying hearers, if you would not stake your salvation on the continuance of any other person's life, why will you stake it on the continuance of your own? Yet this you evidently do when you resolve to defer repentance to a future period; for if you die before that period arrives you die impenitent, unprepared, and perish forever. O, then, play no longer this desperate game; a game in which millions have staked and lost their souls; but if you intend ever to become religious begin to-day, for to-morrow is not."

The Difficulty of Convincing Men of Sin.

"It is always exceedingly difficult to convince a man against his will, to convince him of any unwelcome or disagreeable truth; and the more disagreeable any truth is, so much the more difficult it becomes to produce a conviction of it. How difficult it is, for instance, to convince a consumptive man of his danger. How difficult to make men sensible of their own faults, or to make fond and injudicious parents see the faults of their children. But there is no truth more disagreeable to men—no one, therefore, of which they are so unwilling to be convinced—as that which asserts their exceeding sinfulness. To see their sins is mortifying, is painful, is alarming.

They will therefore shut their eyes against the sight as long as possible. Many sins they will deny themselves to be guilty of; what they cannot deny they will extenuate; and for those which they cannot extenuate, they will make a thousand excuses. If the fallacy of one excuse is shown they will fly to another, and from that to a third, and fourth; and when all their pleas and excuses are answered, they will return and urge them all a second time with as much confidence as at first."

Compassion for the Perishing.

"My arm is too weak to draw you out of that fatal current which is rapidly sweeping you away to destruction. I can only sit on the bank and weep, as I contemplate the increasing strength of the current, and breathe out in agony cries to that God who can alone rescue you from its power, and prevent it from hurrying you into that bottomless gulf in which it terminates. And come you, my Christian hearers, come all, who have been rescued from this fatal current; all, who can feel compassion for perishing immortals, come and assist in crying to Him for help. That you may be excited to this, look at the scene before you. Look around, and see how many of your children, acquaintances, and friends are swept away toward perdition, while they sleep and know it not, and no voice, but that of God, can rouse them. Do you know whither they are hastening? Do you know what hell is? Do you consider how improbable it is that they will escape its condemnation? Do you consider, that unless grace prevents they will, in a few years, be lifting up their eyes in torment and despair? Surely, if you know and consider these things, one universal cry of 'God have mercy upon them!' will burst from every Christian heart."

The Strange Contrast.

"See Jesus adorned with every possible excellence and perfection, uttering the kindest invitations, and bestowing freely the richest blessings—blessings which cost him labors, privations, and sufferings, the greatness of which we can never estimate. See him, in return for these blessings, treated with the most cruel unkindness, ingratitude, and neglect; wounded in the house of his friends by those who have eaten at his table, and trespassed against, on every side, by multitudes in ten thousand ways. See him still forgiving all these trespasses, repeating his forgiveness a thousand and ten thousand times; maintaining, as it were, a contest as to which shall exceed, they in trespassing or he in pardoning."

Thanksgiving in Paradise.

"These sacred and delightful services being ended, they prepare to feast before their Benefactor; but this preparation is made, and the feast itself is participated in with the same feelings which animated their devotions; for whether they eat, or drink, or whatever they do, they do all to the glory of God. On such an occasion they may, perhaps, place upon their board a greater variety than usual of the fruits of Paradise; but if so, it is not so much with a view to gratify their appetites as to exhibit more fully the various and ample provision which God has made for them; and thus, through the medium of their senses, to affect their hearts; for man has not yet begun to consume the bounty of Heaven upon his lusts. He has not yet yielded himself a willing, but ignoble, slave to his corporeal appetites; nor, we may add, has he yet learned, as too many of his posterity have since done, to sit down to the table of Providence, and rise from it refreshed, without acknowledging the Hand that feeds him. No, the blessing of God is implored and his presence desired, as the crowning joy of their feast, without which even the fruits of Paradise would be insipid, and the society of Paradise uninteresting. And while they sit around his table, the viands which nourish their bodies furnish their minds with new food for devotional feeling; for in every fruit before them they see the power, wisdom, and goodness of their Benefactor embodied, and made perceptible to their senses; they see that his goodness prompted him to give them that gratification, that his wisdom devised it, and that his power gave it existence. Thus while they feast upon the fruits of his bounty their souls feast upon the perfections which those fruits display. Thus God is seen and enjoyed in every thing, and every thing leads up their thoughts and affections to him, while he sits unseen in the midst of them, shedding abroad his love through all their hearts, and rejoicing with benevolent delight in the happiness which he at once imparts and witnesses. Meanwhile their conversation is such as the attending angels, who hover around, would not be ashamed to utter; nay, such as God himself is well pleased to hear. The law of kindness is on all their lips, for the law of love is in all their hearts.

"But we can pursue this part of our subject no

further. This must suffice as a specimen of the manner in which sinless creatures would keep a feast unto the Lord; indeed, of the manner in which all their days would be spent. And if so, may we not well exclaim, O sin, what hast thou done! What beauty, what glory, what happiness hast thou destroyed! How hast thou embittered our food; poisoned our cup; darkened the eye which once saw God in all his works; polluted and rendered insensible the heart which once bore his image and was filled with his love; and by one fatal, accursed blow, murdered both the body and the soul of man! Who can wonder that God hates—who can refrain from hating —the destroyer of so much good, the cause of so much evil? Were it not for sin, we should observe this day in a manner as holy and as happy as has now been described. We have the same powers and faculties which were possessed by our first parents in Paradise. And if we may believe the declarations of Scripture, or the testimony of good men, God's glory still shines as brightly in his works as it did then. There is nothing but our own sinfulness to prevent us from seeing it as clearly as it was seen by our first parents, and from being affected by the sight as they were affected."

How Christians Should Keep Thanksgiving Day.

"Even while observing a joyful festival, tears, the fountain of which is supplied by godly sorrow for sin and gratitude to the Redeemer—tears, which it is delightful to shed—are seen on the same countenances which glow with love and hope, and beam with holy, humble joy in God.

"And when they sit down to the table of Providence to feast upon his bounty, the exercise of these emotions is not suspended. They feel there as pardoned sinners ought to feel, and as they would wish to feel at the table of Christ, for the table of Providence is become to them his table; they remember him there; they remember, that whenever their daily food was forfeited by sin, and the curse of Heaven rested upon their basket and store, he redeemed the forfeiture, and turned the curse into a blessing. Hence they feast upon his bounty with feelings resembling those which we may suppose to have filled the bosoms of Joseph's brethren when they ate and rejoiced before him. They had, you recollect, hated him, persecuted him, conspired to effect his death, and sold him for a slave. But by the providence of God he was exalted to power, and had the satisfaction, not only of seeing them humbled at his feet, but of saving them and their families from death. After he had made himself known to them, assured them of his forgiveness, and showed them that though they meant evil against him God had overruled it for good, he invited them to a feast, and richly loaded their table with provisions from his own. We may, in some measure, conceive what their feelings must have been on such an occasion. Though they feasted and rejoiced before their highly exalted, but generous, forgiving, and affectionate brother, yet feelings of sorrow and shame could not but mingle with their joy, and they must often have felt as if they wished to rise from their table, throw themselves at his feet, and once more ask his forgiveness. Well, then, may the redeemed sinner feel thus, while he feasts and rejoices before that much injured, exalted, and compassionate Saviour who is not ashamed to call him brother, and who has not only redeemed and forgiven him, but called him to share in all his possessions and glories. And while such emotions toward the Saviour fill the heart, his name cannot be absent from the tongue. Husbands and wives will speak of him to each other; parents will speak of him to their children; his person, his character, his offices, and his works, will furnish the subject of their conversations and instructions; and a realizing apprehension of his unseen presence, far from damping their joy, will only chastise, and purify, and exalt it."

The State of the World at the Second Coming of Christ.

"'When the Son of man cometh,' says our Saviour, 'will he find faith on the earth?' That is, will he find many who believe in him and expect his coming? a mode of expression which forcibly intimates that he will not. In another passage he teaches us that, at his second coming, he will find the world in the same situation in which it was found by the flood in the days of Noah, and in which Sodom was in the days of Lot. 'As it was,' says he, 'in the days of Noah and of Lot, so shall it be in the day when the Son of man is revealed,' or appears. 'They ate, they drank, they bought, they sold, they planted, they builded, and knew not, till the day in which Noah entered into the ark, and the flood came and destroyed them all.'

"From these, and other passages, it is evident that at the second coming of Christ there will be very little religion, very few pious men found in the world.

But it may be asked, How does this representation agree with the many predictions which assure us that religion is yet to prevail, in a far greater degree than it ever has done, and that the knowledge of God shall fill the earth, even as the waters cover the sea? We shall find an answer to this question in the twentieth chapter of Revelation. We are there taught that the great tempter and deceiver of mankind, who deceiveth the whole world, shall be bound for a thousand years; that is, during that period he shall not be permitted to tempt or deceive mankind, and in consequence religion will almost universally prevail. To this period, all the passages which speak of the great extension of Christ's kingdom refer. But after the expiration of this period, the great adversary will be released for a season; in other words, he will be suffered to renew his temptations; the consequence will be a great and almost universal apostasy. Religion will be ridiculed and opposed, and its friends persecuted with peculiar rancor; the Church will be compassed about with enemies, and on the very point of being swallowed up; and then, in the critical moment, will be seen the signs of the Son of man coming in the clouds of heaven."

Christ's Second Coming Described.

"Let all who are dazzled or fascinated by the pomp and splendor of the world, come and contemplate a scene which stains the pride of all human glory, and throws far back into the deepest shade every thing which men call great, or splendid, or sublime. What are the pompous triumphs, the gaudy pageants, the long processions on which men gaze with eager delight, compared with the descent of the Creator, the Judge, from heaven, surrounded by all the seraphic hosts, and bearing with him the final sentence, the eternal, unchangeable destiny, of every child of Adam? Pause, then, for a moment, and contemplate with the eye of faith, or, if you have no faith, with the eye of imagination, this tremendous scene. Look at that point, far away in the ethereal regions, where the gradually lessening form of our Saviour disappeared from the gaze of his disciples when he ascended to heaven. In that point see an uncommon, but faint and undefined, brightness just beginning to appear. It has caught the roving eye of yon careless gazer, and excited his curiosity. He points it out to a second and a third. A little circle soon collects, and various are the conjectures which they form respecting it. Similar circles are formed, and similar conjectures made, in a thousand different parts of the world. But conjecture is soon to give place to certainty—awful, appalling, overwhelming certainty. While they gaze, the appearance which had excited their curiosity rapidly approaches, and still more rapidly brightens. Some begin to suspect what it may prove; but no one dares to give utterance to his suspicions. Meanwhile, the light of the sun begins to fade before a brightness superior to his own. Thousands see their shadows cast in a new direction, and thousands of hitherto careless eyes look up at once to discover the cause. Full clearly they see it; and now new hopes and fears begin to agitate their breasts. The afflicted and persecuted servants of Christ begin to hope that the predicted, long-expected day of their deliverance is arrived. The wicked, the careless, the unbelieving, begin to fear that the Bible is about to prove no idle tale. And now fiery shapes, moving like streams of lightning, begin to appear indistinctly amid the bright dazzling cloud, which comes rushing down as on the wings of a whirlwind. At length it reaches its destined place. It pauses; then, suddenly unfolding, discloses at once a great white throne, where sits, starry resplendent, in all the glories of the Godhead, the man Christ Jesus. Every eye sees him, every heart knows him. Too well do the wretched, unprepared inhabitants of earth now know what to expect; and one universal shriek of anguish and despair rises to heaven, and is echoed back to earth. But louder, far louder than the universal cry, now sounds the last trumpet; and far above all is heard the voice of the Omnipotent summoning the dead to rise and come to judgment.

"New terrors now assail the living; on every side, nay, under their very feet, the earth heaves, as in convulsions, graves open, and the dead come forth; while at the same moment a change, equivalent to that occasioned by death, is effected by almighty power on the bodies of the living. Their mortal bodies put on immortality, and are thus prepared to sustain a weight of glory or of wretchedness which flesh and blood could not endure. Meanwhile, legions of angels are seen darting from pole to pole, gathering together the faithful servants of Christ from the four winds of heaven, and bearing them aloft to meet the Lord in the air, where he causes them to be placed at his own right hand, preparatory to the sentence which is to award to them everlasting life. Such, my brethren, is the scene which you will one day witness. And where now are the pomps, the honors, the riches, and pleasures of this world, which yesterday appeared so dazzling? Has not all their brightness faded, even in your estimation? Ought they not to appear, must they not appear, as less than nothing and vanity to him who looks for, who firmly believes, that he shall see such a spectacle as this? Can you wonder that faith in such truths—the faith of the Christian—should overcome the world? Christian, if you gain more and greater victories over the world than you ever have done, bring this scene often before the eye of your mind, and gaze upon it till you become blind to all earthly glory. He who gazes long at the sun becomes unsusceptible of impression from inferior luminaries; and he who looks much at the Sun of Righteousness will be little affected by any alluring object which the world can exhibit."

Man Capable of Equality with Angels.

"Man is capable of being raised to an intellectual equality with the angels, or being made equal to them in wisdom and knowledge. The image of God, in which he was created, included knowledge as well as righteousness and true holiness. And while he retained this image—while he stood crowned by his Maker's hand with glory and honor, and invested with the dominion of the world in which he dwelt—he was, as inspiration informs us, but little lower than the angels. The inferiority here intended must, it is acknowledged, have been an intellectual inferiority. But this small intellectual inferiority on the part of man may be satisfactorily accounted for without supposing that his intellectual faculties are essentially inferior to those of angels, or that his mind is incapable of expanding to the full dimensions of angelic intelligence. It may be accounted for by difference of situation, and of advantages for intellectual improvement. Man was placed on the earth, which is God's footstool; but angels were placed in heaven, which is his throne, his palace, and the peculiar habitation of his holiness and glory. They were thus enabled to approach much nearer to the great Father of lights than could earth-born man; and their minds were, in consequence, illuminated with far more than a double portion of that divine, all-disclosing radiance which diffuses itself around him. While man was compelled to drink from the streams, they could repair at once to the fountain. Nor must it be forgotten that man was encumbered with a body which demanded daily supplies of food; while angels, free from all these incumbrances, and upborne on wings which never tire, were able to maintain an uninterrupted and unceasing flight. Who, then, will wonder that man, thus situated, thus encumbered, should be a little lower than the angels in the intellectual scale? But free him, as he will hereafter be freed, from all the weights and fetters with which a gross, material body encumbers his immortal mind; place him, as the good will hereafter be placed in heaven, fast by the throne of an irradiating God; let him, instead of seeing all things as through a glass darkly, behold his Creator face to face; and who will undertake to prove, who will venture to assert, that he will remain even a little lower than the angels; that he will not, in wisdom and intelligence, soar to an equal height with them? Such an assertion, if made, must be entirely without support; for we know, we can conceive, of no intellectual faculties possessed by angels which are not possessed by man; we neither know nor can conceive of any assignable limits either to the advancement of the human mind in knowledge or to the possible expansion of its faculties. So far as we know, or can conceive, it is capable of every thing of which any created mind can be capable. If the mind of an infant can expand, during the lapse of a few years, to the dimensions of a Newton's mind, notwithstanding all the unfavorable circumstances in which it is here placed, why may it not, during an eternal residence in heaven, with the omniscient, all-wise God for its teacher, expand so far as to embrace any finite circle whatever? Who can place his finger on any assignable spot, and say, Thus far can it go and no farther? We seem, then, to have sufficient reason for believing that man is capable of being raised to an intellectual equality with the angels."

Man's Capabilities Invest the Cross with Sublimity.

"How inestimable does the worth of the human soul appear—how clearly is it seen to exceed that of the whole world—when we view it as endued with a capacity of being made equal to the angels! How momentous an event occurs when such a soul is born into the world! When an immortal being commences a flight through endless duration; a flight which will raise him high to an equality with angels, or plunge him low among malignant demons and fiends! Think of this, ye parents! ye, to whom is committed the care of giving to this flight its earliest direction, and on whom it much depends, under God, what its termination shall be. How grand, let me further remark, how Godlike, how every way worthy of himself, does the object of our Saviour's interposition in behalf of ruined man appear when viewed in the light of this subject! In this light, how clearly is his Gospel seen to be glad tidings. What moral glory and sublimity surround his cross, when we contemplate him as voluntarily suspended there for the purpose of raising such a creature as man from the depravity, degradation, and wretchedness of apostate spirits, to an equality with the angels in God's presence! And how evident does it appear, that the reward which raised them to such a height must be conferred on them from respect rather to their Saviour's merits than to their own!"

Motives to Imitate the Angels.

"What can be more obvious, more undeniable, than the conclusion, that if you hope to be made equal to the angels hereafter you ought to imitate, so far as is practicable, angels now? That you may be induced to imitate them, and to climb with greater diligence and alacrity the steep ascent before you, let me persuade you to fix your eyes upon its summit. A dense, impenetrable cloud appears, indeed, to conceal it from mortal eyes; but inspiration speaks, and the cloud is dissipated; faith presents her glass, and the sun-bright summit is seen. On Him who sits enthroned upon it you cannot, indeed, gaze. His glories, though you shall see them unvailed hereafter, are too insufferably dazzling for mortal eyes to sustain. But contemplate the resplendent forms which float around him in an atmosphere of pure, celestial light. See their bodies, resembling sunbeams seven times refined. See their countenances, beaming with intelligence, purity, benevolence, and felicity. Through their transparent bodies look in, and contemplate the souls which inhabit them, expanded to the full dimensions of angelic minds, bearing the perfect image of their God, and reflecting his glories as the polished mirror reflects the glories of the noonday sun. This, O Christian, is what thou shalt hereafter be! These dazzling forms were once sinful dust and ashes, like thyself. But grace, free, rich, sovereign, almighty grace, has made them what they now are. It has washed, and justified, and sanctified, and brought them to glory. And to the same glory, O Christian, it is bringing thee! And canst thou, then, sleep, canst thou be slothful, canst thou complain of the difficulties which attend, of the obstacles which oppose, thy ascent to such glory and felicity as this? O let gratitude, let duty, let shame, if nothing else, forbid! Lift up, ye embryo angels, lift up the heads which hang down, and let the drooping spirit revive! Read, hear, meditate with prayer, deny yourselves, mortify sin but a little longer, and you shall mount up, not on eagles' but on angels' wings, and know what is meant by being made equal to resplendent intelligences!"

The Pangs of Remorse in Eternity.

"The gnawing worm of which our Saviour speaks includes the consciences of sinners. The sufferings inflicted by conscience will be even more painful than those which are occasioned by the sinner's passions;

for terrible as are the gnawings of passion, those of conscience are still more so. Her scourge draws blood at every stroke. Even in this world she has drawn many, as she did Judas, to despair, madness, and suicide. But her loudest rebukes, her keenest reproaches here, are mere whispers compared with the thundering voice in which she will speak hereafter. Here she speaks only at intervals. There she will speak without intermission. Here the sinner has various ways of stifling her reproaches or diverting his attention from them. He may rush into scenes of business or amusement; he may silence her with sophistical arguments and excuses, or with promises of future amendment; and, when all other means fail, he may drown her for a season in the intoxicating bowl, as too many, alas! madly do. But there, he will have no means of silencing, or escaping from, her reproaches for a moment. Here she knows comparatively little of God, of duty, or of sin, and therefore often suffers the sinner to escape when she ought to scourge him. But there she will see every thing in the clear light of eternity, and in consequence, instead of a whip of small cords, will chastise the sinner as with a scourge of scorpions. There the sinner will clearly see what a God he has offended, what a Saviour he has neglected, what a heaven he has lost, and into what a hell he has plunged himself. All the sins which he has committed, with all their aggravations and consequences; all the Sabbaths he enjoyed, the sermons which he heard, the warnings and invitations which he slighted, the opportunities which he misimproved, the serious impressions which he banished, will be set in order before him and overwhelm him with mountains of conscious guilt. And O, the keen, unutterable pangs of remorse, the bitter self-reproaches, the unavailing regrets, the fruitless wishes that he had pursued a different course, which will be thus excited in his breast! The word remorse is derived from a Latin word which signifies *to gnaw again* or *to gnaw repeatedly;* and surely no term can more properly describe the sufferings which are inflicted by an accusing conscience. Well, then, may such a conscience, when its now sleeping energies shall be wakened by the light of eternity, be compared to a gnawing worm. The heathen made use of a similar figure to describe it. They represented a wicked man as chained to a rock in hell, where an immortal vulture constantly preyed upon his vitals, which grew again as fast as they were devoured. Nor is this representation at all too strong. Even in this world, where conscience is comparatively weak, I have often seen the bed, and the whole chamber of the sick man, shake under the almost convulsive agonies which her lash inflicted. I have been told by persons suffering under most painful diseases, that their bodily sufferings were nothing to the anguish of mind which they endured. I have seen a man of robust constitution, vigorous health, strong mind, and liberal education, tremble like an aspen leaf, and scarcely able to sustain himself under the pressure of conscious guilt and pungent remorse. A man in similar circumstances has been known to rise in winter at midnight, and run for miles with naked feet over the rough and frozen ground, in order that the bodily pain thus occasioned might, if possible, divert his attention for a time from the far more intolerable anguish of his mind. And a dying infidel has been known to exclaim, Surely there is a God, for nothing less than omnipotence could inflict the pangs which I now feel! What, then, must be the pangs inflicted by a gnawing conscience in eternity?"

An Unquenchable Fire.

"Our Saviour speaks not only of the gnawing worm, but of an unquenchable fire. What reference this may have to the corporeal sufferings of the wicked I shall not pretend to decide, but it appears evident, from other passages, that so far as the soul is concerned it refers to a keen and constant sense of God's presence and righteous displeasure. He says of himself, 'I am a consuming fire; and a fire is kindled in mine anger, which shall burn even to the lowest hell.' These expressions evidently intimate that a view of his perfections and constant presence, combined with a sense of his displeasure, will affect the soul as fire does the body, withering its strength and drying up its spirits. Some of you have formerly known a little of this; and you know, or at least will easily conceive, that no fire can torture the body more keenly than a sense of God's displeasure does the soul. But to those of you who know nothing of this experimentally, it will be more difficult to convey any clear apprehension of this subject. The following supposition may perhaps assist in doing it. Suppose that when Washington was the commander of our armies you had been a soldier under him, and had been detected in a plot to betray your country. Suppose yourself to be brought before him, surrounded by the whole army, and compelled by some means to fix your eyes steadily several hours on his, encountering during the whole time his stern, indignant, and withering glances. Would you not soon have found your situation intolerably painful? Would not his glance seem to thrill through your soul, and almost scorch it like fire or blast it like lightning? What, then, must it be to see yourselves surrounded by a just and holy God, to meet his heart-searching, heart-withering eye, wherever you turn, fixed full upon you; to see the Author of your being, the Sovereign of the universe, the great, the glorious, the majestic, the omnipotent, the infinite Jehovah regarding you with severe displeasure; to see his anger burning against you like fire! O, this will be indeed a fire to the soul! a fire which will be felt in all its faculties, and fill them to the brim with anguish—anguish as much greater than any which could be occasioned by material fire as the Creator is superior to his creatures. It is, then, O it is a fearful thing to fall into the hands of the living God; that God who is a consuming fire to the workers of iniquity!"

Objections to Future Punishment Answered.

"The incarnation of the Son of God, the tears which he shed for sinners, the blood which he poured out for sinners, the joy which angels feel when one sinner repents, and the unutterable anxiety which inspired men felt for the conversion of sinners—all conspire to prove that the fate of those who die without repentance, without conversion, must be inconceivably dreadful. Will you then say, such a punishment cannot be just? It is impossible that I should deserve it? But remember, that you know nothing of your sins, or of what sin deserves. Were you properly acquainted with your own sinfulness, you would feel convinced that it is just. All true penitents feel and acknowledge that it would have been perfectly just to inflict this punishment upon them. Were not you impenitent you would feel the same. Besides, this punishment, dreadful as it is, is nothing more than the natural, necessary consequence of persisting in sin. The corroding passions, the remorse of conscience, and the displeasure of God, which will constitute the misery of sinners, are all the results of sin. Every sinner has the seeds of hell already sown in his breast. The sparks which are to kindle the flames of hell are already glowing within him. Christ now offers to extinguish these sparks. He shed his blood to quench them. He offers to pour out his Spirit as water to quench them. But sinners will not accept his offer. They rather fan the sparks, and add fuel to the fire. How then can they justly complain, when the fire shall break out into an unquenchable conflagration and burn forever! As well might a man who should put vipers into his bosom complain of God because they stung him. As well might a man who has kindled a fire and thrown himself into it complain of God because the flames scorched him. But I can spend no more time in answering objections, or in defending the justice of God against the complaints of his creatures. I cannot stand here coolly arguing and reasoning while I see the pit of destruction, as it were, open before me, and more than half my hearers apparently rushing into it. I feel impelled rather to fly, and throw myself before you in the fatal path, to grasp your hands, to cling to your feet, to make even convulsive efforts to arrest your progress, and pluck you as brands out of the burning. My careless hearers, my people, my flock, death, perdition, the never-dying worm, the unquenchable fire, are before you! Your path leads directly into them! Will you not, then, hear your friend, your shepherd? Will you not stop and listen, at least for a moment? Will you, O will you, refuse to believe that there is a hell, till you find yourselves in the midst of it? O be convinced, I conjure you, be convinced by some less fatal proof than this! Yet how can I convince you? How can I stop you? My arm is powerless; yet I cannot let you go. I could shed tears of blood over you would it avail. Gladly, most gladly, would I die here on the spot, without leaving this sacred desk, could my death be the means of turning you from this fatal course. But what folly is this, to talk of laying down my worthless life to save you! Why, my friends, the Son of God died to save you—died in agonies—died on the cross; and surely that doom cannot but be terrible, to open a way of escape from which he did all this. And it is dreadful. The abyss into which you are falling is as deep as the heaven from which he descended is high. And will you then rush into it, while he stands ready to save you? Shall he, as it respects you, die in vain? Will you receive the grace of God in vain? Shall those eyes which now see the light of the Sabbath, glare and wither in eternal burning? Shall those souls, which might be filled with the happiness of heaven, writhe and agonize forever under the gnawings of the immortal worm? Shall I, must I, hereafter see some who are dear to me, for whom I have labored and prayed and wept, weltering in the billows of despair, and learning, by experience, how far the description comes short of the terrible reality? But I cannot proceed. The thought unmans me. I can only point to the cross of Christ, and say, There is salvation, there is blood, which, if applied, will quench the fires that are already kindling in your breasts. There is deliverance from the wrath which is to come."

Benefits of the Universal Spread of Christ's Kingdom.

"Let righteousness, peace, and joy in the Holy Ghost universally prevail, and sin and misery will be banished from the world. By righteousness, is here intended a temper and conduct conformable to our Saviour's rule of equity—'Whatsoever ye would that men should do to you, do ye even so to them.' By peace is intended peace with God, peace of conscience, and peace with our fellow-creatures. By joy in the Holy Ghost is intended those divine consolations which God imparts to his people, and which often cause them to rejoice, as the apostle expresses it, with a joy unspeakable and full of glory.

"Now were these things universally prevalent, what evil could remain to infest the world? Universal righteousness would banish all those evils which spring from fraud, injustice, and oppression; all the crimes which now disturb the peace of society; all causes of contention between nations and individuals. Peace with God would deliver mankind from the heavy judgments and calamities with which he is now constrained to afflict them on account of their opposition to his authority, and from all the unhappiness occasioned by want of resignation, by anxiety, and discontent. Peace of conscience would entirely free them from that guilty fear, remorse, and dread of death which now often embitter their choicest comforts. Peace with each other would destroy at once the innumerable evils which arise from public and private wars, disputes, and dissensions, while the consolations of the Holy Spirit would fill them with that peace which passeth all understanding, and give them, while on earth, a continual foretaste of the joys of heaven, toward which they will be constantly advancing, and at which they would at length arrive, there to live and reign throughout eternity with Him in whose presence is fullness of joy, and at whose right hand are pleasures for evermore. Such are the benefits which would result to mankind from the universal spread of Christ's kingdom—such the glorious effects which it naturally tends to produce."

"*For in Him Dwelleth all the Fullness of the Godhead Bodily.*"

"The original word here rendered fullness, signifies that by which any thing is filled, completed, or made perfect. Thus when it is said, 'The earth is the Lord's, and the fullness thereof,' by the fullness of the earth is evidently meant all those things with which the earth is filled, or every thing which it contains. So by the fullness of the Godhead is meant, all that the Godhead contains, all the natural and moral attributes of Deity; every thing, in short, which renders the divine nature perfect and complete. This phrase, then, includes in its import the whole deity or divinity, with its attributes of infinity, eternity, immutability, omnipotence, omniscience, omnipresence, holiness, justice, goodness, mercy, faithfulness, and truth. Should it be thought that the word fullness does not necessarily mean so much as this, yet it must, I think, be allowed that all the fullness of the Godhead cannot mean any thing less; for if any one perfection or attribute of divinity be taken away all the fullness of the Godhead would not remain. There would be something wanting. The divine nature would not be full; or in other words, perfect and complete. Wherever, then, all the fullness of the Godhead dwells, there every natural and moral attribute of divinity will be found.

"Let us next inquire what is meant by the assertion that all this fullness dwells in Christ. There are, in the original, two words which, in our translation, are rendered *to dwell*. The first literally signifies to reside, as in a tent or tabernacle, and is used to denote a temporary residence. This word is used by St. John when he says, 'The Word was made flesh, and dwelt among us;' literally, resided among us, as in a tabernacle or temporary habitation. The other word signifies to dwell as in a house, or fixed habitation, and is always used to signify a more permanent residence; because a house is permanent compared with a tent. Now it is the latter word, the word that signifies a permanent residence, which is used in our text. The import of the assertion which it contains, then, is this: All the fullness of the Godhead resides in Jesus Christ, as in its permanent or fixed habitation."

Habitually at Ease in Zion.

"If there is any truth in the Scriptures it is certain that all who are habitually at ease in Zion know nothing of true religion. They are either careless sinners or self-deluded hypocrites. The pious man, the true Christian, is described by the inspired writers as one who mourns for sin, who is engaged in a spiritual warfare, who is fighting the good fight of faith, who crucifies the flesh with its affections and lusts, who is running the Christian race, who is engaged in subduing and mortifying his sinful propensities, who denies himself, takes up his cross daily and follows Christ; who, as a pilgrim, a stranger, a traveler, is seeking another and better country; one who works out his own salvation with fear and trembling. Now is it possible that a man who is doing all this can be at ease, in the sense of our text? A soldier on the field of battle at ease! a man running a race at ease! a traveler, toiling up a steep ascent, bearing the cross, at ease! a man crucifying sinful propensities, dear as a right hand or right eye, at ease! a man working out his salvation with fear and trembling at ease! a man who hates and mourns for sin, loves God, and feels concerned for his perishing fellow-creatures, at ease in a world lying in wickedness, where God is dishonored, where Christ is neglected, where immortal souls are perishing by millions; where there is so much to be done, so much to be suffered, so much to be guarded against and resisted; where death stands at the door, ready every moment to summon him to his great account! My friends, it is impossible. No Christian can be habitually easy, careless, and indolent in such a situation as this. He may, perhaps, slumber for a moment, but even then he is not at ease."

The Alarm Sounded.

"Like the inhabitants of the old world, you are eating and drinking, and planting and building, and marrying and giving in marriage, while death, like the flood, is constantly approaching and threatening to sweep you away with resistless violence to the judgment-seat. God hearkens and hears, but you speak not aright. Almost no one repents of his wickedness, saying, What have I done? This insensibility must be removed, this fatal peace destroyed. In God's name, then, I must sound an alarm. In his name, and as his watchman, who must answer for your souls if they perish through my neglect, I set the war-trumpet of Jehovah to my lips, and cry, Woe, woe, woe, to you that are at ease in Zion! Thus saith Jehovah, the great, the mighty, the terrible God, Tremble ye that are at ease; rise up and be troubled, ye careless ones, and listen to my voice; for while ye say Peace and safety, sudden destruction cometh upon you, and ye shall not escape. Your peace is delusive; your ease is full of danger; it is the stagnant calm which precedes the hurricane and the earthquake; it is the ease which the diseased patient feels when raging inflammation terminates in gangrene—the symptom, the immediate forerunner of death. No further evidence of your guilt and danger is requisite; nothing more is necessary to secure your condemnation than the very ease which you feel and the false confidence which confirms it.

It is your not fearing the woe which brings the woe upon you. It is your very insensibility to your danger which proves your danger to be great; it is your unconcern for your sins which proves that they have never been pardoned."

Fearful Consequences of Not Punishing Sin.

"Inspiration teaches us that the happiness of heaven consists in knowing, loving, serving, and praising God. It is his glory, we are told, which constitutes the light of the heavenly world above. But there would be no happiness in knowing, serving, or praising him, should he lose the perfections which compose and adorn his moral character. Take away his truth, his justice, his holiness, and all the glory which illuminates heaven would vanish into night. But should God renounce his determination to punish sin, he would stain all these perfections; nay, he would cease from that moment to possess them. He would no longer be true; for he has not only said but sworn, sworn by himself, that sinners shall not go unpunished. Where, then, would be his truth should they escape? He would no longer be holy; for holiness implies hatred or opposition to sin. He would no longer be just; for justice consists in executing his law, and rewarding every one according to his works. In short, he would become altogether such an one as ourselves. Who then could find everlasting happiness in seeing and praising through eternity such a being as this? a being without truth, or holiness, or justice. Who could either respect or love him? How instantaneously would the praises of heaven cease! How would their golden harps drop from the hands of its now happy inhabitants; and how would angels be compelled to stop in the midst of their unfinished song, 'Just and true are all thy ways, O King of saints!' The sun of the moral world would be forever eclipsed, and a black, endless night would shroud the universe. But this is not all. Were sin unrestrained, unpunished, it would soon scale heaven, as it has once done already in the case of the apostate angels; and there reign and rage with immortal strength through eternity, repeating in endless succession, and with increased aggravation, the enormities which it has already perpetrated on earth. We may add, that, after God had once surrendered his truth, his justice, and holiness, and laid aside the reins of government, he could never more resume them. Nor could he ever give laws, or make promises to any other world, or any other race of creatures, which would be worthy of the least regard. It would be instantly and properly said, He has once violated his word and his oath, and he may do it again. He has once shown himself fickle, unjust, and unholy, and what security can we have that he will not do it again. Should he silence these clamors by an exertion of his almighty power, he might indeed have slaves to cringe before him, but he could never have affectionate subjects who would serve him with cheerfulness and confidence; nor could he, after once allowing sin to go unpunished, ever punish it again, without exposing himself to the charge of partiality and injustice."

Superior Advantages of the Christian Dispensation.

"The very rolls which Jeremiah wrote by God's command, in which he expresses so clearly his indignation against sin, and which it was so criminal in the king of Judah and his princes to disregard—forms a part of this volume. Nor is this all. The same God who spoke to them by his prophet, has, in these latter ages, spoken to you by his Son. By him he has revealed himself to us in the most interesting attitudes; he has addressed us in the most impressive language; he has addressed us as the God and Father of our Lord Jesus Christ; in the attitude of taking from his bosom his only begotten and well-beloved Son, that he might give him up for us all, to bear our sins on the cross. In the instructions, in the Gospel of that Son, he has set before us denunciations of vengeance far more tremendous—invitations and offers of mercy far more tender—proofs of his goodness far more affecting—motives to love and obedience far more powerful—than were ever exhibited to his ancient people. He has brought life and immortality more clearly to light; he has rent asunder the vail which concealed the eternal world from the view of mortals; he has made the glories of heaven to blaze down upon our eyes; he has caused the unquenchable flames of hell to flash up before our faces; he has caused the groans of the latter, the songs of the former, the blast of the last trumpet, and the sentence which the final Judge will pronounce upon the righteous and upon the wicked, to resound in our ears. In fine, all that he has done, all that he designs to do, he has recorded in the

Scriptures. He has dictated them by his own Spirit; he has subscribed them with his own name; he has stamped upon them the broad seal of heaven; he has authenticated them by fulfilling many of the prophecies which they contain, and, addressing them to us as it were by name, has caused them to drop from heaven into our hands."

Despair: Its Nature and Effects.

"The ancient divines were accustomed to call despair one of the seven deadly sins. That it well deserves this character is evident from its nature and effects. It is directly contrary to the will of God. He, we are told, taketh pleasure in them that fear him, and hope in his mercy. He must, therefore, be displeased with them that refuse to do this. It is also a great insult to the character of God. It calls in question the truth of his word; nay, it gives him the lie; for he has told us that whosoever cometh to him he will in nowise cast out. But the language of despair is, He will cast me out, though I should come to him. It calls in question, or rather denies, the greatness of his mercy. He has told us that his mercy is infinite; that it is from everlasting to everlasting; but the language of despair is, My sins are beyond the reach of God's mercy, and therefore it is not infinite. It also limits the power of God. He has said, Is any thing too hard for me? With God nothing is impossible. But despair says, There are some things which are too hard for God; some things which it is impossible for him to perform. It is impossible that he should renew my heart, subdue my will, and make me fit for heaven. Thus despair limits or denies all God's perfections, and, of consequence, greatly insults and provokes him. Despair is also contrary to the Spirit of God. The three principal graces of the Spirit are faith, hope, and love. But despair is opposed to them all. That it is opposed to faith in God's promises, we have already seen; that it is opposed to hope, is evident from its very nature; and a little reflection will convince us that it is equally inconsistent with love. To sum up all in one word, despair includes in itself the very essence both of impenitence and unbelief. It contains in itself the essence of impenitence, for it seals up the heart in a sullen, obstinate, unyielding frame, so that those who are under its influence cannot breathe one penitential sigh, or shed a single penitential tear. This effect it has on the devils. This effect it will produce in all the wicked at the judgment-day. Hence it is directly opposed to that broken heart and contrite spirit in which true repentance essentially consists. It also contains in itself the very essence of unbelief, for it shuts up the heart against all the promises of the Gospel, against all the invitations of Christ, against all the revelations which God has made of mercy, and represents him as a severe, inexorable, arbitrary tyrant, whom it is vain to endeavor to please. But unbelief and impenitence are every-where represented as sins exceedingly great and provoking to God. How offensive, how provoking, then, must be that despair which includes in itself the essence of both these aggravated sins!"

God Listening to the Afflicted Penitent.

"'I have surely,' says God, 'heard Ephraim bemoaning himself.' So he does still. As an affectionate parent, after confining a stubborn child to a solitary apartment, sometimes stands at the door without, secretly listening to his complaints, that he may release him on the first symptom of submission, so when God puts us into the prison of affliction he invisibly, but attentively, listens to catch the first penitential sigh, and hear the first breathings of prayer which escape us; and no music, not even the halleluias of angels, is more pleasing to his ears than are these cries and complaints of a broken heart; nor can any thing more quickly or more powerfully excite his compassion. Agreeably he represents himself as strongly affected by the complaints of Ephraim: 'My bowels,' says he, 'are troubled for him.' My friends, what astonishing compassion and love is this, that the infinite, eternal Jehovah should represent himself as troubled and grieved for the sufferings of penitent sinners under those afflictions which their sins had brought upon them! Certainly nothing in heaven or earth is so wonderful as this; and if this language does not affect us and break our hearts, nothing can do it."

All Classes Invited to the Gospel Feast.

" Our Creator, our God, has made a great feast, a marriage feast for his Son; a feast for the entertainment of sinners; a feast in which all his inexhaustible stores, all the celestial dainties which infinite wisdom could devise, which almighty power could create, are set forth. To this feast you are now invited. No tickets of admission are necessary. The Master of the feast stands at the door to receive you, declaring that not one who comes shall be cast out; and as his servant, sent forth for this very purpose, sent especially to you, I now invite you to come. I invite you, children, for there is a place for you. Leave your toys and follies, then, and come to Christ. I invite you who are young, for your presence is especially desired. Leave your sinful amusements and companions, then, and come to the Saviour. I invite you who are in the meridian of life. To you, O men, I call, and my voice is to the sons of men. Particularly do I invite you who are parents to come, and to bring your children with you to the Saviour's feast. I invite you who are aged to come, and receive from Christ a crown of glory, which your gray hairs will be if you are found in the way of righteousness. I invite you to come, ye poor, and Christ will make you rich in faith and heirs of his kingdom. I invite you to come who are rich, and bring your wealth to Christ, and he will give you durable riches and righteousness. I invite you who are ignorant to come, and Christ will impart to you his treasures of wisdom and knowledge. I invite you who possess human learning to come, and Christ will baptize your knowledge, and teach you to employ it in the most advantageous manner. I invite you who are afflicted to come, for my God is the God of all consolation, and my Master can be touched with the feeling of your infirmities. I invite you who feel yourself to be the greatest of sinners to come, for you will find many there whose sins once equaled your own, now washed and made white in the blood of the Lamb. I invite you who have long despised, and who still despise this invitation, to come, for Christ's language is, Hearken to me, ye stout-hearted and far from righteousness. And if there be any one in this assembly who thinks himself overlooked—if there be one who has not yet felt that this invitation is addressed to him—I now present it to that person, particularly, and invite him to come."

Moral Sublimity of Christ's Invitations.

"'Look unto me, and be ye saved, all ye ends of the earth.' 'If any man thirst, let him come unto me and drink.' 'Whosoever will, let him come, and him that cometh I will in nowise cast out.' And who is he that dares utter such language as this? Who dares thus stand in the midst of the world, of such a world as this, a thirsty, perishing world, and invite all, all its dying inhabitants without exception, to come to him and drink the waters of life and salvation? Can he have room sufficient for such an innumerable multitude? Has he not reason to fear that his treasures will be exhausted? Does he know what he says? Yes, my friends, he does know what he says; and he may well say it, for in him dwells all the fullness of the Godhead bodily. He has enough, and more than enough, for ten thousand such worlds as this. And, my hearers, this is saying much; for reflect a moment how much is necessary to supply the wants of a single immortal soul through time and through eternity. Think how many souls there are, have been, and shall be, in the world. Think of the innumerable criminals—criminals of the most abandoned kind—of the murderers, the robbers, the conquerors, the blasphemers, the adulterers, the harlots, the impious, hardened wretches who neither fear God nor regard man, that have been, and still are, to be found among mankind. What an ocean of mercy is necessary to wash away their sins, to make the deep crimson white as snow! What an omnipotence of grace is requisite to fit such wretches for admission into a heaven of spotless purity, and make them holy as God! Yet all such Christ invites, all such he is able to save, all such he would save, would they come to him. Who, then, can describe, who can conceive, the ten thousandth part of that grace and mercy which must be in Christ; or of the love which renders him thus willing to scatter that grace and mercy round him upon the worthless and undeserving? Is there not something inexpressibly grand, sublime, and affecting in the idea of a being whose fullness enables him, whose generosity prompts him, to throw wide open the door of his heart, and invite a dying world to enter in, and drink and be satisfied, and live forever;—of a being from whom flows light, holiness, and happiness sufficient to fill to overflowing all that come to him, be their numbers ever so many, their sins and wants and miseries ever so great;—of a being, of whose fullness myriads of immortal beings may drink through a whole eternity without exhausting, or even diminishing, it in the smallest degree?"

Merely Human Instrumentalities Ineffectual.

"As the tempest, the earthquake, and the fire roused the prophet, and prepared him to attend to what God would say to him, so the works and dispensations of Providence are used to rouse thoughtless sinners, and awaken their attention to the still, small voice of Jehovah. But they communicate no specific instruction or reproof. They do not tell the sinner in what respect he has done wrong, nor what it is to do right. They may amaze him, they may frighten him, they may plunge him into distress and despondency. But they leave him there. After they have done their utmost, the sinner is still left without God in the world, and without knowledge of the way in which God may be found. The same may be said of other means. Ministers may give voice and utterance to the Bible, which is the word of God. Like James and John, they may be sons of thunder to impenitent sinners. They may pour forth a tempest of impassioned, eloquent declamation. They may proclaim all the terrors of the Lord; represent the earth as quaking and trembling under the footsteps of Jehovah; flash around them the lightnings of Sinai; borrow, as it were, the trump of the archangel, and summon the living and the dead to the bar of God; kindle before their hearers the conflagration of the last day and the fires of eternity, and show them the Judge descending, the heavens departing as a scroll, the elements melting, the earth with its works consuming, and all nature struggling in the agonies of dissolution;—and still God may not be there; his voice may not be heard either in the tempest, the earthquake, or the fire; and if so, the preacher will have labored but in vain; his hearers, though they may for the moment be affected, will receive no permanent salutary impressions. Nothing effectual can be done unless God be there, unless he speaks with his still, small voice. By this still, small voice we mean the voice of God's Spirit; the voice which speaks not only to man but in man; the voice, which in stillness, and silence, whispers to the ear of the soul, and presses upon the conscience those great, eternal truths, a knowledge and belief of which is connected with salvation."

How to Prolong the Visits of the Saviour.

"If we would prolong the Saviour's gracious visits, we must furnish him with opportunities of doing good, and keep him constantly employed in this blessed work. We must bring to him ourselves, our children, our friends and acquaintances, to be pardoned, instructed, sanctified, and saved. We must not leave him without employment for a single day; and if he begins to withdraw, we must lay the sick, the dying, and the dead across his path; for nothing will stop his departure like such an obstacle as this. Omnipotent as he is, he cannot step over a perishing soul laid by faith across his way. As unbelief can paralyze his arm, so faith can constrain him to work, and with gentle, but irresistible force, arrest his progress, even when he has begun to withdraw."

Christ's Absence from the Church.

"Christ is constituted head over all things to his Church, and therefore the effects which a Church experiences on his departure from it are similar to those which would result to a human body from the loss of its head. For instance, the head is the seat of intelligence, the palace, the presence-chamber of the soul, where she holds her court, and from whence she issues forth her counsels and commands to the members of the body. Take away the head, and the tongue loses its eloquence, the right hand its cunning, and the feet their director. It is the same in the body of which Christ is the head. It has no wisdom, nor knowledge, nor intelligence, without him. Its members know not what to do; they have, in a spiritual sense, neither eyes nor ears, without their head; and, therefore, infallibly wander, and stumble, and fall. We have no sufficiency of ourselves.

"The head is the bond of union. Take away the head from a human body, and the members soon separate and molder into dust. So Christ is the only bond of union to his members. While he remains with them they are firmly united, but when he departs the connecting tie is broken; jealousies, dissensions, and divisions arise; the Church becomes like a rope of sand; its members are easily separated and split into parties, and every one's heart, and hand, and tongue, is turned against his brother.

"The head is necessary to the growth of the body. Without the head the body can receive no nourishment, and consequently no strength; its growth is immediately suspended. It is the same with the body of Christ. His presence always causes its increase both in numbers and in graces. But when he departs its growth ceases. Spiritual nourishment is no longer received, and the whole body declines.

"The head is the seat of life and sensation. Take away the head and death ensues. The body becomes insensible as the clod of earth from which it was formed. It is the same with the Church. Take away Christ, its head, its life, and it dies. Nothing remains but a lifeless, insensible, putrefying carcass, fit only to produce and become food for worms. Well, therefore, might the Saviour say to his disciples, 'Without me ye can do nothing;' for as the body without the spirit is dead, so the Church without Christ is also dead; and nothing but his return can restore it to life."

The Believer's Foretastes of Heaven.

"The apostle, after informing us 'that eye hath not seen, nor ear heard, nor the heart of man conceived of those things which God has prepared for them that love him,' adds, 'but God hath revealed them unto us by his Spirit.' Of the truth of this assertion every Christian, who walks in the fear of God, is convinced by happy experience. Like the blessed inhabitants of heaven, such persons are enabled by the Holy Spirit to enjoy fellowship with the Father, and with his Son Jesus Christ; to participate in the joy that is felt in heaven when sinners repent; and to unite with the spirits of the just made perfect in ascribing blessing, and glory, and power, unto God and the Lamb. At intervals, which return more or less frequently in proportion to their diligence, zeal, and fidelity, God is pleased to grant them still greater consolation, to lift upon them the light of his countenance, and cause them to rejoice in his salvation. He sheds abroad his love in their hearts, makes them to know the great love wherewith he has loved them, shines in upon their souls with the pure, dazzling, transforming beams of celestial mercy, truth, and grace; displays to their enraptured view the ineffable beauties and glories of Him who is the chief among ten thousand, and enables them in some measure to comprehend the lengths and breadths, the heights and depths, of that love of Christ which passeth knowledge. While the happy Christian, in these bright, enraptured moments, sinks lower and lower in self-abasement and humility, the Spirit of God, stooping from his blessed abode, raises him, as it were, on his celestial wings, and places him before the open door of heaven, and enables him to look in and contemplate the great I AM, the Ancient of days, enthroned with the Son of his love, the brightness of his glory. He contemplates, he wonders, he admires, he loves, he adores. Absorbed in the ravishing, the ecstatic contemplation of uncreated loveliness, glory, and beauty, he forgets the world, he forgets himself, he almost forgets that he exists. His whole soul goes forth in one intense flame of admiration, love, and desire, and he longs to plunge into the boundless ocean of perfection which opens to his view, and to be wholly swallowed and lost in God. With an energy and activity of soul unknown before, he roams and ranges through this infinite ocean of existence and happiness, of perfection and glory, of power and wisdom, of light and love, where he can find neither bottom nor shore. His soul dilates itself beyond its ordinary capacity, and expands to receive the tide of felicity which fills and overwhelms it. No language can do justice to his feelings, for his joys are unspeakable; but with an emphasis, a meaning, an energy, which God only could excite, and which God alone can comprehend, he exclaims in broken accents, My Father and my God! Thus by the agency of the Spirit is he filled with all the fullness of God, and rejoices with joy unspeakable and full of glory, till his wise and compassionate Father, in condescension to the weakness of his almost expiring child, graciously draws a vail over glories too dazzling for mortal eyes long to sustain; leaving him still, however, in the enjoyment of that peace of God which passeth all understanding. Such, my friends, are the joys which the Spirit of God occasionally imparts to those who walk in his fear; or rather, such is the exceedingly imperfect description of them which we are able to give."

The Sufferings of Christ a Proof of his Love.

"Other things being equal, we consider that love as the greatest which induces a willingness to suffer the greatest degree of pain. And this is just reasoning; for self-love makes us unwilling to suffer. Of course, when we are willing to suffer for the sake of another, it proves that we love him as we love ourselves; nay, that our love for him is sufficiently strong to counteract the influence of self-love. Let us, then, inquire what Christ's love for us led him to suffer for our sakes. But here we labor under a difficulty; a difficulty arising from our ignorance. We know but little even of the bodily sufferings which he endured for our salvation. We know, indeed, that he was scourged till the naked bones appeared through his mangled flesh; that he was buffeted, or beaten upon the face; that his temples were pierced with thorns; that he was fastened to the cross by nails driven through his hands and feet, and that, with his whole weight thus suspended, he hung for six hours, bleeding, parched with thirst, and agonizing in the pangs of death. But though we know these facts, we know but little of his bodily sufferings. It is one thing to read or hear of what he suffered, and quite another thing to form a just conception of it. By what effort either of our understandings or of our imaginations are we to conceive of tortures which we never felt—to conceive of the pangs of crucifixion—to conceive of the agonies inflicted by hanging with the whole weight of the body suspended on nails driven through the hands and feet—parts of the frame which are, perhaps above others, endowed with the most exquisite sensibility. One stroke of the scourge, one thorn piercing our temples, one of the many repeated blows by which the nails were urged home, would probably give us more lively ideas of what our Saviour suffered than all our efforts can excite. And yet the tortures which his body endured were but a part, and incomparably the smaller part, of his sufferings. They wrung from him no groan, no expression of anguish. But his mental sufferings did more. They wrung from him not only groans, but great drops of blood. Before he was arrested, and while his body was free from pain, he was, we are told, in an agony—he exclaimed, 'My soul is exceeding sorrowful, even unto death;' and his sweat was as great drops of blood falling down to the ground. Is it asked, what occasioned this mental agony? I answer, it was the curse of the law, which, we are told, he bore for us. It was the hand of his Father, the hand of Omnipotence, which, as the prophet informs us, bruised him and put him to grief. The burden of man's guilt which he bore, the weight of divine wrath which we deserved, was what crushed him down. He drank the cup which we were doomed to drink, that cup into which, an apostle tells us, was poured the fierceness of the wrath of Almighty God. It was of this he said, 'Father, if it be possible, let this cup pass from me.' It was the agonies occasioned by drinking this cup which made him cry out, 'My God, my God, why hast thou forsaken me?' Now if we cannot conceive the full extent of his bodily sufferings, how much less can we conceive of the nameless anguish of his soul? Who, on this side everlasting burnings, can conceive what it is to drink the fierceness of the wrath of Almighty God, poured out without mixture into the cup of his indignation? Yet under the united pressure of all these inconceivable corporeal and mental agonies he consented to die, and it was love, love for us, which induced him to consent. Well, then, may we exclaim, while standing by his cross, Behold how he loved us!"

A Striking Illustration.

"Still more loudly does the professing Christian declare that he regards his God and Redeemer as a wilderness, when he repairs, in search of happiness, to the scenes of worldly pleasure, or to the society of worldly-minded men. He then says to them in effect, The ways of wisdom are not ways of pleasantness; a religious life is a life of constraint and melancholy; I should die with hunger and thirst did I not occasionally forsake the wilderness in which I am doomed to live, and refresh myself with the fruits on which you are feasting. Suppose, my hearers, that while Adam resided in Paradise the world had been filled, as it now is, with sinful inhabitants. Had he, in these circumstances, frequently, or occasionally, forsaken the garden of God, and wandered out into the world to seek happiness in the society or in the pursuits of sinful men, would not his conduct have seemed to say, Paradise is a wilderness, a land of darkness, in which happiness is not to be found? I am weary of the presence of God, which is there manifested, and am constrained to come to you in search of pleasures which my place of residence does not afford? Just so, when the professed friends of God wander from him, and from the path of duty, in search of happiness, they practically say, He is a wilderness, a land of darkness, in which I find nothing pleasant, nothing to allure, nothing which satisfies my desires."

The Oracles of God.

"That this title is given to the Scriptures with perfect truth and propriety no one who acknowledges their divine inspiration will, it is presumed, deny. They do not, indeed, and it is one of their chief excellences that they do not, resemble in all respects the heathen oracles. They neither answer, nor profess to answer, such questions as were usually proposed to them. They inform no man what will be the duration of his life, nor by what means it will be terminated. They will not predict to us the result of any particular private or public enterprise. They will not aid the politician in devising, nor the soldier in executing, schemes for the subjugation of his fellow-creatures. They were never designed to gratify a vain curiosity; much less to subserve the purposes of ambition or avarice; and this is, probably, one reason why many persons never consult them. But though they give no answers to such questions as these passions suggest, they answer questions incomparably more important, and communicate information infinitely more valuable. If they inform no man when or how his life will be terminated, they inform every man, who rightly consults them, how both its progress and termination may be rendered happy. If they inform no man how he may prolong his existence in this world, they will inform every man how he may secure everlasting life in the world to come. If they give no information respecting the result of any particular enterprise, they will teach us how to conduct all our enterprises in such a manner that the final result shall be glory, and honor, and immortality. And while they inform individuals how they may obtain endless felicity, they will teach nations how to secure national prosperity. In fine, whatever a man's situation and circumstances may be, whatever offices or relations he may sustain; this oracle, if consulted in the manner in which God has prescribed, will satisfactorily answer every question which it is proper for him to ask; every question, an answer to which is necessary either to his present or future well being; for it contains all the information which our most wise and benevolent Creator sees it best that his human creatures should, at present, possess. Indeed, we have reason to believe that should he now condescend to visit and converse with us in a visible form, he would answer all our inquiries by referring us to the Scriptures; for when our Saviour, in whom are hidden all the treasures of wisdom and knowledge, resided on earth, he pursued this course with respect to such questions as had been already answered in the Old Testament. To such as proposed any of those questions his usual answer was, What saith the Scripture? What is written in the law? How readest thou? And if he pursued this course while the Scriptures contained the Old Testament only, we may presume that he would now pursue it exclusively, since the revelation which God designed for men is completed by the addition of the New. In possessing the Scriptures, then, our country possesses every real advantage that would result from the establishment of an oracle among us, where God should give answers to his worshipers by an audible voice, as he formerly did to the Jews. Indeed, we possess advantages in some respects far greater than would result from such an establishment; for wherever the oracle might be placed, it would unavoidably be at a distance from a large proportion of those who wished for its advice; to consult it, a long and expensive journey would often be necessary; and, in many cases of frequent occurrence, an answer, thus obtained, would come too late. But in the Scriptures we possess an oracle which may be brought home to every family and every individual; which may be placed in our habitations, in our closets, and consulted daily or hourly, without fatigue, expense, or delay; nay more, which may be made the companion of the traveler on his journey and of the mariner on his voyage. In this oracle we possess all, and much more than all, that was possessed by the ancient Church in its urim and thummin, its ephod and its sanctuary. By placing it in our closets, and consulting it aright, we may make them to us all that the Holy of Holies was to the pious Moses; a place where God will meet us, converse with us, answer our inquiries, and accept our offerings. In fine, we have in this oracle the very mind and heart of our Creator. The thoughts and purposes of his mind, and the emotions of his heart, lie here in silence, waiting an opportunity to make themselves known. Hence, whenever we open the Scriptures, we do in effect open the lips of Jehovah, and the words of eternal truth burst at once upon our ears; the counsels of unerring wisdom address our understandings and our hearts."

The Inquirer at the Oracle.

" It is also true, that in consequence of having been familiar from our childhood with much of the information which these oracles impart, we are generally far from being sensible how deeply we are indebted to them, how great is their value, and how deplorable our situation would be rendered by their loss. If we would form just conceptions of these several particulars, we must place ourselves, for a moment, in the situation of a serious, reflecting inquirer after truth, who has reached the meridian of life without any knowledge of the Scriptures. Let us suppose such a man to have diligently studied himself, his fellow-creatures, and the world around him; and to have made use of all the assistance which heathen philosophy can afford. Let us suppose that he has pursued his inquiries as far as unassisted human intellect can go, and that he now finds himself bewildered in a maze of conflicting theories, and enveloped by all that distracting uncertainty, perplexity, and anxiety into which the researches of men unenlightened by revelation inevitably plunge them. To such a man what would the Scriptures be worth? What would he give for a single hour's opportunity of consulting an oracle which should return such answers to his inquiries as they contain? Would you rightly estimate the information which he might derive from such an oracle during that short period? See him, then, approach it, and listen while he consults it. Perplexed by the numberless questions which impatiently demand a solution, and agitated by an undefinable awe of the invisible, mysterious Being whom he is about to address, he scarcely knows how, or where, to commence his inquiries. At length he hesitatingly and tremblingly asks, 'To whom are the heavens above me, the world which I inhabit, and the various objects with which it is filled, indebted for their existence?' A mild, but majestic voice replies from the oracle, In the beginning, God created the heavens, and the earth, and all that is therein. Startled by the scarcely expected answer, but soon recovering his self-possession, the inquirer eagerly exclaims, 'Who is God—what is his nature, his character, his attributes?' God, replies the voice, is a spirit: he is from everlasting to everlasting, without beginning of days or end of years; and with him is no variableness nor shadow of turning; he fills heaven and earth; he searches the hearts and tries the reins of the children of men; he is the only Wise, the Almighty, the High, and Holy, and Just One; he is Jehovah, Jehovah God, merciful and gracious, longsuffering, and abundant in goodness and truth, keeping mercy for thousands, forgiving iniquity, transgression, and sin; but one who will by no means clear the guilty. A solemn pause ensues. The inquirer's mind is overwhelmed. It labors, it sinks, it faints, while vainly attempting to grasp the illimitable, incomprehensible Being, now for the first time disclosed to its view. But a new and more powerful motive now stimulates his inquiries and, with augmented interest he asks, 'Does any relation or connection subsist between this God and myself?' He is thy Maker, returns the oracle, the Father of thy spirit, and thy Preserver; he it is who giveth thee richly all things to enjoy; he is thy Sovereign, thy Lawgiver, and thy Judge; in him thou dost live, and move, and exist, nor can any one deliver thee out of his hands; and when, at death, thy dust shall return to the earth as it was, thy spirit will return to God who gave it. 'How,' resumes the inquirer, 'will he then receive me?' He will reward thee according to thy works. 'What are the works,' the inquirer asks, 'which this Sovereign requires of me?' Thou shalt love the Lord thy God with all thy heart, and with all thy soul, and with all thy mind, and with all thy strength. Every transgression of this law is a sin; and the soul that sinneth shall die. 'Have I sinned?' the inquirer tremblingly asks. All, replies the oracle, have sinned, and come short of the glory of God. The God, in whose hand thy breath is, and whose are all thy ways, thou hast not glorified. A new sensation, the sensation of conscious guilt, now oppresses the inquirer, and with increased anxiety he asks, 'Is there any way in which the pardon of sin may be obtained?' The blood of Jesus Christ, replies the oracle, cleanseth from all sin. He that confesseth and forsaketh his sins shall find mercy. 'But to whom shall I confess them?' the inquirer resumes; 'where shall I find the God whom I have offended, that I may acknowledge my transgressions, and implore his mercy?' He is a God at hand, returns the voice; he is not far from thee; I, who speak to thee, am he. 'God be merciful to me a sinner!' exclaims the inquirer, smiting upon his breast, and not daring to lift his eyes toward the oracle. 'What, Lord, wilt thou have me to do?' Believe on the Lord Jesus Christ, answers the voice, and thou shalt be saved. 'Lord, who is Jesus Christ, that I may believe on him?' He is my beloved Son, whom I have set forth to be a propitiation through faith in his blood; hear thou him, for there is salvation in no other. Such are, probably, some of the questions which would be asked by the supposed inquirer; and such are, in substance, the answers which he would receive from the oracles of God."

Nature and Effects of Godly Fear.

"By the fear of God is meant, not that guilty, slavish fear, which impenitent sinners often feel, but the holy, filial fear, which is peculiar to real Christians. This fear is every-where represented by the inspired writers as one of the most essential parts of true religion, and is, indeed, not unfrequently used by them to denote religion itself. It is produced and maintained in the heart by the agency of the divine Spirit. It arises from a believing apprehension and an experimental knowledge of the existence, character, perfections, and constant presence of Jehovah;

it is occasioned by a spiritual discovery, made to the soul, of his awful, adorable, and infinite perfections; and its natural effects are, veneration for God, submission to his will, obedience to his commands, and a holy, watchful care to avoid every thing which may grieve, displease, or provoke him to forsake us."

The Fear of God Controlling the Imagination.

"The fear of God controls, in some measure at least, the imagination. It is true that this lawless, and almost untamable power seems to be less influenced by the fear of God than any other faculty of the soul. Still, wherever the fear of God exists, the imagination will be constrained, in some degree, to submit to it. Its sallies will be carefully watched, its excursive wanderings will be checked; it will be speedily recalled when it roams into forbidden ground, and be often compelled to assist the Christian in his meditations on death, judgment, and the realities of eternity. Knowing that the thought of foolishness is sin, he who fears God will at least strenuously endeavor to prevent vain thoughts from lodging within him, and his endeavors will gradually be crowned with success. Such is that submission of the soul to God which walking in his fear implies."

The Duty of the Church toward Children.

"A duty incumbent on every Church, considered as such, is to take care of the religious education of its children. It is true that the religious education of children is a duty more immediately incumbent on their parents; but it is incumbent on Churches to take care that such of their members as are parents perform this duty. The neglect of it ought to be regarded as a subject of Church discipline. Addressing his ancient Church as an individual, God says, Thou hast taken my sons and my daughters which thou hast borne unto me, and hast sacrificed them unto idols to be devoured. Is this a small matter, that thou hast slain my children? But it is evident that the Jewish Church did not actually sacrifice children to idols in its collective capacity. This was the act of individual parents. Yet because the Church did not interpose to prevent the sacrifice, it is charged upon it as the act of the whole. And so if children of the Church are now sacrificed to Satan on the altar of the world by their parents, the Church itself is answerable, so far as their own neglect was the cause."

The Gospel Glad Tidings.

"Do you demand evidences that the Gospel is glad tidings? You shall have them. Come with me to the garden of Eden. Look back to the hour which succeeded man's apostasy. See the golden chain which bound man to God sundered, apparently forever, and this wretched world, groaning under the weight of human guilt and of its Creator's curse, sinking down, far down, into a bottomless abyss of misery and despair. See that tremendous Being who is a consuming fire, encircling it on every side, and wrapping it, as it were, in an atmosphere of flame. Hear from his lips the tremendous sentence, Man has sinned, and man must die. See the king of terrors advancing, with gigantic strides, to execute the awful sentence, spreading desolation through the vegetable, animal, and rational kingdoms, and brandishing his resistless dart in triumph over a prostrate world. See the grave expanding her marble jaws to receive whatever might fall before his wide-wasting scythe, and hell beneath yawning dreadfully to engulf forever its guilty, helpless, despairing victims. Such was the situation of our ruined race after the apostasy. There was nothing before every child of Adam but a certain fearful looking-for of judgment and fiery indignation. There was but one road through this world, but one gate that opened out of it—the wide gate and the broad way that leads to destruction.

"My friends, endeavor to realize, if you can, the horrors of such a situation. I am aware that to do this is by no means easy. You have so long been accustomed to hear the tidings of salvation that you can scarcely conceive of what would have been our situation had no Saviour appeared. But endeavor, for a moment, to forget that you ever heard of Christ or his Gospel. View yourselves as immortal beings hastening to eternity, with the curse of God's broken law, like a flaming sword, pursuing you; death, with his dart dipped in mortal poison, awaiting you; a dark cloud, fraught with the lightnings of divine vengeance, rolling over your heads; your feet standing in slippery places in darkness, and the bottomless pit beneath, expecting your fall. Then, when not only all hope, but all possibility of escape seemed taken away, suppose the flaming sword suddenly extinguished, the sting of death extracted, the Sun of righteousness bursting forth, painting a rainbow upon the before threatening cloud, a golden ladder let down from the opening gates of heaven, while a choir of angels swiftly descending, exclaim, 'Behold, we bring you glad tidings of great joy, which shall be to all people; for unto you is born a Saviour who is Christ the Lord.' Would you, could you, while contemplating such a scene, and listening to the angelic message, doubt it communicated glad tidings? Would you not rather unite with them in exclaiming, Glad tidings, glad tidings, glory to God in the highest, that there is peace on earth and good-will to men?"

The Gospel Glorious Glad Tidings.

"The Gospel is not only glad tidings, but glorious glad tidings. St. Paul, contrasting the Gospel and the Law, with a view to show the superiority of the former, observes that if the ministration of death was glorious, the ministration of the Spirit must be still more glorious; for if the ministration of condemnation be glory, much more doth the ministration of righteousness exceed in glory. Glory is the display of excellence, or perfection. That the Gospel contains a grand display of the moral excellences and perfections of Jehovah will be denied by none but the spiritually blind, who are ignorant of its nature. But to give only a general view of this grand display of God's character in a single discourse, or even in a volume, is impossible. With less difficulty might we inclose the sun in a lantern. We shall not, therefore, attempt to describe a subject which must forever be degraded, not only by the descriptions, but by the conceptions, I will not say of men, but of the highest archangel before the throne. On no page less ample than that of the eternal, all-infolding mind, which devised the Gospel plan of salvation, can its glories be displayed, nor by any inferior mind can they be fully comprehended. Suffice it to say, that here the moral character of Jehovah shines full-orbed and complete : here all the fullness of the Godhead, all the insufferable splendors of Deity, burst at once upon our aching sight : here the manifold perfections of God, holiness and goodness, justice and mercy, truth and grace, majesty and condescension, hatred of sin and compassion for sinners, are harmoniously blended, like the parti-colored rays of solar light in one pure blaze of dazzling whiteness. Here, rather than on any of his other works, he founds his claims to the highest admiration, gratitude, and love of his creatures :—here is the work which ever has called forth, and which through eternity will continue to call forth, the most rapturous praises of the celestial choirs, and feed the ever-glowing fires of devotion in their breasts ; for the glory which shines in the Gospel is the glory which illuminates heaven, and the Lamb that was slain is the light thereof. To the truth of these assertions all will assent who can say with the apostle, 'God, who commanded the light to shine out of darkness, hath shined in our hearts, to give us the light of the knowledge of the glory of God in the face of Jesus Christ ; and we beheld his glory, the glory as of the only begotten of the Father, full of grace and truth.'"

An Appeal to Christian Ministers.

" Heathen writers inform us of a soldier who, when sent out by his general with tidings of a victory, would not stop to extract a thorn which had deeply pierced his foot until he had delivered his message to the Senate. And shall we, then, when sent by Jehovah with such a message—a message the faithful delivery of which involves his glory and the eternal happiness of our fellow-creatures—shall we linger, shall we suffer any personal inconveniences, any difficulties, any real or fancied dangers, to interrupt or retard us in the execution of our work? Shall we, with the true water of life, the true elixir of immortality in our possession, suffer our own private concerns to divert us from presenting it to the dying, and forcing it into the lips of the dead? Shall we, with Aaron's censer in our hands, hesitate whether to rush between the living and the dead, when the anger of the Lord is kindled, when the plague has already begun its ravages, and thousands are falling at our right hand, and ten thousand at our left? Shall we wait till to-morrow to present the bread of life to the famished wretch, who, before to-morrow arrives, may expire for want of it? Surely if we can do this—if we can be so regardless of our obligations to God and of our duty to man—the least punishment which we can expect is to be debarred from that salvation which we neglected to afford to others, and to be made answerable for the blood of all the souls who, in consequence of this neglect, perished in their sins. Let us, then, my fathers and brethren, never forget that the King's business requireth haste, and that who or whatever stands still, we must not. Let the sun pause in his course, though half the world should be wrapped in frost and darkness by his delay; let rivers stagnate in their channels, though an expecting nation should perish with thirst upon its flood-forsaken banks; let long-looked-for showers stop in mid-air, though earth, with a thousand famished lips, invoke their descent; but let those who are sent with the life-giving tidings of pardon, peace, and salvation to an expiring world never pause, never look or wish for rest till their Master's welcome voice shall call them from their field of labor to everlasting repose; to that world where those, who, as burning or shining lights, have turned many to righteousness, shall shine as the stars, and as the brightness of the firmament for ever and ever."

Christ as a Citizen of our World.

"It must have been exceedingly painful to such a person as Christ to live in a world like this. He was perfectly holy, harmless, and undefiled. Of course, he could not look on sin but with the deepest abhorrence. It is that abominable thing which his soul hates. Yet during the whole period of his residence on earth he was continually surrounded by it, and his feelings were every moment tortured with the hateful sight of human depravity. How much sorrow the sight occasioned him, we may in some measure learn from the bitter complaints which similar causes extorted from David, Jeremiah, and other ancient saints. They describe, in the most striking and pathetic language, the sufferings which they experienced from the prevalency of wickedness around them, and often wished for death to relieve them from their sufferings. But the sufferings of Christ from this cause were incomparably greater than theirs. He was far more holy than they, his hatred of sin incomparably more intense, and the sight of it proportionably more painful. In consequence of his power of searching the heart, he saw unspeakably more sin in the world than any mere man could discover. We can discover sin only when it displays itself in words and actions. But he saw all the hidden wickedness of the heart, the depths of that fountain of iniquity from which all the bitter streams of vice and misery flow. Every man that approached him was transparent to his eye. In his best friends he saw more sin than we can discover in the most abandoned reprobates. He saw also, in a far clearer light than we can do, the dreadful consequences of sin, the interminable miseries to which it is conducting the sinner, and his feelings of compassion were not blunted by that selfish insensibility which enables us to bear with composure the sight of human distress. On the contrary, he was all sympathy, compassion, and love. He loved others as himself, and therefore felt for the sufferings of others as for his own. If Paul could say, Who is weak and I am not weak? who is offended and I burn not? much more might Christ. In this, as well as in a still more important sense, he took upon himself our griefs, and bore our sorrows. As he died for all, so he felt and wept for the sufferings of all. The temporal and eternal calamities of the whole human race, and of every individual among them, all seemed to be collected and laid upon him. He saw at one view the whole mighty aggregate of human guilt and human wretchedness, and his boundless benevolence and compassion made it by sympathy all his own. It has been said by philosophers, that if any man could see all the misery which is daily felt in the world he would never smile again. We need not wonder, then, that Christ, who saw and felt it all, never smiled, though he often wept. We may add, that the perfect contrast between the heavens which he had left and the world into which he came, rendered a residence in the latter peculiarly painful to his feelings. In heaven he had seen nothing but holiness, happiness, and love. In this world, on the contrary, he saw little but wickedness, hatred, and misery in ten thousand forms. In heaven he was crowned with glory, and honor, and majesty, and surrounded by throngs of admiring, adoring angels. On earth, he found himself plunged in poverty, wretchedness, and contempt, and surrounded by malignant, implacable enemies. My friends, think of a prince educated with care and tenderness in his father's court, where he heard nothing but sounds of pleasure and praise, and saw nothing but scenes of honor and magnificence, sent unattended to labor as a slave in a rebellious province, where himself and his father were hated and despised; think of a person of the most delicate and refined taste going from the bosom of his family, and the magnificent abodes of a polished city, to spend his life in the filthy huts of the most degraded and barbarous savages, and compelled daily to witness the disgusting scenes of cruelty and brutality which are there exhibited; think of a man endowed with the tenderest sensibility, compelled to live on a field of battle, among the corpses of the dead and the groans of the dying, or shut up for years in a madhouse with wretched maniacs, where nothing was to be heard but the burst of infuriated passions, the wild laugh of madness, and the shrieks and ravings of despair. Think of these instances, and you will have some conception, though but a faint one, of the scenes which this world presented to our Saviour, of the contrast between it and the heaven he left, of the sorrows which embittered every moment of his earthly existence, and of the love which induced him voluntarily to submit to such sorrows.

"Another circumstance which contributed to render our Saviour a man of sorrows, and his life a life of grief, was the reception he met with from those whom he came to save. Had they received him with that gratitude and respect which he deserved, and permitted him to rescue them from their miseries, it would have been some alleviation of his sorrows. But even this alleviation was in a great measure denied him. Some few, indeed, received him with affection and respect, though even they often grieved him by their unkindness and unbelief; but by far the greater part of his countrymen he was treated with the utmost cruelty and contempt. Many of them would not allow him even to remove their bodily diseases, and still greater numbers were unwilling that he should save them from their sins. Now to a noble, ingenuous mind, nothing is so cutting, so torturing, as such conduct. To see himself despised, slandered, and persecuted with implacable malice, by the very beings he was laboring to save; to see all his endeavors to save them frustrated by their own incorrigible folly and wickedness; to see them, by rejecting him, filling up to the brim their cup of criminality and wrath, and sinking into eternal perdition within reach of his vainly-offered hand —to see this, must have been distressing indeed.

Yet this Christ saw. Thus he endured the contradiction of sinners against himself; and how deeply it affected him, we may infer from the fact, that though his own sufferings never wrung from him a tear, he once and again wept in the bitterness of his soul over rebellious Jerusalem, exclaiming, 'O that thou hadst known, even thou, at least in this thy day, the things that belong to thy peace; but now they are hid from thine eyes!'

"Another circumstance that threw a shade of gloom and melancholy over our Saviour's life was, his clear view and constant anticipation of the dreadful agonies in which it was to terminate. He was not ignorant, as we happily are, of the miseries which were before him. He could not hope, as we do, when wretched to-day, to be happier to-morrow. Every night, when he lay down to rest, the scourge, the crown of thorns, and the cross were present to his mind; and on these dreadful objects he every morning opened his eyes, and every morning saw them nearer than before. Every day was to him like the day of his death, of such a death, too, as no one ever suffered before or since. How deeply the prospect affected him is evident from his own language: 'I have a baptism to be baptized with, and how am I straitened till it be accomplished!'"

The Meekness and Patience of Jesus in Crucifixion.

"'He was oppressed and afflicted, yet he opened not his mouth. He was brought as a lamb to the slaughter, and as a sheep before his shearers is dumb, so he opened not his mouth.' Never was language more descriptive of the most perfect meekness and patience; never was prediction more fully justified by the event than in the case before us. Christ was indeed led as a lamb to the slaughter. Silent, meek, and unrepining he stood before his butchers, at once innocent and patient as a lamb. No murmurs, no complaints, no angry recriminations escaped from his lips. If they were opened, it was but to express the most perfect submission to his Father's will, and to breathe out prayers for his murderers. Yes, even at that dreadful moment, when they were nailing him to the cross—when nature, whose voice will at such a time be heard, was shuddering and convulsed in the prospect of a speedy and violent death—when his soul was tortured by the assaults of malignant fiends, and his Father's face hidden from his view—even then he possessed his soul in patience to such a degree as to be able to pray for his murderers. My friends, we must attempt to bring the scene more fully to your view. Come with us, a moment, to Calvary. See the savage, ferocious soldiers seizing with rude violence his sacred body, forcing it down upon the cross, wresting and extending his limbs, and with remorseless cruelty forcing through his hands and feet the ragged spikes which were to fasten him on it. See the Jewish priests and rulers watching with looks of malicious pleasure the horrid scene, and attempting to increase his sufferings by scoffs and blasphemies. Now contemplate attentively the countenance of the wonderful sufferer, which seems like heaven opening in the midst of hell, and tell me what it expressed. You see it, indeed, full of anguish, but it expresses nothing like impatience, resentment, or revenge. On the contrary, it beams with pity, benevolence, and forgiveness. It perfectly corresponds with the prayer which, raising his mild, imploring eye to heaven, he pours forth to God, 'Father, forgive them, for they know not what they do!' Christian, look at your Master and learn how to suffer. Sinner, look at your Saviour and learn how to admire, to imitate, and to forgive."

Christ's Mediatorial Kingdom.

"The laws of this extensive kingdom are recorded in the Gospel. The subjects of it may be divided into two grand classes—those who are obedient and those who are rebellious. The former class is composed of good men and angels; the latter, of wicked men and devils. The former serve Christ willingly and cheerfully. He rules them with the golden scepter of love; his law is written in their hearts; they esteem his yoke easy and his burden light, and habitually execute his will. All the bright armies of heaven, angels and archangels, who excel in strength, are his servants, and go forth at his command, as messengers of love to minister unto the heirs of salvation, or as messengers of wrath to execute vengeance on his enemies. Nor are his obedient subjects to be found only in heaven. In this rebellious world also the standard of the cross, the banner of his love, is erected, and thousands and millions who were once his enemies have been brought willing captives to his feet, have joyfully acknowledged him as their Master and Lord, and sworn allegiance to him as the Captain of their salvation. Nor is his authority less absolute over the second class of his subjects, who still persist in their rebellion. In vain do they say, We will not have this man to reign over us. He rules them with a rod of iron, causes even their wrath to praise him, and makes them the involuntary instruments of carrying on his great designs. He holds all the infernal spirits in a chain, governs the conquerors, monarchs, and great ones of the earth, and in all things wherein they did proudly is still above them. None are too small to escape his notice, none are too great to be controlled by his power."

The Progress and Prospects of Christ's Kingdom.

" By the progress of this kingdom, we do not mean the increase of Messiah's power—for, as we have just seen, this is already unlimited and universal—but we mean the spread of the Gospel, and the increase of the number of Christ's obedient subjects. In this respect the progress of the kingdom has hitherto been comparatively small; for though thousands and millions have submitted to his arms, yet many millions are still in arms against him. Satan still apparently reigns as the prince and god of this ruined world. Darkness still covers the earth, and gross darkness the people; and by far the greater part of our race are still the wretched captives of idolatry, vice, and superstition. But it shall not always, it shall not long, be thus. The promise of Him who cannot lie assures us that it shall not. His word abounds with the most explicit and animating predictions of the future spread and approaching glories of Messiah's reign. The stone which the king of Babylon saw in his dream cut out of a mountain without hands, shall spread and fill the earth. In the days of these kings, that is, of the Roman emperors, says the prophet Daniel, in expounding this dream, shall the God of heaven set up a kingdom which shall never be destroyed; it shall never be left to other people, but it shall break in pieces and consume all these kingdoms, and it shall stand forever. The fulfillment of these predictions the same prophet elsewhere describes. 'I saw in the night visions,' says he, 'and behold, one like the Son of man came with the clouds, and came to the Ancient of days, and there was given him dominion and glory and a kingdom, that all people, nations, and languages should serve him. His dominion is an everlasting dominion, and his kingdom, that which shall not be destroyed.' In addition to this, the prophecies of Isaiah and the minor prophets are filled with predictions of the same import. We are there assured, that in the last days the mountain of the Lord's house shall be established upon the top of the mountains, and all nations shall flow unto it; that the knowledge of the Lord shall fill the earth; that Ethiopia shall stretch out her hands unto God, and that the Jews shall be brought in with the fullness of the Gentiles. It is, however, needless to insist on these predictions, for we are assured that Christ shall reign till all enemies are put under his feet; and we are also informed that Jehovah has sworn by himself that every knee shall bow to Jesus, and every tongue confess that he is Lord. In vain will any strive to prevent the fulfillment of this declaration. Those who refuse to confess him cheerfully, shall be compelled to do it reluctantly; those who will not bend shall break; for God has declared that he will overturn, overturn, and overturn, till He shall come whose right it is, and the dominion shall be given to him, and that all the kingdoms of this world shall become the kingdoms of our Lord and of his Christ. Nor will it be long ere these predictions are fulfilled. Already is the banner of the cross unfurled. Already are the soldiers of Christ going forth to subdue the nations, with weapons which are mighty to the pulling down of strongholds. Already does a voice begin to be heard throughout the world, saying, 'Repent, for the kingdom of heaven is at hand.' Already has Christ ascended the chariot of his salvation, and is riding forth, conquering and to conquer, arrayed in meekness, and truth, and righteousness, while God overturns, overturns, and overturns the nations which oppose him, and dashes them in pieces against each other like a potter's vessel. Already is the cry heard from Asia and Africa, Come over and help us; and soon will Ethiopia stretch out her hands to God, and the isles of the Southern ocean wait for his law. Soon will the cry be heard, Alleluia, for the Lord God omnipotent reigneth. He who sits on the throne is exclaiming, Behold, I create all things new; I create new heavens and a new earth. Behold, the Lord God shall come with a strong arm, his reward is with him, and his work before him. Prepare ye, then, the way of the Lord, make straight in the desert a highway for our God. But what tongue can describe the happiness which is approaching? who can paint the glories of Messiah's reign? In his days shall the righteous flourish, and abundance of peace, so long as the moon endureth. His name shall endure as long as the sun, and men shall be blessed in him, and all nations shall call him blessed. The wilderness and the solitary place shall be glad, and the desert rejoice and blossom as the rose. Then shall the eyes of the blind be opened, and the ears of the deaf unstopped; then shall the lame man leap as a hart, and the tongue of the dumb sing. Nations shall not lift up sword against nation, nor learn war any more. The wolf also shall dwell with the lamb, and the leopard lie down with the kid, and the calf and the young lion and the fatling together, and a little child shall lead them. And the cow and the bear shall feed; their young ones shall lie down together. Thus that paradisaical state which was destroyed by the first Adam shall be restored by the second; and love, peace, and happiness, which sin had banished from the world, shall again return under the mild reign of Him who is emphatically styled the Prince of Peace. Who, in view of these glorious prospects, can avoid exclaiming,

> 'O long expected day begin;
> Dawn on this world of death and sin!
> Come the great day, the glorious hour,' etc.?"

Christ's Ascension.

"That we may look at this scene aright, it is desirable to view it as it appeared to his disciples. In order to do this, we must, by the aid of the imagination and a strong faith, place ourselves as it were in their circles, and look at it through their eyes. Finding them assembled in Jerusalem, their Master, for the last time, calls them to follow him. They obey, and he leads them out of the city to the Mount of Olives. There, standing on an eminence, where they can all see him, he gives them his last instructions and his parting promises. Then, lifting up his hands, he pronounces upon them a blessing, and while he pronounces it, they see him rise from the earth, self-moved, self-supported, and begin to ascend. Reclining as on the bosom of the air he rises higher and higher, with a gentle, gradual motion, his countenance, beaming compassion and love, still fixed on his disciples, and his hands extended, still scattering blessings on them as he ascended. Now he rises above the groves by which they are surrounded; now he mounts to the middle region of the air; now he reaches the clouds, and still they see him. But there a cloudy vehicle receives him, conceals him from their eyes, and rises with him. With eager eyes they still follow the ascending cloud as it mounts toward the skies, lessening to their sight till it becomes only a small speck, and at length wholly disappears, far away in the ethereal regions.

"But though their eyes could follow him no further, we need not stop here. Borrowing the glass of revelation we may see him still ascending, reaching, and entering the wide, unfolded gates of heaven, sitting down at the right hand of the throne of God, far above all principalities, and powers, and might, and dominion, and every name which is named, not only in this world but in the world to come; and there receiving the scepter of universal empire, and exercising all power in heaven and on earth. Assisted by revelation faith may also see the employments in which our ascended Saviour is engaged. She may see him appearing in the presence of the Father as the Advocate of his people, and continuing to make intercession for all that come unto God by him. She may see him entering with his own blood into the heavenly temple, and there presenting a full atonement for the sins of men. She may see him receiving gifts for men, and sending down those gifts to the successive generations of mankind. Finally, she may see him fulfilling his dying declaration to his disciples: In my Father's house are many mansions, I go to prepare a place for you."

The Human Soul a Palace.

"The human soul may be justly compared to a palace; for it is a most beautiful, noble, and magnificent edifice; an edifice formed of imperishable materials; an edifice fearfully, admirably, wonderfully made. It is a house not made with hands, a building of God, the masterpiece of the all-wise and all-powerful Architect, who formed and adorned it for his own use. It is sufficiently capacious to contain not only the whole creation, but even the Creator himself; for it was especially designed to be the earthly residence of that high and holy One who fills immensity and inhabits eternity. Even now, debased, disfigured, and polluted as it is by sin, it bears the evident marks of original grandeur and beauty; and, as the poet observes of Beelzebub, is majestic though in ruins."

Satan's Code of Laws.

"Should the foe of God and man publish a revelation of his own mind and will, issue his own orders, and promulgate his decrees to mankind, would he not urge them to live just as they now do? Would he not tell the young to put off the thought of death, to neglect religion, to conform to the world, to give themselves up without restraint to the pursuit of frivolous pleasures and amusements, serving divers lusts and vanities? Would he not charge the middle-aged to seek first the good things of this life, instead of the kingdom of God and his righteousness; to lay up treasures on earth and not in heaven; to rise early, sit up late, and eat the bread of carefulness; and put off religion to old age? Would he not command all ages and ranks in society to spend the Sabbath in idleness; in reading foolish, frivolous, or pernicious books; in transacting, or at least thinking of, their worldly business; in unprofitable visits or useless conversation; instead of employing it in attending to the great things which concern their everlasting peace? Would he not charge them when in the house of God to let their thoughts wander after vanities, to neglect or forget the truth which is proclaimed, or to apply it to their neighbors instead of themselves? Would he not enjoin it upon them to neglect the word of God, and to trust in their own righteousness; or assure them, as he did our first parents, that though they transgress and eat forbidden fruit, yet they shall not surely die? Would he not especially charge those who begin to think seriously of religion to dismiss all such melancholy and superstitious fancies, and either to give themselves no concern respecting eternity, or at least defer it to a more convenient season? In a word, would he not direct mankind to love themselves supremely, to do their own pleasure, obey their own inclinations, seek their own exaltation, profit, and honor; and, without regarding what God has said, to cast off his fear and restrain prayer before him, walking in the way of their own hearts, and according to the sight of their own eyes? Yes, my friends, these are the secret wishes of Satan, these would be his commands, should he publish a code of laws; and hence it is but too evident that mankind obey him, that he is the god of this world, and keeps entire possession of every unconverted soul."

Satan's Armor.

"He has his armor both offensive and defensive, and with this he defends and fortifies his palace in the soul, and attempts to make it strong against the Captain of our salvation. This armor is directly the reverse of that Christian armor which St. Paul describes in his Epistle to the Ephesians. Instead of being girded with the girdle of truth, he girds the sinner with a girdle of error, falsehood, and deceit. Instead of the breastplate of Christ's righteousness, he furnishes him with a breastplate of his own fancied righteousness, goodness, and morality. Instead of the shield of faith, which the Christian possesses, the sinner has the shield of unbelief; and with this he defends himself against the threatenings and curses of the law, and all the arrows of conviction which are aimed at him by the ministers of Christ. Instead of having on for a helmet the hope of salvation, by faith in the Saviour's blood, Satan furnishes his subjects with a false hope of obtaining salvation at last, let them live as they please; and instead of the sword of the Spirit, which is the word of God, he teaches them to wield the sword of a tongue set on fire of hell, and furnishes them with a magazine of cavils, sneers, excuses, and objections, with which they attack religion and defend themselves. He also builds for them many refuges of lies, in which, as in a strong castle, they fondly hope to shelter themselves from the wrath of God."

The False Peace of the Sinner.

"The peace which the subjects of Satan enjoy consists in these two particulars: 1. They are seldom if ever alarmed respecting their own salvation. Like madmen, who fancy themselves kings and emperors, the sinner thinks that he is rich and increased in goods, and has need of nothing; and does not in the least suspect that he is poor, and miserable, and blind, and naked. He has a good opinion of himself, suspects no danger, thinks little of death or eternity; or if he does, fancies that he is already prepared, and that there is no cause of anxiety or alarm. True, he may occasionally, notwithstanding his armor, be slightly wounded by the arrows of conviction, or he may hear the curses and terrors of the law proclaimed by God's ministers when they lift up their voices as a trumpet to warn him of his transgressions; but he listens to them as to the noise of distant thunder, which, though it roll over the heads of others, disturbs not himself, and is quickly forgotten amid the hurry and bustle of worldly pursuits.

2. The sinner enjoys peace, because there is nothing in his soul to take the part of God against Satan, and thus produce intestine war and commotion. All his powers and faculties are leagued against God on the side of sin, unless we except his conscience, and

this soon becomes seared and stupefied, so that its voice is seldom heard. There is consequently in the sinner's breast none of that inward warfare which the Christian feels, no lusting of the flesh against the Spirit, and of the Spirit against the flesh. In this respect all is calm and peaceful within, but, alas! it is the calmness and peace of spiritual death.

His understanding, his will, his affections, his imagination are all chained up in spiritual bondage, darkness, and death. The foe of God and man reigns supreme and uncontrolled on the throne of his heart; all his mental and corporeal faculties are so many instruments of unrighteousness to displease and dishonor his Maker; yet he is careless and secure, suspects no danger, and, while hardening himself against God, hopes to prosper."

The Sinner's Substitute in the Hands of Justice.

"But the proofs of Christ's love do not end here. He also gave himself up to the wrath of God, to the curse of his broken law. He surrendered himself as a sinner into the hands of incensed justice; and while he thus stood in the sinner's place, God treated him as if he had been a sinner. He hid his face from him; set the terrors of his wrath in array against him; made him the mark of those arrows, the poison of which drinks up the spirits; and plunged the flaming sword deep in his inmost soul. In this the very essence of his sufferings consisted. All that men and devils could do he bore without a groan. But when the weight of divine wrath crushed him down, when his Father's face was hidden from his view, and he beheld him only in the character of an awful, holy, avenging God, as a consuming fire to sinful creatures, then his anguish could no longer be concealed, but burst forth in that heart-rending exclamation, 'My God, my God, why hast thou forsaken me!'"

Man Lost to God.

"Should a man by any means be deprived of sight, he might be said to be lost to the sun, though this luminary would still shine around him, warm him with its beams, and produce the fruits which preserved his life. But he would have lost all views of its brightness, and of those objects which it discovers to others; its light would no longer guide him, nor enable him to discern the dangers which might be in his path. In a similar manner are men lost with respect to God. Though his glory shines around them, and his power preserves their lives and gives them all the blessings they enjoy, yet they realize not his presence; they are blind to his perfections; they see not his glory in his works; they hear not his voice in his word; they are not guided by his light, they discern not the objects which he reveals. In a word, the Father of lights, the great sun of the universe, has no existence in their apprehensions. And when they look up to heaven all is dark, and the eternal throne appears empty. When they contemplate the visible creation they see only a fair but lifeless body; for of God, the animating, guiding soul, who fills, upholds, and directs every part, they perceive nothing. Even when they look into the volume of his word, it is to them only a dead-letter, and they find there nothing of God, though he lives and speaks in every line. Having thus lost the knowledge of the true God, they turn, of course, to some created idol, and transfer to it that affection, confidence, and dependence which belong to him. Forsaking the fountain of living waters, they have hewed out to themselves cisterns, broken cisterns, which can hold no water. Thus they are lost to God, as this world would be lost to the sun should it fly off into the regions of eternal frost and darkness."

Man Lost to Holiness and Happiness.

"Being thus lost to God, mankind are, of course, lost to holiness. In forsaking him, they forsake the path of duty and become sinners. In forsaking him, they forsake also the Author of all holiness in the hearts of creatures. Turn a mirror from the sun, and it ceases at once to reflect his image. Place it in darkness, and it emits not a gleam of light. So when a creature turns from God, he loses at once his holy image. Forsaking the fountain of good, he becomes wholly destitute of goodness. Should the most perfect created spirit in heaven wander from God, he would cease to be holy; he would become wholly depraved; he would be a devil. Agreeably, the Scriptures invariably represent mankind as by nature entirely destitute of holiness; as alienated from the life of God through the ignorance that is in them, because of the blindness of their hearts; in a word, as dead in trespasses and sins, and, of course, as devoid of holiness as a dead man is of life. In consequence of being thus lost to God and holiness, mankind are consequently lost to happiness. God is the fountain of felicity, the only source of real happiness to intelligent creatures. He is the proper element of the soul, as the ocean is the element of its inhabitants, and as well might the inhabitants of the ocean be happy in the burning sands of Arabia, as man can be happy in a state of absence from God."

The Penal Consequences of Sin.

"By the penal consequences of sin we mean those present and future miseries which the justice of a holy God has attached to its commission. Among those miseries may be mentioned those guilty fears and reproaches of conscience which, in a greater or less degree, all sinners experience. If you will look into your own breasts, my friends, and consider how much you suffer from fears of death, apprehensions of God's anger, and self-reproach; if you reflect how often these things haunt you in secret, and how often they render you unhappy in society even, when an aching heart is concealed by a smiling countenance, you will feel convinced, that if other men are like you, they must feel much more unhappiness than they appear to feel, or than they are willing to confess. And, my friends, other sinful men are like you, and the mental sufferings which agitate your breasts are a faithful counterpart to those which they experience; and never do these sufferings cease till the sinner becomes holy, or his conscience is seared and he is given up of God.

"In the next place, among the penal consequences may be reckoned death, with all the diseases, pains, and sufferings which precede it, and the heart-rending anguish which it often occasions when it deprives us of our children and friends. By sin death entered into the world, and it passes upon all men, because all have sinned. Were there nothing else to render sinful men unhappy, the certainty of death would alone be sufficient to do it; for the more happy they were in other respects, the more would their happiness be disturbed by a dread of that awful hour which must put an end to it; and if their happiness depended on the enjoyment of friends, the uncertainty of their life would furnish new cause for anxiety and alarm.

"But these things, though sufficient to render men strangers to happiness, are not all the penal consequences of sin. On the contrary they are but the beginning of sorrows, for the wages of sin is death, including not the death of the body only, but the death, the eternal death, of the soul. By the broken law of God all sinners are doomed to be cast into the lake of fire, which, says an inspired writer, is the second death; there to sink deeper and deeper through eternity in the abyss of wretchedness and despair, lost, forever lost, to God, to holiness, to happiness, and hope."

The Light that Guides us Back to God.

"Should this world, which now revolves round the sun, wander from it so far as to lose sight of its beams, it is evident that it could never again find its way back to the sun. It could hold up no light by which to discover this luminary; for the sun can be seen only by its own rays, and if the world should once lose sight of these rays, and be lost in the regions of eternal night, there would be nothing to guide it back, nothing to direct its course toward the sun. Then the only way to secure its return would be for a ray of light, proceeding from the sun, to follow the lost planet through all its wanderings, and thus point out the way to the luminary from which itself emanated. Such is the situation of mankind with respect to God, the Sun of the universe. They have wandered from him so far that they have lost sight of his beams, all knowledge of his character, and of the way to find him.

"Now Christ, considered as the Son of man, is a ray of light from this Sun sent to find and guide us back to God. This, we are told, is the brightness, the effulgence, the shining forth, of his Father's glory, the true light which enlighteneth every man who cometh into the world. To find lost man he undertook a long and toilsome journey, even a journey from heaven to earth, and at his return to heaven he pointed out the way, and commanded, invited, and encouraged man to follow."

The Marshaled Hosts.

"Other books, even the most interesting, contain only accounts of human wars, terrestrial enterprises, and expeditions for the conquest or deliverance of nations, and the struggles of the oppressed for liberty, or of the daring exploits, perilous achievements, and hairbreadth escapes of the falsely brave. But the Bible, independently of many other most interesting subjects, gives us an account of a war between good and evil, between God and the powers of darkness; of an expedition, undertaken for the deliverance of a ruined, lost, enslaved world—an expedition planned in heaven, devised in the remote ages of eternity, and finally accomplished in the most successful manner by the eternal Son of God. In this war we behold sin and Satan, and death and hell, with all the power of earth, marshaled on one side ; and on the other, the Seed of the woman, the Son of man, going forth unarmed and alone to certain victory and not less certain death ; to victory which could be obtained only by his death, but which was completed by his triumphant resurrection and ascension to heaven. As the prize contended for in this warfare, we see millions of immortal souls, the least of which is of far more value than this world, with the worlds around it ; souls whom the Son of man is seeking to raise to heaven, while his foes wish only to sink them deep in hell. Such is the war which the word of God describes, such the combatants, such the spoils of victory."

God's Highest Claims.

"It has ever been allowed that there is something venerable, as well as affecting, in the sorrows of suffering greatness ; and that a wise and good monarch reduced to poverty and distress is a spectacle which no man, not wholly devoid of feeling, could contemplate without feeling emotions of respectful sympathy. How venerable, how grand, how dignified, then, were the sorrows and sufferings of the Son of God ! sorrows and sufferings brought upon him, not by his own misconduct and imprudence, but by his own boundless benevolence. Who, then, would not have expected that these sorrows should have been held sacred ? Who does not perceive that God on the throne of the universe has, if I may so speak, less claims upon the reverence, gratitude, and affection of his creatures, than God manifest in the flesh in the form of a servant? Who does not see that God, appearing as Immanuel—God with us—has more numerous and more powerful claims upon mankind than God in any other form? If, then, Jehovah is worshiped and adored with rapturous affection by angels in heaven, much more might it be expected that he should be loved and praised by men, when for their sakes he appeared as a man of sorrows on earth."

Goodness of Heart and Greatness of Mind.

"In the character of the man Christ Jesus, goodness of heart and greatness of mind were combined. He possessed, in the highest possible degree, every estimable moral and intellectual quality. He was the only perfect man which the world has seen since the fall. He exhibited human nature in the highest degree of perfection to which it can be raised. In him goodness and greatness were not only personified, but, if I may so express it, concentrated and condensed. He was light and love clothed with a body. Qualities which are never seen united in men, and which seem almost incompatible with each other, were in him sweetly and harmoniously blended. Seldom, indeed, do we see the qualities of the lion and the lamb, of the serpent and the dove, uniting together in the same person. Those who are distinguished for benevolence, gentleness, condescension, meekness, compassion, sympathy, and sweetness of temper, are usually deficient in magnanimity, courage, and fortitude. And on the contrary, those who are remarkable for possessing the qualities last mentioned are usually destitute of the mild and amiable virtues. But Christ possessed them all. He displayed, in the highest degree, magnanimity, firmness, courage, and fortitude; and those heroic virtues were shaded and softened by all that is mild, and amiable, and attractive. While he far excelled all the heroes, conquerors, and great ones of the earth in those qualities of which they boast, he rivaled the smiling infant in tenderness and sweetness of disposition. In a word, he was the lion of the tribe of Judah, and he was the lamb of God. Here, then, was such a character as men had never seen before; a character with which even the holy, omniscient Judge of excellence was pleased and delighted. Surely, then, it might have been reasonably expected that when such a character was presented to the wondering eye of mankind, they would receive him with reverence and affection; that all the praises which they had for ages lavished on far inferior excellence would at once have been given to him."

A Startling View of the Sinner's Guilt.

"Though the measure of every impenitent sinner's iniquity is constantly filling up, it fills much more rapidly in some cases, and at some seasons, than at others. Some sinners appear to sin with great eagerness, boldness, and diligence; to sin with all their heart, and soul, and might, and strength, as if they were determined to see how much guilt they can contract in a short space. Others, who are apparently much less vicious and abandoned, fill up the measure of their sins with equal rapidity, in consequence of enjoying and abusing great religious privileges, opportunities, and means of grace. Indeed, it may be laid down as a general rule, from which there are no exceptions, that the measure of every impenitent sinner's guilt fills rapidly in proportion to the light, the conviction, and the means of moral improvement against which he sins. As the productions of the earth ripen most speedily where they enjoy in the greatest degree a rich soil, frequent showers, and the genial beams of the sun, so sinners ripen most speedily for destruction when they are favored, in the greatest degree, with religious privileges and opportunities. When a sinner is visited by some dangerous disease—is brought apparently near to death—is in consequence awakened, alarmed, and led to promise, that should his life be spared he will devote it to God—and when, on being restored to health, he forgets his promises and returns to his sinful courses—he adds very largely to his former guilt; more, perhaps, than he could have done in whole years of uninterrupted health. Similar remarks may be made respecting those who lose their possessions, their children, or near friends, without deriving any spiritual advantage from the loss. There are, perhaps, no threatenings in the Bible more terrible than those which are denounced against such as do not repent when under the stroke of God's correcting hand. To some who were guilty of this conduct God says, 'Surely this iniquity shall not be purged from you till ye die.' But never do sinners fill up the measure of their guilt more rapidly than when they sin against conviction; against the remonstrances of an enlightened conscience, and the influences of the Spirit of

God. Sinners who are guilty of this conduct, who stifle or lose religious impressions, do more, perhaps, to fill up the measure of their iniquities, than they had previously done during the whole course of their lives."

The Safe Side.

"When we love any person supremely, we are careful to avoid not only those things which we know will displease him, but such as we suspect may do it. We always think it best, in such cases, to be on the safe side, and to avoid every thing which we do not feel confident will not be displeasing. It is the same with respect to God. Those who love him supremely will avoid not only what they know to be sinful, but what they suspect may be sinful; they will abstain not only from evil, but from the very appearance of evil; and if they are not certain that any proposed indulgence is wrong, yet if they do not know it to be right they will reject it. They will say, There can certainly be no sin in not pursuing this offered pleasure, but there may be something wrong in pursuing it, and thus God may be displeased, and we will therefore keep on the safe side, and not even incur the risk of offending him, for the sake of any earthly gratification whatever."

Repentance a Cause of Rejoicing with God.

"God rejoices when sinners repent, because it gratifies him to see them escape from the tyranny and from the consequences of sin. God is light; perfect holiness. God is love; pure benevolence. His holiness and his benevolence both prompt him to rejoice when sinners escape from sin. Sin is that abominable thing which he hates. He hates it as an evil or malignant, and as a bitter, or destructive, thing. It is, indeed, both. It is the plague, the leprosy, the death, of intelligent creatures. It infects and poisons all their faculties; plunges them into the lowest depths of guilt and wretchedness, and pollutes them with a stain which all the waters of the ocean cannot wash away, which all the fires of hell cannot remove; from which nothing can cleanse them but the blood of Christ. Such is the malignity of its nature, that could it gain admittance into the celestial regions it would instantly transform angels to devils, and turn heaven into hell. That this is no exaggerated representation melancholy experience but too clearly evinces. Already has sin transformed angels to devils; already has it converted this world from a paradise to a prison; from a habitation of immortals to an Aceldama and a Golgotha, a place of skulls and a field of blood. Already has it poisoned not only our bodies but our souls; it has brought death into the world and all our woe, and,

> 'In one hour,
> Spoiled six days' labor of a God.'

Even now it stalks through our subjugated world with gigantic strides, spreading ruin and wretchedness around in ten thousand forms. Strife and discord, war and bloodshed, famine and pestilence, pain and sickness, follow in its train; while death, mounted on his pale horse, with the grave and hell, follow in the rear. Such are the miseries which sin has introduced into this once happy world; such the evils which attend its progress here, notwithstanding the various restraints which are employed to check its career. Would we see these evils consummated, and learn the full extent of that wretchedness which sin tends to produce, we must follow it into the eternal world, descend into those regions where peace, where hope never comes; and there, by the light of revelation, behold sin tyrannizing over its wretched victims with uncontrollable fury; fanning the inextinguishable fire, and sharpening the tooth of the immortal worm. See angels and archangels, thrones and dominions, principalities and powers, stripped of all their primeval glory and beauty, bound in eternal chains and burning with rage and malice against that Being in whose presence they once rejoiced, and whose praises they once sung. See multitudes of the human race in unutterable agonies of anguish and despair cursing the gift, the giver and prolonger, of their existence, and vainly wishing for annihilation to put a period to their miseries. Follow them through the long, long ages of eternity, and see them sinking deeper and deeper in the bottomless abyss of ruin; perpetually blaspheming God because of their plagues, and receiving the punishment of these blasphemies in continual additions to their wretchedness. Such are the wages of sin; such the inevitable doom of the finally impenitent. From these depths of anguish and despair look up to the mansions of the blessed, and see to what a height of glory and felicity the grace of God will raise every sinner that repenteth. See those who are thus favored in unutterable ecstasies of joy, love, and praise, contemplating God face to face, reflecting his perfect image, shining with a splendor like that of their glorious

Redeemer, filled with all the fullness of Deity, and bathing in those rivers of pleasure which flow forever at God's right hand. Follow them in their endless flight toward perfection. See them rapidly mounting from height to height, and darting onward with increasing swiftness and unwearied wing toward that infinity which they will never reach. View this, and then say whether infinite holiness and benevolence may not with propriety rejoice over every sinner that by repentance escapes the miseries, and secures the felicity, here so imperfectly described."

Why the Son of God Rejoiceth Over Repentant Sinners.

"Why does a mother rejoice over her infant offspring? Is it not because she has given them existence and support? Why does a father rejoice over and press to his heart with new fondness the child whom he has just rescued from the flames which consumed his habitation? Is it not because he has saved the object of his affections at the peril of his own life? So if it be asked why Christ rejoices over repenting sinners, we reply, because he has given them spiritual life and nourishment; because he has redeemed them with his own precious blood from eternal wretchedness and despair. In the joy arising from other sources he participates with his Father and the Holy Spirit; but this is a cause of joy almost peculiar to himself. It was long since predicted respecting him, that he should see of the travail of his soul and be satisfied; in other words, that he should see the effects of his sufferings in the repentance and salvation of sinners, and consider this as a sufficient recompense for all the toils and sorrows through which he was called to pass. This prediction is daily fulfilling. Our Immanuel sees the fruit of the travail of his soul in every sinner that repenteth, and rejoices that his agonies were not endured in vain. There are, we trust, not a few in this assembly over whom he has thus rejoiced. And O! with what affectionate emotions must he regard them. You can in some degree conceive, my friends, what your feelings would be toward a trembling dove that should fly into your bosom for protection from the talons of a vulture. You can form some conception of the feelings with which David contemplated the helpless lamb which he had rescued, at the peril of his own life, from the paw of the lion and the jaws of the bear. But who can conceive of the emotions with which the Son of David must contemplate an immortal soul drawn down to his feet by the cords of love, whom he has rescued from the roaring lion at such an infinite expense? If we love, and prize, and rejoice in any object in proportion to the labor, pain, and expense which it has cost us to obtain it, how greatly must Christ love, and prize, and rejoice in every penitent sinner! His love and joy must be unutterable, inconceivable, infinite. Compared with his, even a mother's love must be cold. My friends, for once I rejoice that our Saviour's toils and sufferings were so great, since the greater they were, the greater must be his love for us and his joy in our conversion. And permit me to add, if he thus rejoices over one sinner that repenteth, what must be his joy when all his people are collected out of every tongue, and kindred, and nation, and people, and presented spotless before his Father's throne! What a full tide of felicity will pour in upon him, and how will his benevolent heart expand with unutterable delight, and swell almost to bursting, when, contemplating the countless myriads of the redeemed, he says, Were it not for my sufferings, all these immortal beings would have been throughout eternity as miserable, and now they will be as happy, as God can make them. It is enough. I see of the travail of my soul and am satisfied. My friends, how great must that joy, that happiness be, which satisfies the benevolence of Christ."

Similarity the Basis of Communion with God.

"The original word in the Scriptures which is sometimes rendered fellowship, and sometimes communion, signifies that reciprocal intercourse or communion which subsists between beings who are partakers of the same nature, whose moral characters are similar, and who mutually know and esteem each other. It is an observation no less just than common, that like rejoices in like, and where there is no likeness there can be no communion. Thus, for instance, there can be no communion between the inhabitants of the water and those of the air; for what is life to the one is death to the other. There can be no communion, in the proper sense of the term, between mankind and the brutal world, because the former are endowed with reason and the latter are not. It is the same, in a less general sense, with respect to men of different ages, characters, and situations in life. The old cannot enjoy communion with the young in the pleasures of youth, nor the philosopher with the ignorant savage in the pursuits of the chase. The blind can enjoy no fellowship with those who see, in the beauties of vision, nor the deaf, with those who hear, in the harmony of sounds. Unless persons resemble each other, therefore, in a greater or less degree, there can be no mutual communication of joys and sorrows between them; they cannot enter into each other's views and feelings, clearly understand each other's language, enjoy each other's society, or form an intimate, happy, and lasting union. But, on the other hand, when persons meet who resemble each other in temper, character, age, and situation—who love and hate the same things, and pursue and avoid the same objects—they readily unite, like drops of dew when brought into contact, and appear to compose but one soul in different bodies. Similitude, similarity of nature, of character and pursuits, must therefore be the basis of all true fellowship or communion. Hence it appears, that no creatures can enjoy communion with God and his Son but those who are partakers of his divine nature, who resemble him in their moral character, and who love, hate, and pursue those things which are respectively the objects of his love, hatred, and pursuit."

In What Communion with God Consists.

"This communion consists in a mutual giving and receiving, which is constantly maintained between God and the soul, and which is carried on through the medium of the Lord Jesus Christ; who being Head over all things to his Church, and uniting God and man in one person, is admirably qualified to discharge the office of mediator between God and his people. This is he of whom Jacob's ladder was a type. By him all temporal and spiritual blessings descend from Heaven to his people, and through him all their prayers, and praises, and thanksgivings come up for a memorial before God, being perfumed with the incense of his precious blood. In him all fullness dwells, and of this fullness all his friends receive, and grace for grace. As the sun is continually pouring forth a flood of light, and heat, and sweet attractive influences on the planets which harmoniously revolve around him, rejoice in his beams, and by reflection return them again to their source, so the Sun of righteousness, whose riches of grace and glory are unsearchable and inexhaustible, is continually pouring forth enlightening, purifying, and life-giving influences into the souls of believers, while they revolve around him, receive and rejoice in his beams, and return them back to him in grateful ascriptions of thanksgiving and praise. He gives himself and all that he has to his people, engaging to be their God, their father, their friend and protector, and their exceeding great reward; and promising to love them, keep and guide them, even unto death; to watch over them as the apple of his eye, to gather them with his arm, and carry them in his bosom; to cause all things, both in time and eternity, to work together for their everlasting good. His people, on the other hand, humbly, gratefully, and joyfully receive him as their God and portion, and in return give up themselves and all that they have to him, without reserve, as his people, engaging to love him, trust in him, worship him, to spend and be spent in promoting his cause, honor, and interest in the world."

The Christian Joy in Communion with God.

"God is pleased at other times to revive and strengthen Christians' fainting spirits with the cordials of his love. He sends down the Spirit of adoption into their hearts, whereby they are enabled to cry, Abba, Father; and to feel all those filial affections of love, joy, trust, hope, reverence, and dependence which is at once their duty and their happiness to exercise toward God. By the operation of the same Spirit he shines into their minds, to give them the light of the knowledge of the glory of God in the face of Jesus Christ; opens and applies to them his exceeding great and precious promises; makes them to know the great love wherewith he has loved them; and reveals to them those unutterable, inconceivable, and unheard-of things which he has prepared for those who love him. He also shines in upon their souls with the pure, dazzling, melting, overpowering beams of celestial mercy, grace, and love; displays to their enraptured view the glories and beauties of Him who is the chief among ten thousand and altogether lovely; and gives them to know the heights and depths, the lengths and breadths, of that love of Christ which passeth knowledge. Thus he gives them as great foretastes of heaven as their feeble natures can support, fills their souls to the very brim with all the fullness of God, and makes them understand that peace of God which passes all understanding.

"On the other hand, the happy Christian in these bright, enraptured moments, while he is thus basking in the beams of celestial light and splendor, forgets the world, forgets himself, forgets his existence, and is wholly absorbed in the ravishing, the ecstatic contemplation of uncreated loveliness, glory, and beauty. He contemplates, he wonders, he admires, he loves, he adores. His whole soul goes forth in one intense flame of gratitude, admiration, love, and desire; and he longs to plunge himself into the boundless ocean of perfection which opens to his view, and to be wholly swallowed up and lost in God. With an energy and activity unknown before, he roams and ranges through this ocean of perfection and glory, of power and wisdom, of truth and justice, of light and love, where he can find neither a bottom nor a shore. His soul dilates itself beyond its ordinary capacity, and expands to receive the flood of happiness which overwhelms it. All its desires for earthly happiness are dried up, and it no longer inquires, Who will show me any good? The scanty thirst-producing streams of earthly delight only increase the feverish desires of the soul; the noisy, tumultuous transports, and fancied raptures of the enthusiast, the visionary, and fanatic, which proceed merely from the fervor of the passions and affections, soon die away, and leave no fruit behind; but the tide of joy which flows in upon the Christian, when he thus enjoys communion with God, is as full, as constant, as unfathomable as the source from whence it flows. No language can do justice to his feelings, for his happiness is unutterable; but with an emphasis, a meaning, an expression which God only could excite, and which none but God can comprehend, he exclaims, in broken accents, My Father, my God! whom have I in heaven but thee, and what can a miserable worm of the dust desire besides thee?"

Reasons for Family Worship.

"Walking in all God's ordinances and commandments blamelessly, implies the maintaining of the worship of God in the family. It is acknowledged that there is no command which, in so many words, says, Worship God in your families, or, Maintain family prayer. Yet that this is a duty incumbent on heads of families is, perhaps, as clearly taught in the Scriptures as if it were the subject of an express command. We have, for instance, the example of good men in favor of it. God expresses full confidence that Abraham would maintain religion in his family. Joshua's resolution was, 'As for me and my house, we will serve the Lord.' David, after the public exercises of religion were finished, returned to bless his household; that is, to unite with them in an act of worship; and our Saviour often prayed with his little family of disciples. Families that call not upon God's name are classed among the heathen, and it is intimated that God will pour out his fury upon them. Besides, we are commanded to pray always, on all occasions and in all circumstances; of course, in our families. And St. Peter exhorts husbands and wives to live together as heirs of the grace of life, that their prayers may not be hindered—an expression which evidently refers to united prayers, and intimates that he thought it very important that such prayers should not be hindered; and that he took it for granted that Christian families would offer such prayers. Besides, the reasonableness, the propriety, and the happy effects of family worship, show it to be a duty. It is reasonable and proper, for families have mercies in common to ask for, and they receive favors in common for which they should unite in expressing their gratitude. And the happy effects which result from a right performance of this duty are innumerable and inestimable. It has a happy effect upon the head of the family himself. It tends to make him circumspect, to produce watchfulness over his temper and conduct through the day; for how can he indulge sin or give vent to angry passions in presence of the family, when he recollects that he is a priest in his own house; that he prayed with them in the morning; and that he will again be called to pray with them at night? He cannot but feel that, if the rest of his conduct is not of a piece with this, his own children and servants will despise him for his inconsistency. This practice has also a most salutary influence upon the happiness of domestic life. If any unpleasant feelings arise between members of the same household, such feelings can scarcely outlive the return of the next season for family devotion. Affection and peace must return when they next meet around the family altar, unless one or the other is a hypocrite. Thus dissensions are prevented, and domestic peace and harmony are perpetuated. I may add, that it always tends to produce, and often does produce, the most happy effects upon the children of the family. At least, it is certain that a much larger proportion of children are moral, and become pious, in families where this duty is properly performed than in those where it is wholly neglected, or only occasionally attended to."

The Picture Not Overdrawn.

"Who that believes there is a God would not have his family one of the few faithful families on which God looks with approbation? Who would not wish that the eye of God should discover in it nothing displeasing to him?

"Consider how much it would promote your present happiness to possess such a character. Where can happiness be found on earth, if not in such a family as has now been described? Mutual affection and harmony, peace and contentment, would dwell in it. All the gifts of Providence would be enjoyed with a double relish, because they would be received as the gifts of a Father, and be sanctified by his word and prayer. Almost every cause of domestic unhappiness would be excluded. There would be no room for anxiety, uneasiness, and alarm; for such a family could cheerfully trust in God to supply all its real wants, and to shield it from all real evils. Even if afflictions came, they would come as mercies, and deprived of their stings. In short, such a family would be of one heart and of one soul; that heart and that soul would be devoted to God, and God in return would devote himself to them. And O, how pleasant, how soothing, how refreshing would it be to the husband, the father, to return at evening to such a house after the labors and fatigues of the day, to be greeted with affectionate smiles and to return them; to shut out the world with its follies and cares, and to feel, while rejoicing in the circle of those whom he loved, that God was looking down upon them with approbation and delight; that an unseen Saviour was rejoicing in the midst of them to see the happiness which he had purchased, and which his religion bestowed! How sweet to close an evening thus pleasant, and a day spent in the service of God, by uniting around the family altar in an offering of prayer and praise to their great Benefactor, and then lie down to rest with that feeling of sincerity and safety which filial confidence in Heaven inspires! Some may, perhaps, choose to call this representation religious romance; but it is sober reality; it is no more than has been actually enjoyed; and if we see few families in which it is realized, it is only because there are few in which both heads of the family walk in all the commandments and ordinances of the Lord blameless.

"Permit me to remind you how greatly such a family would honor God and adorn religion. It would, indeed, in such a world as this, be like one of those ever-verdant islands which rise amid the wide ocean of Arabian sands, and whose constant verdure leads the weary and thirsty traveler to seek for the hidden spring which produces it. It is, perhaps, impossible for an insulated individual to exhibit all the beauty and excellence of Christianity; because much of it consists in the right performance of those relative duties which he has no opportunity to perform. But in a religious family—a family where both husband and wife are evidently pious—religion may be displayed in all its parts, and in the fullness of its glory and beauty; and one such family will do more to recommend it, and to soften the prejudices of its enemies, than can be effected by the most powerful and persuasive sermon."

Solemn Questions to Parents.

"For whom are you educating your children? We ask not this question as having authority to call you to an account; we ask it not with a view to pry into the state of your families; we ask it not to condemn you; but we ask it merely with a view to call your attention to the subject, and to lead conscience to give an answer. Say then, my friends, for whom are you educating your children? for God or for his enemies? Do you consider your children as a sacred gift, intrusted to you only for a short period, and which the Donor expects to be employed in his service, and returned to him more valuable than when it was bestowed? Do you recognize God's right to dispose of them according to his good pleasure, and to take them from you whenever he shall see best? Have you sincerely and solemnly surrendered them to God, and dedicated them to his service? Are you governed by a supreme regard to the glory of God in all your efforts for their improvement, and in all the labors, cares, and sufferings which you undergo on their account? Do you educate them for the service of the King of kings, daily laboring to convince them of the infinite importance of securing his favor, and of avoiding his displeasure; conducting every part of their education with ultimate reference to this end; endeavoring to cultivate all those tempers and dispositions which are agreeable to his will, and to prepare them, as far as in your power, for the employments of heaven? Do you study the directions which God has given you in his word, and frequently implore the assistance of his

Holy Spirit in performing your arduous and responsible duties? Do you pay more attention to the souls than to the bodies of your children? do their spiritual maladies occasion you more distress than any infirmities of body, and are you more pained by observing in them wrong tempers and sinful passions than by seeing them awkward and unpolished in their intercourse with society? Not only so; do you esteem the education of the heart more important than that of the mind, and labor more earnestly to cherish correct moral feelings and suitable affections than to impart intellectual acquirements? In a word, do your children see in your daily deportment, in your conversation, in your very looks, that all your aims and wishes respecting them are centered in the one great wish for their conversion; that in comparison with this, you regard no other object as of any importance, and that you would be content to see them poor, despised, and contemned in this world, if they might but secure eternal riches and an unfading crown in that which is to come? If you are not at least attempting to do all this, you are not educating your children for God."

A Whirlpool.

"If those whose example is only negatively bad, are guilty of the sin mentioned"—the sin of preventing children from coming to Christ—"much more are those guilty whose example is positively bad. In this class are included all who profess wrong principles, or openly indulge in vicious practices. The open infidel, who denies or calls in question the divine authority of revelation; the conceited infidel, who ridicules or explains away the most important doctrines; the scoffer or profane swearer, who familiarizes the infant ear to the language of impiety, and teaches the untutored tongue to utter it; the Sabbath-breaker, who tramples on the barrier with which God has encircled the sacred day; the liar or slanderer, who by his example leads the young to trifle with truth and with the reputation of their fellow-creatures; the slave to intemperance and sensuality, who seduces others into the paths of dissipation and excess, are all, I will not say indirectly, but directly, preventing the young from coming to Christ. Every such character does much to bar up the way of life, or is a stumbling-block over which many will stumble and fall to rise no more. And if he be one whose talents, wealth, learning, rank, or vivacity of manner gives him extensive influence in society, the pernicious effects of his example will be incalculable. Under his deadly shade no plants of purity will flourish, no flowers of virtue bloom. He breathes around contagion, pestilence, and death, and while he sinks into the abyss of vice and infidelity, the whirlpool which he forms will ingulf every thing that comes within its action.

"But if he be a parent what shall we say? If there be a sight on earth at which humanity must shudder—over which angels might weep—it is the sight of a young, a numerous family following with unsuspecting confidence a ruthless fiend in the shape of a parent, who extends the hand of a guide only to lead them far from Him who would gather them in his arms and carry them in his bosom; and betrays the helpless lambs to that roaring lion who goes about seeking whom he may devour."

The Power of Example Illustrated.

"Mr. Baxter relates a story of a shepherd driving his flock over a high and narrow bridge built across a torrent. The foremost of the flock, terrified by some accidental occurrence, leaped over the bridge into the flood below; the others, not seeing the danger into which their leaders had fallen, and supposing they might safely follow them, leaped after them, one by one, till all were destroyed. In a similar manner, I suppose, generations of mankind perish. We have all, says the prophet, gone astray like sheep, and turned every one to his own way. The end of this way is destruction. Into this destruction all past sinners, who died impenitent, have already fallen. But we see not the gulf into which they have plunged; and, like the foolish sheep, pursue with headlong impetuosity the same road. Our children, supposing that they may safely follow where we lead the way, rush after us, and find too late we have guided them to their ruin: while their children in turn, unless grace prevent, will follow them in like manner to perdition. Thus, like a river whose waters are successively swallowed up in the ocean, one generation of men after another is led on blindfold by the influence of example, and plunged into the gulf which has no bottom. Need any thing more be said to show the infinite importance of setting a good example before our children, and leading them after us in the path of life?"

An Appeal to Baptized Children.

"In giving you pious parents God has conferred on you one of the greatest blessings which he could bestow. He might have caused your souls to inhabit bodies among the heathen, where you would never have heard of a Saviour, where your parents would have dedicated you to false gods, and perhaps have offered you in sacrifice upon their altars! And will you requite him for this favor by practically saying, I regret that my parents were pious, or that they dedicated me to God; would I had been born in an irreligious family, where I should never have been troubled with religion or prayer, but where I might have indulged in the pursuit of worldly pleasures without interruption or restraint? Will you ungratefully undo all that your parents have done for your salvation, and tear yourselves out of the arms of the Saviour in which they have placed you? Will those of you whose parents have ascended to heaven, do this? If so, remember that as your guilt will be no common guilt, so your punishment will be no common punishment. How awfully aggravated it will be, you may learn from the terrible threatenings denounced against the unbelieving Jews, who like you were children of the covenant. Christ declares that the very heathen will rise up against them in the day of judgment and condemn them; that it will be more tolerable for Sodom and Gomorrah in that day than for them; and that while many shall come from the east and the west, and the north and the south, and sit down in the kingdom of God, the children of the kingdom shall be cast into outer darkness, where shall be weeping and gnashing of teeth. In a word, he tells us that they who know their Lord's will and do it not shall be beaten with many stripes. And will you, then, by refusing to turn from your iniquities, pull down upon yourselves this terrible fate? Shall all the tears, prayers, and exertions of your parents only serve to increase your condemnation? Shall the baptismal water with which you have been sprinkled be converted into drops of liquid fire? Shall the blessings which Christ was sent to bring be transformed into curses; and will you, to whom they are first offered, be the first to reject them? You are like Capernaum, raised, as it were, to heaven by your privileges. Will you, by abusing or neglecting them, be yourselves cast down to hell, to the lowest hell?"

Children Welcomed to the Fold of Christ.

"Some of you, I hope, are ready to say to Christ's Church, as did Ruth to Naomi, Entreat us not to leave you, nor to return from following after you; for where you go, we will go; where you dwell, we will dwell; your people shall be our people, and your God our God. The Lord do so to us, and more also, if aught but death part you and us. Farewell, vain world! farewell, sinful pleasures! farewell, sinful companions! Our fathers' God calls us, our Saviour invites us, and we have determined to comply with the call, and cast in our lot among his people. And is this your determination? this the sincere language of your hearts? Welcome, then, ye once wandering lambs of the flock; welcome to the fold of Christ; welcome to his Church; welcome to the good and great Shepherd, who gathers the lambs with his arms and carries them in his bosom! We bid you a thousand and a thousand welcomes to the ark of safety; and while we congratulate you on your happy escape from the snares of the world and the toils of the tempter, we would unite with you in blessing Him who has set your sin-entangled feet at liberty, and inclined you to choose the wise, the better part. You now ratify what your parents have done in your name; you consent to take their God for your God, and to give yourself up to him in the bonds of his everlasting covenant."

Parents Guilty of the Sin of Eli.

"Eli's sons made themselves vile and he restrained them not. It is not said that he set them a bad example. It is evident, on the contrary, that his example was good. Nor is he accused of neglecting to admonish them; for we are told that he reproved them in a very solemn and affectionate manner, and warned them of the danger of continuing to pursue vicious courses. In this respect he was much less culpable than many parents at the present day; for not a few set before their children an example positively bad, and still more entirely neglect to admonish and reprove them. But though Eli admonished, he did not restrain his children. He did not employ the authority with which he was clothed as a parent, to prevent them from indulging their depraved inclinations. This is the only sin of which he is accused; and yet this was sufficient to bring guilt and misery upon himself, and entail ruin upon his posterity.

"Of the same sin those parents are now guilty who suffer their children to indulge, without restraint, those sinful propensities to which childhood and youth are but too subject; and which, when indulged, render them vile in the sight of God. Among the practices which thus render children vile are, a quarrelsome, malicious disposition; disregard to truth; excessive indulgence of their appetites; neglect of the Bible and religious institutions; profanation of the Sabbath; profane, scurrilous, or indecent language; willful disobedience; associating with openly vicious company; taking the property of their neighbors; and idleness, which naturally leads to every thing bad. From all these practices it is in the power of parents to restrain their children, in a very considerable degree, if they employ the proper means; at least, it is in the power of all to make the attempt, and to persevere in it so long as children remain under the paternal roof; and those who neglect to do this, those who know, or who might know, that their children are beginning to practice any of these vices without steadily and perseveringly using all proper exertions to restrain and correct them, are guilty of the sin of Eli. Nor will a few occasional reproofs and admonitions given to children free parents from the guilt of partaking in their sins. No, they must be restrained; restrained with a mild and prudent, but firm and steady hand; restrained early, while they may be formed to habits of submission, obedience, and diligence; and the reins of government must never for a moment be slackened, much less given up into their hands, as is too often the case. Nor will even this excuse those parents who neglect family religion, and the religious instruction of their children, and who do not frequently pray for the blessing of Heaven upon their endeavors. If we neglect our duty to our heavenly Father, we surely cannot wonder or complain if he suffers our children to neglect their duty to us ; nor, if we do not ask his blessing, have we any reason to complain should it be withheld. In this, as in other cases, exertion without prayer, and prayer without exertion, are equally vain. To sum up all in a word, every parent who is not as careful of the morals as he is of the health of his children ; every one who takes more care of the literary than of the moral and religious education of his children, is certainly guilty of the sin we are condemning. How much more criminal, then, are those parents who set before their children an irreligious or vicious example ; who join with the great enemy of their peace in tempting them to sin ; and thus, instead of restraining, inflame and strengthen their sinful propensities. The parent who starves or poisons his children is innocent, in the sight of God, compared with one who thus entices them into the path of ruin."

Consequences of Parental Unfaithfulness.

"If parents indulge their children in infancy and childhood, and do not restrain them when they make themselves vile, it is almost impossible that they should not pursue courses and contract habits which will render them as bitterness to their fathers, and a sorrow of heart to those who bore them. If such parents are pious, their hearts will probably be grieved, and their eyes consumed with tears, to see their children rebelling against God and plunging into eternal ruin. If they are not pious, and care nothing for the future happiness of their children, they will still probably have the grief of seeing them idle, dissolute, undutiful, bad husbands, bad fathers, and bad members of society; for it can scarcely be expected that he who is a bad son will act his part well in any other relation of life. Especially will such parents usually meet with unkindness and neglect from their children if they live to be dependent on them in their old age. It is in this, as in almost every other instance, the case that as a man sows so he must reap. They that sow the seeds of vice in the minds of their children, or who suffer them to be sown by others, and to grow without restraint, will almost invariably be compelled to reap, and to eat, with many tears, the bitter harvest which those seeds tend to produce."

God's Moral Government Over Nations.

"It is indispensably necessary to the perfection of God's moral government that it should extend to nations and communities as well as to individuals. This, I conceive, is too evident to require proof; for how could God be considered the moral governor of the world if nations and communities were exempt from his government? Again, if God is to exercise a moral government over nations and communities, by rewarding or punishing them according to their works, the rewards and punishments must evidently be dispensed in this world; for nations and communities will not exist, as such, in the world to come. In that world God must deal with men considered simply as individuals. Further, it seems evidently proper that communities as well as individuals should have a time of trial and probation allowed them; that if the first generation prove sinful the community should not be immediately destroyed, but the punishment suspended, till it be seen whether the nation will prove incorrigible, or whether some succeeding generation will not repent of the national sins and thus avert national judgments. Now it is evident that if God thus waits upon nations, as he does upon individuals, and allows them a season of probation, a space for repentance, he cannot destroy them until many generations of sinners are laid in their graves. Besides, by thus suspending the rod or the sword over a nation, he presents to it powerful inducements to reform. He appeals to parental feelings, to men's affection for their posterity, and endeavors to deter them from sin by the assurance that their posterity will suffer for it. In connection with these remarks, we must recollect, what has been already stated, that God never punishes a generation for the sins of its ancestors, unless it imitates their conduct, unless it is guilty of similar or more aggravated offenses, and thus justifies the wicked conduct of preceding generations. Besides, as sinful nations, like individuals, if they do not reform usually become worse, it will ever be found that the last days of a nation are its worst days, and that the generation which is destroyed is more abandoned than all preceding generations. I will only add, that when God forsakes or destroys a nation for its national sins, he does not inflict more upon that generation which is destroyed than its own sins deserve, though he punishes them more severely than he would have done were it not for the guilt which had accumulated by the preceding generations."

The Crime of Perjury a National One.

"No other nation can boast of such ancestors, to no other nation has so small a share of guilt been transmitted by its founders. But it is too evident to require proof, that our immediate ancestors have sunk very far below the standard of their forefathers. The progress of those vices which principally tend to draw down divine judgments upon a people has been constant, rapid, and highly alarming. Dissipation, intemperance, profanation of the Sabbath, neglect of divine institutions, and profane language, have burst in upon us like an overwhelming flood. The prevalence of perjury, or false swearing, is, if possible, still more alarming. To say nothing of the little regard paid in many cases to oaths of office, how terribly have our commercial transactions, for some years, been polluted by this crime! Of what palpable perjuries have great numbers of our fellow-citizens been guilty, both at home and in foreign lands; and how largely have those who employed them participated in the guilt! We may think little of this, and flatter ourselves that customary oaths are trifles; but be assured, my hearers, that when God is, on any occasion, called to bear witness to a transaction, he witnesses it; and woe be to the wretch who calls upon the God of truth to bear witness to a lie! God will not hold him guiltless who taketh his name in vain; nor will he hold a nation or community guiltless in which this sin prevails. Even you, my hearers, would think it the greatest of insults should a man impudently call upon you to testify to the truth of a known lie. With what feelings, then, must the God of truth hear himself so frequently called upon to bear such testimony?"

A Solemn Caution to Young Men.

"Look around, and you will see on every side young men whom appetites and passions are plunging into intemperance, sensuality, and every species of vicious excess, and thus ruining them, not only for the future but for the present world. You see them forming habits whose chains it will be exceedingly difficult for them to break, and which, unless broken, will drag them away to destruction. And no young man can have any security that he shall not be left to form such habits, unless he obtains that security which is afforded by God's sanctifying grace and pardoning mercy; unless he early commits himself to that great and good Shepherd who has engaged to preserve all his sheep. Until this is done he is at the mercy of every gust of temptation, every sudden sally of appetite and passion. It is in vain that in his sober moments he resolves not to yield to temptation. How little such resolutions, how little any human restraints, avail to secure him, melancholy observation but too clearly shows. How many promising young men have we seen who, while they remained under the parental roof, were moral, correct, and apparently fortified against temptation; but who, when they were removed from it, fell an easy prey to temptation, and sunk into the arms of vicious indulgence! And how many have we seen who, after passing safely through the dangerous period of youth, became the wretched victims of intemperance in manhood. Presume not then, young man, upon thine own strength. When so many others have fallen thou mayest fall. Against such a fall thou canst have no security until thou obtainest the protection of God."

Evils Avoided by Early Piety.

"A man who does not become religious till the season of youth is passed away must of course spend all the early part of life in sin. And what will be the consequence? He will commit many sins, the recollection of which must be painful to him as long as he lives; he will lose much time and many precious opportunities of improvement and of doing good, which he will afterward regret; he will afford his sinful propensities an opportunity to become strong; and it will, of course, be more difficult to subdue them, and his future conflicts will be more severe. His imagination will be polluted, and the consequences will trouble him as long as he lives.

"He will, probably, in some degree at least, be a tempter of others, and the recollection of this will be bitter as wormwood and gall. He can never have the satisfaction of reflecting that he gave God his first, and earliest, and best, affections; that when the world was all fresh and gay, and smiling around him, he cheerfully forsook all to follow Christ. On the contrary, it must pain him to reflect that he did not forsake the world till he had proved its emptiness; that he did not follow Christ until experience taught him that there was nothing else worth following. We may add, that the man who is not converted until a late period will, more than probably, indulge in vices, or form habits which will cause him much unhappiness through life. Nay more, it will not be at all strange should he injure his health and undermine his constitution, and have nothing left to offer to God but a diseased body and an enfeebled mind."

The Sublime Contrast.

"How noble, how dignified, how sublime, does the character of Daniel appear! That you may see this in its true light, bring him forward and compare him with the nobles, princes, and great ones of Babylon. See them indulging in sensual pleasures, proud of their wealth and birth, panting for riches, honor, and applause; seeking these transitory trifles by every possible means, neglecting immortal honors and glories, and meanly envying and hating that excellence which they could not reach. See Daniel, on the contrary, calm, firm, and self-collected; with an eye fixed on God and heaven, despising the trifles which they pursued, aiming at the glory of his Maker and the happiness of his fellow-creatures, and following, with unconquerable, undeviating resolution the path of duty. While they groveled on the earth, his head and his heart were in heaven;—while their minds were darkened by the clouds of ignorance and prejudice, and their breasts convulsed by the storms of ambition, avarice, envy, and revenge, his exalted soul dwelt in regions of eternal day, far above the clouds of mental ignorance and the storms of contending passions. That you may still more clearly discern the superiority of his character, compare him with the kings whom he served. See Belshazzar, making a great feast to a thousand of his lords, and surrounded by every thing which could dazzle or delight the senses. See Nebuchadnezzar, walking in the midst of his palace, reflecting with self-complacency on the nations he had subdued, and proudly exclaiming, 'Is not this great Babylon that I have built, for the house of the kingdom, by the might of my power, and for the honor of my majesty?' Then turn your eyes to the prophet. See him, with that heroic boldness which nothing but true piety can give, reproving the pride of one of these kings, and the impious extravagance of the other; see him, in defiance of threats and impending danger, bending his knees to the only Being whom he feared; see him, with unshaken calmness and serenity, sitting in the midst of ravenous lions, who, like lambs, crouch at his feet;—and then say which was the more dignified character, he or the proud kings of Babylon. Nay more, say which possessed the more enviable titles and honors; he or they? They were styled princes on earth. But he, as a prince, had power with God and prevailed. They were honored, admired, and applauded by their fellow-worms; but he was greatly beloved by his God. Who would not be Daniel in the lion's den, rather than Belshazzar at his feast, or Nebuchadnezzar on his golden throne? O how evidently does it, in this instance, appear, that the righteous is more excellent than his neighbor!"

Sound and Important Views for Voters.

"Subjects who have the privilege of choosing their own rulers and magistrates make themselves partakers of all their sins when they give their votes for vicious or irreligious characters. I hope, my hearers, it is not necessary to assure you that this remark has no party political bearing. In making it I certainly do not mean to censure one party more than another, nor do I intend the most distant allusion to any of our rulers or magistrates; for I am taught not to speak evil of dignities. I merely state it as an abstract principle, which cannot be denied without denying the truth of Scripture, that when we vote for vicious or irreligious men, knowing them, or having good reason to suspect them to be such, we make ourselves partakers of all their sins. If Timothy made himself a partaker of the sins of every unworthy character whom he carelessly admitted into the ministerial office, then we certainly make ourselves partakers of the sins of every improper character whom we voluntarily assist in appointing to any public office. But as many, even among good men, do not appear to think sufficiently of this truth, it may not be improper to insist upon it more particularly.

"In the first place, God has plainly described the characters whom we ought to choose for rulers and magistrates. 'Thou shalt provide out of all the people able men, such as fear God, men of truth and hating covetousness, and place such to be rulers.' And again, 'He that ruleth over men must be just, ruling in the fear of God.' He has also told us, that when the righteous are in authority the people rejoice, but that when the wicked bear rule the people mourn. If, then, we choose different men for our rulers, we slight God's counsels and disobey his commands.

"Again: We are taught in the Scriptures that we must give an account to God of the manner in which we employ the talents and improve the privileges with which he favors us. Now the right of choosing our own rulers is undoubtedly a most precious privilege. This, I presume, you will readily acknowledge; for we frequently hear of the precious right of suffrage. Now what account of this privilege can they give to God who have abused it, by assisting to place in authority such characters as he has forbidden us to appoint?

"Once more; rulers and magistrates are servants to the public. Now it is an admitted axiom that what a man does by his servant he does by himself. If, then, we voluntarily assist in appointing vicious or irreligious rulers, we make ourselves partakers of all their sins, and must account for all the good which might have been done had we chosen different characters."

Responsibility of Legislators and Magistrates.

"Their responsibility is greater than that of other men. They have greater opportunities of doing both good and evil than other men. If they do good, they will do much good. If the influence of their example and their exertions be thrown on the side of truth and goodness, no one can compute how great or how lasting may be the salutary effects which they will produce. On the contrary, if they do evil they will do much evil. They will, like Jeroboam, make people to sin. We are informed by an inspired writer that one sinner destroyeth much good. This remark is true of every sinner; but it is most emphatically true of sinners who are placed in authority. One such sinner may destroy more good, and prove the cause of more evil, than a whole generation of sinners who are placed in a lower sphere. And even if they do not actually do evil, they may occasion great guilt, by neglecting to do good. Says the voice of inspiration, 'To him that knoweth to do good, and doeth it not, to him it is sin.' In another place we are taught that men partake in the guilt of all those sins which they might have prevented. Legislators, rulers, and magistrates, then, are answerable to God for all the possible good which they neglect to do; and they share in the guilt of all the sins which they might, but do not, prevent. So far as those who are invested with authority neglect to prevent, to the utmost of their power, open impiety, irreligion, disregard of the Sabbath and of divine institutions, profanation of God's name, intemperance, and other similar evils, they share in the sinfulness and guilt of every Sabbath-breaker, profane swearer, and drunkard, among those over whom they are placed.

"How great, then, is the responsibility of all who are invested either with legislative, judicial, or executive authority! How aggravated will be their guilt, how terrible their punishment, should they prove unfaithful to their country and their God!"

Mutual Love Between Christ and his People.

"He knows that his people love him, and he knows how much they love him. He knows that he is precious to their souls; more precious than the air they breathe, than the light of heaven. He knows that they love him better than father or mother, husband or wife, brother or sister, son or daughter, yea, far better than their own lives; and that for his sake they are ready to renounce and forsake them all. He knows that his love sweetly constrains them to live to his service, and that they rejoice when they are counted worthy to suffer pain and shame for his name. He knows that they look upon him as their Redeemer, their Friend, their Shepherd, their Physician, their Advocate, their Wisdom, their Strength, their Life, and their All; that the enjoyment of his presence and favor constitutes all their felicity; that they consider no earthly affliction comparable to his absence or displeasure, and that the weakness of their love to him is their constant grief and shame. He knows that they prefer him to themselves, that they wish for a heavenly crown only that they may throw it down at his feet; and that the principal reason why they desire heaven is, that they may see, and serve, and praise him, and ascribe all the glory of their salvation to him. And how then can he refrain from loving those who thus love him; whom he has himself taught to love him. With what an unutterable emotion of mingled pity, sympathy, and love must he look down on those who are thus attached to him in the midst of a rebellious world, and who for his sake are denying themselves, taking up the cross, and striving to follow him in defiance of all the inward and outward opposition which they are called to encounter? Hear what he says to such: 'I know thy works, I have set before thee an open door, and no man can shut it; for thou hast a little strength, and hast kept my word, and hast not denied my name. Because thou hast kept the word of my patience, I also will keep thee in the hour of temptation which will come on all the earth, and I will cause thine adversaries to come and worship before thy feet, and to know that I have loved thee.'"

The Happiness of Loving and Being Loved.

"How happy are they who love. It has been often and justly observed, that to love and to be beloved by a deserving earthly friend affords the greatest happiness which the world can give. What happiness, then, must they enjoy who love and are beloved by the infinite fountain of love,—God's eternal Son, the brightness of his glory, the possessor of all power in heaven and earth; source of every thing amiable and excellent in the universe. What pure, ineffable, exalted delight must they find in communion with such a friend; and what indescribable benefits must they receive from his love! What can created minds conceive of, what can the heart form a wish for, beyond the friendship of such a being? Nay, what creature could have dared to raise his wishes so high, had not God himself encouraged us to do it? O, it is too, too much! not too much, indeed, for God to give, but far too much for man to deserve. But in vain do we attempt to give you adequate ideas of the happiness resulting from the love of Christ. It is one of those things which it is impossible for man to utter; and the joy which it produces is a joy unspeakable. If any would know it, they must learn it, not from language, but from their own experience, for language sinks under the weight of a subject which it was never intended to describe. We can only say, that to love and be beloved by Christ is the very essence of heaven."

The Infidel Met on his Own Ground.

"It is *safe* to believe that the Scriptures are a revelation from God, and that those who wrote them were inspired. This, it is presumed, no infidel will deny. No infidel will pretend that we expose ourselves to any evil or danger in a future state by believing the Scriptures to be the word of God, even though it should prove that they are not so; for believing them does not lead to the neglect of any duty which infidels regard as necessary to the attainment of future happiness. Allowing, then, for argument's sake, that they should prove not to be a revelation from God; those who believed that they were so will still stand on as safe ground as those who rejected them. It is, then, safe to believe the Scriptures. But it is not safe to disbelieve them; for if they are the word of God, all who do not receive them as such will perish. And no one will deny that it is possible they may be the word of God. No one can, with the least shadow of reason, pretend that it is not probable they are so. A book which thousands of the learned and the wise, after a thorough examination, have received as a revelation from Heaven, must be supported by proofs of no common strength. Taking the infidel, then, on his own ground, it is by no means safe to reject the Scriptures. He who rejects them is far from walking safely.

"It is *safe* to believe in the immortality of the soul, and in a future state of retribution. This assertion requires no proof; for it is impossible that any future evil or danger should result from believing these doctrines, even if they are not true. If the soul is not immortal, if there is no future state, they who believed and they who disbelieved these doctrines will alike cease to exist at death. On the other hand, it is not safe to disbelieve these doctrines. Even those who disbelieve them must allow that they may possibly be true; nay, that there is some probability of their truth. And if they are true, the consequences of disbelieving them will be terrible; for he who does not believe that his soul is immortal will take no care of it; and he who does not believe in a future state of retribution will make no preparation for it, and will, of course, die unprepared. He, then, who disbelieves these doctrines does not walk safely."

Safety of Believing in the Divinity of Christ.

"It is *safe* to believe in the proper divinity of Jesus Christ. Some may deny this assertion, on the ground that if Christ is not God, to worship him as such will involve us in the guilt of idolatry. But whether he is or is not God, it is certainly our duty to worship him. We are commanded to honor him even as we honor the Father; and we are told that when the Father brought him into the world, he said, 'Let all the angels of God worship him.' If it is the duty of all the angels to worship him, much more, we may conclude, is it ours. Nor among all the cautions which are given us in the Scriptures, is there the least intimation that we must beware of loving and honoring Christ too much, or that there is any danger of placing him too high. Indeed, it would be strange if there were such intimation, for why should we be cautioned against worshiping one who is worshiped in heaven, and who shares with his Father the praises of its inhabitants? In fine, if it is safe to obey God, to imitate the apostles, to utter the language of heaven, then it is safe to worship Jesus Christ. And if it is safe to worship him, it cannot be unsafe to believe that he is God. You cannot suppose that any man will be condemned at the judgment day for thinking too highly of his Saviour, or loving and honoring him too much. But if Christ is God, it is by no means equally safe to disbelieve that he is so. If the doctrine of his proper divinity is true, it must be a fundamental doctrine, a doctrine the belief of which is necessary to render us Christ's. This Dr. Priestly, the great apostle of Unitarianism, has acknowledged. 'If you are right,' said he to a distinguished clergyman in this country, who believed our Saviour's divinity—'if you are right, we are not Christians at all, and I do not wonder in the least at the bad opinion you entertain of us.' And is there not at least a probability that those who believe Christ's divinity are right? Do not many inspired passages appear to assert it in the most unequivocal terms? And since no evils can result from believing it, even though it should not prove to be true, while the most terrible evils will be the consequence of disbelieving it, if it is true, is it not the safer and wiser course to believe it?"

An Objection Answered.

"It is *safe* to believe that Christ has made an atonement for sin, and that we must be justified by faith in him, and not by our own works. From a belief of these doctrines, rightly understood, no evil or danger can result, even if they are not true. It has, indeed, been asserted that these doctrines are unfavorable to morality, but the assertion is groundless; for all who believe that we are justified by faith in Christ believe that this faith will produce good works, and that a faith which does not produce them cannot be genuine. They believe that good works are as necessary to our salvation as if we were actually justified by performing them. In fine, they believe that without holiness no man shall see the Lord. This being the case, it is impossible that their reliance on the atonement and righteousness of Christ should make them negligent of moral duties. Nor can it be shown that the belief of these doctrines occasions any other evil, or exposes them that believe, either here or hereafter, to any danger. It is, then, safe to believe them even if they are not true. But it is very unsafe to disbelieve them if they are true. A mistake respecting the terms of acceptance, the way of salvation, must be fatal, if any mistake can be so. Those who make the mistake incur the guilt, and expose themselves to the fate, of the Jews, who, being ignorant of God's righteousness, went about to establish their own righteousness, and thus failed of salvation. One of the most zealous advocates of the doctrine that we are justified by our own works, after writing a large volume in support of it concludes with this remarkable concession, 'Nevertheless, since we are prone to estimate our good works too highly, and fancy that they are sufficient for our justification when in fact they are not so, the safer way is to renounce all dependence on them, and rely on the righteousness of Christ alone.'"

The Safe Side.

"It is *safe* to believe that all men will not be saved, and that without repentance, faith, and holiness, none will be saved. To prove this little need be said. If the doctrine that all men will inherit salvation is true, those who deny are as safe as those who believe it. If it is not true, those who trust in it trust to a lie, and will utterly perish in their own deceivings. And even its warmest advocates must allow that there is at least a possibility of its proving false. No man then walks safely who ventures his soul, his all, upon its truth."

"*How Can a Man Be Too Religious?*"

"How can a man be too religious? How can any man go beyond the precepts which require him to love God with all his heart; to do every thing to his glory; to renounce every thing which causes him to sin, though dear as a right hand or a right eye; to crucify the affections and lusts; to deny himself, take up the cross, and to be holy as God is holy? How can any man be more humble, prayerful, thankful, and heavenly-minded than the Scriptures require him to be? And even if it were possible to do more than our duty, could any harm result from doing it? Would God punish a man for being too religious, for loving him too well, and serving him too faithfully? Did you ever hear of a man who, on his dying bed, repented of having paid so much attention to religion, or who expressed any fears that God would be displeased with him on account of his zeal and devotion? Did you ever hear of a man's saying, in such circumstances, Were I to live my life over again, I would be less strict and scrupulous than I have been, in obeying the divine commands? On the contrary, do not even the most pious reproach themselves in a dying hour for their deficiencies; and say, Were we to pass through the world again, we would strive to be more faithful and more devoted to God? Surely, then, there is no danger of being too religious. Surely the strict course is the safe course. Even if those who pursue it go further than is absolutely necessary, yet their salvation is sure. In a word, they are safe, even if their opponents are right. But the same cannot be said of the opposite course. If the former are right, the latter are fatally wrong. Though it is not easy to conceive of a man having too much religion, we can easily conceive of a man having too little. Though it is impossible to believe that any one will be punished for going beyond what God requires of us, it is very possible that many may be punished for falling short of it. He only, then who walks strictly, walks safely."

The World We Live In.

"We live in a changeable world, where nothing is stable, where nothing is certain, where every thing is changing, or dissolving, or passing away; a world which, with all its works, is destined to be burned up, and from which we must soon be removed. And is such a world a suitable portion for immortal beings; a proper place in which to lay up treasures, or on which to rest our hopes? Might we not as easily employ our time and exertions in building upon a quicksand, or upon ice which the summer's sun will melt away? Again, the world in which we live is a sinful, and of course a dying, world, which lies in wickedness under its Maker's curse, on which the vials of his wrath are constantly poured out, and from which thousands are daily swept away to the retributions of eternity. We live in a prison, where rebels against heaven's King are awaiting their sentence; in a place of execution, where fire and sword, pestilence and famine, disease and death, have for ages been employed in executing the sentence of God's law upon transgressors; in a grave-yard, where lie buried the many successive generations of sinners upon whom the sentence has been executed. We live surrounded by the dying and the dead; we strive to enrich ourselves with treasures which they have left behind; treasures for which many of them bartered their salvation, and which are, therefore, the price of blood, the blood of immortal souls. We live in a world in which multitudes of intelligent beings are daily commencing their existence, an existence which is never to end; in which still greater multitudes are constantly ripening for heaven or for hell; and from which thousands are daily going to one or the other of those endless abodes. And is such a world a proper place in which to seek great things for ourselves? Can the fires of avarice or ambition glow in the midst of so many things which are calculated to extinguish them? We sometimes read of wretches who, when a city is wrapped in flames or overturned by an earthquake, rush among the blazing ruins or the falling houses in search of plunder. We read of others, who follow the march of armies, and hover around a field of battle with a view to strip the bodies of the dying and the dead. We wonder at their insensibility; but alas! my friends, our conduct, while we seek great things for ourselves in such a world as this, proves that we are equally insensible. We rush on in the mad pursuit of worldly objects, surrounded by dangers, diseases, and death, with the earth trembling, and the grave ready to open under our feet. We follow in the rear of an immense army of our fellow-creatures, who have all advanced to grapple with the king of terrors, and have all fallen in the unequal combat. We are hastening to encounter the same enemy, with an assurance of meeting the same fate; yet we eagerly seize the spoils which the dead have left scattered on the field of battle; we are ready to contend and quarrel for their possessions, and take no means to prepare for the contest in which we must soon engage with the last enemy, who will strip us of all we have so hardly and laboriously acquired."

Christmas Thoughts.

"That a Being possessed of infinite wisdom, power, and goodness should create a world, or many worlds, is nothing very wonderful or surprising. But that after he had created it, and after its inhabitants had revolted from him, he should visit it—visit it in a human form, in the likeness of sinful flesh—that he should enter it, not as the Ancient of Days but as an infant—live in it, not as its Sovereign and Proprietor but as a servant, a dependent on the bounty of his own creatures—and above all that he should die in it, die in it as a malefactor, on a cross, between two thieves—that this earth should not only have been pressed by its Creator's footsteps, but wet with his tears, and stained with his blood—these are wonders indeed; wonders which would be utterly incredible had not God himself revealed them; wonders which will still be regarded as incredible by all who forget that God is wonderful in working, and that as high as the heavens are above the earth, so high are his ways above our ways, and his thoughts above our thoughts. No wonder that angels should desire to look into these things. No wonder that they left heaven in multitudes to visit our world when their Creator and their Lord lay an infant in a manger. No wonder that raptures and ecstasies unfelt before swelled their bosoms, and called for new songs to express them. The wonder is that man, stupid, insensible man, should be no more affected by this event; that he should regard it without interest, and almost fall asleep while he hears it described. It is not thus, when events comparatively trifling solicit his attention. Let the King of Great Britain visit his Irish and Scottish dominions, and the whole world rings with it. Let the President of these States come among us, and every house pours out its inmates to welcome or to gaze. Let a comet blaze athwart the sky, and thousands of sleepless eyes are open to watch the ethereal stranger. But let the Creator, the Eternal Sovereign of the universe, by whom and for whom all things were made, come in the most interesting form to visit this rebellious province of his dominions, and how few are found who even trouble themselves to ask whence he comes or what is his object; how much fewer to give him the welcome which he had a right to expect! My hearers, how strange is this: and how strange it is that we cannot see and blush at our own stupidity. Why is this event, which will cause the name of our world to resound through the whole created universe of God, and to be had in everlasting remembrance, regarded with such indifference? This world itself will soon, with all its works, be burned up. Its place in the heavens will know it no more. Not even a wreck will remain to remind future orbs that here once rolled the planet called Earth; and its very existence would at length fade away from the memories of all except its former inhabitants! but the fact mentioned in our text will preserve its name from oblivion, and through eternal ages it will be remembered as the world which its Creator visited and for which he died. And for similar reasons its inhabitants, the posterity of Adam, will be objects of intense interest and curiosity to holy beings through interminable ages. Show me a man, show me one of that race for which my Creator died! show me one of those he redeemed by his blood! will, we may suppose, be one of the first exclamations of all who through the ages of eternity shall from various parts of Jehovah's dominions enter heaven."

The Certainty of Unseen Things.

"You sometimes say, at least in your hearts, No man has ever returned from the other world to give us any information of what awaits us there, or even to assure us of its existence. We cannot, then, be certain that there is another world, or a day of judgment, or a heaven, or a hell. If, indeed, one would rise from the dead, and assure us that he had seen and known all these things, we might believe. But, my hearers, something far more satisfactory than this has been done. Not a man merely, but the Son of God, our Creator, our future Judge, has come from the other world to this on purpose to reveal it to us, to bring life and immortality to light. He came directly from the bosom of his Father, and is therefore intimately acquainted with all his counsels and designs. He came from that very heaven which he revealed to us; and lest we should refuse to give him credit, he by his miracles fixed the broad seal of heaven to his doctrines. Lest even this should be insufficient, the eternal Father, by an audible voice from heaven, exclaimed, 'This is my beloved Son; hear ye him!' that is, yield full credit to all which he reveals; yield implicit obedience to all his commands. And how much better, how much more satisfactory is this, than would be the report of some fallible mortal returning from the other world, who might be deceived himself, or willfully deceive us. My hearers, if you will not yield to this evidence, if you will not believe the Lord Jesus Christ who came from heaven, and is returned to heaven, most certainly you would not be persuaded though one rose from the dead. You must, however, do as you please; but for us—I speak in the name of all his real disciples—until you can show us a better, a more infallible Teacher, we must and will follow him. Nor are we ashamed to avow our faith. No; we exult and glory in it. We triumph while we point to the strong foundations of our belief, and build upon them our eternal hopes. We can look up and say to our ascended Saviour, Lord, we believe and are sure that thou art the Christ, the Son of the living God. And we know experimentally the truth of the apostle's assertion, 'He that believeth on the Son of God hath the witness in himself;' a witness which cannot deceive him. Tell us not, then, of the vain opinions, the endless conjectures of ignorant, fallible, short-sighted men, groping in midnight darkness. Tell us not of conjectures when we have certainty. Every thing which Christ has revealed respecting the other world is fixed, established, certain. It is no longer a matter of doubt or dispute. We rely upon it, as if we had ourselves visited the other world and seen all which he reveals. We venture our all upon it. We renounce things which we have seen for things which we have not seen; and while we believe, we find our Saviour's declaration verified, I am come a light into the world, that he who believeth in me should not walk in darkness but have the light of life. Hence, too, we firmly believe that he will again visit our world as its Judge; that to them who look and wait for him he will appear the second time without sin unto salvation. He has assured us that he will, and we can rely confidently upon his word. Nor is it, even humanly speaking, one half so improbable that he will come the second time, as it was that he would come the first. It appears far less astonishing that he should come as God to judge the world, than that he should come as man to die for the world. And being assured that he did come once, we feel assured that he will come again."

"*Holiness to the Lord.*"

"That we may understand the import of this expression, it is necessary to recollect that, when the Jewish high priest was engaged in the duties of his sacred office, and especially when he went into the holy of holies to burn incense, he was commanded to wear upon his forehead a golden miter with the words Holiness to the Lord engraven upon it. By this inscription both the high priest himself, and all who read it, were forcibly reminded that the God whom he served was a holy God, and that holiness becomes his house, his service, and his worshipers forever. If he ever felt serious and devout, it would be when he wore this inscription upon his forehead. But in the day of which we are speaking, this inscription shall be upon the harness of the horses, and upon the utensils employed in domestic life; that is, as we have already observed, upon all the daily business and employments of both sexes. We are not, however, to suppose that the letters which compose these words are actually to be written there. The meaning of this prediction evidently is, that, while persons are engaged in all the common business and concerns of life, whether at home or abroad, whether in the house or by the way, they shall feel as serious, as devout, as much engaged in the service of God, as did the Jewish high priest when he wore that sacred inscription upon his forehead. The merchant at his desk, the mechanic in his shop, the mariner in his vessel, the husbandman in his field, the traveler on his journey, and the female at home shall have such a constant, realizing sense of the presence and perfections of God, and such love, confidence, and reverence in exercise toward him, as will lead them to do every thing in a holy manner and with a view to his glory. Every thing will then be sanctified by the word of God and prayer. Religion will then not be confined, as it too often is now, to the closet and the house of God; but she will walk abroad, pervading every place with her blessed influence, and cheering happy man in all his employments with her heavenly smiles and heart-enlivening consolations. Men will then labor as Adam did in paradise, where labor was rest, and employment, and pleasure. Friends and acquaintances will then meet, as Christians now meet, to serve and praise God; every meeting will be a religious meeting; men will then speak of the things of God, as the Jews were commanded to do, in the house and by the way, when they sit down and when they rise up, and conversation on earth will be like the converse of saints and angels in heaven.

"Then there will be no idle or profane language, no evil speaking or slander heard; for the law of love will be in the heart, and, of course, the law of kindness will dwell on the lips. Then, too, the press, as well as the tongue, will be sanctified. As men will learn war, so the press will tell of war, no more; but periodical publications will then spread abroad the politics, the laws, and the triumphs of the Redeemer's kingdom. Books will no longer contain poison for the soul, or fuel for hateful passions; but be streams flowing from the fountains of life and truth. Then, too, all the domestic relations will be sanctified. Husbands and wives, parents and children, brothers and sisters, masters and servants will then love out of a pure heart fervently, as members of the same body and fellow-heirs of the same heaven. Suffice it to say, that all the common affairs of life will then be performed better than the most sacred religious duties now are. Thus every thing will be turned to gold. Some faint traces of such a state of things, faint however indeed, we find in the better ages of the Jewish commonwealth. For instance, when Boaz visited his reapers in the field, we find him saying to them, The Lord be with you; while they replied to him, The Lord bless thee. Such will be the language universally heard in the day of which we are speaking; and however nauseous and disgusting such expressions may seem, when considered as the cant of formality and hypocrisy, which speaks without feeling, they appear very different, viewed as the real language of the heart. Some such expressions are in common use among ourselves, though the real meaning is unknown, or forgotten, by thousands who adopt them. The term Adieu, for instance, signifies, I commend you to God; and even the common expression, Good-bye, is an abbreviation or corruption of the pious wish, God be with you. We mention these instances merely to show how the influence of religion will pervade even the common forms and ceremonies of society in the day of which we are speaking."

The Nature and Claims of Jehovah.

"Let us inquire what is due to Jehovah on account of his nature. The nature of any being is that, the possession of which constitutes him what he is. Thus the possession of human nature constitutes a man; the possession of angelic nature constitutes an angel; and the possession of a divine nature constitutes God. Now the nature of Jehovah is divine. In what it consists or what is its essence, we cannot, indeed, tell. We only know some of its properties. We know that it is uncreated, self-existent, independent, and eternal. It could have no beginning; for there is no cause which could bring a divine nature into existence. It can have no end; for there is no cause which can put a period to the existence of divinity. And as Jehovah possesses a divine nature, so he alone possesses such a nature. He is not only God, but God alone. There is no God before him, none beside him. In a word, he is the only being of the same kind who now exists, who ever has existed, or who ever will exist. In this respect he differs widely from all other beings. Of those who possess human nature, and of those who possess angelic nature, the number is great. Of course whatever is due to human or angelic nature must be divided among a great number of individuals. Whatever is due to angelic nature must be divided among all the angels. But with respect to Jehovah the case is different. He has no partners in the divine nature. Of course, there are none to share with him in what is due to that nature. All that is due to divinity is due to him alone, without division. Here, then, is a being who deserves something which is due to no other being in the universe, who may justly claim to be regarded with affections to which no other being has any title. He, therefore, who does not give something to Jehovah which he gives to no other being does not give unto him the glory which is his due. If it be asked, What must be given to

Jehovah which is given to no other being? I answer, One thing which must be given to him alone is, religious worship and adoration. Many other things, indeed, are his due, which we shall have occasion to notice; but this is due to him considered simply as a being who is by nature God over all. And the religious worship which is paid him must be suited to his nature. He is by nature a spirit, and must therefore, as our Saviour informs, be worshiped in spirit and in truth. He is also a most holy spirit, and must therefore be worshiped in the beauty of holiness, in the exercise of all those holy affections which constitute moral beauty and excellence. The man who thus worships Jehovah—the man whose body, soul, and spirit all bow down before him in humble prostration—whose understanding acknowledges that he is God alone and whose heart adores him as God alone, gives unto him the glory which is his due on account of his nature."

The Character of Jehovah.

"Let us inquire what is due to Jehovah on account of the character which he possesses. Now the character of Jehovah is absolutely perfect. It is the very standard of perfection. We may safely challenge the whole created universe to mention or conceive of a single beautiful, amiable, admirable, or venerable quality which he does not possess in an infinite degree. Indeed it is certain that no language has even a name for any excellent, moral, or intellectual quality which is not found in the character of Jehovah. And it is worthy of remark, that there is in his character something which is suited to excite every proper affection of which the human soul is capable. Are we, for instance, capable of feeling veneration and awe? There is something in God's character which is suited to excite these emotions. Are we capable of feeling admiration? There is in his character every thing to admire. Are we capable of love? In his character there is sufficient to raise the flame of love to the highest pitch of intensity. Are we capable of exercising confidence? His truth and faithfulness may well lead us to confide in him. Are we capable of hope? His mercy is well suited to excite it. And can it be necessary to remark, that if any being can deserve praise, he who possesses such a character as this deserves it? Is it not most evident that he is worthy to be feared, and venerated, and admired, and loved, and confided in, with all the heart, and soul, and mind, and strength? Now to regard him with all these affections, and to express these affections in fervent, humble praise, extolling him as infinitely great, and powerful, and wise, and good, and merciful, and true, is to give him the glory which is due to his character. Of him who thus offers praise, God says, He glorifieth me."

God's Works of Providence Demand our Praise.

" God's works of providence display infinitely greater wisdom, skill, power, and goodness than all the works of men. We admire the ability displayed by a commander who regulates, without confusion, all the motions of a numerous army; by a monarch who skillfully manages all the concerns of an extensive and populous empire. But what is this compared with the wisdom, knowledge, and power which are exhibited by Jehovah in the preservation, control, and government of all his innumerable hosts, and his almost boundless empire! He must every moment see every thing which takes place in the universe; every feeling, thought, word, and action of each of his creatures, and every motion of each particle of matter. He must not only see all these things, but he must never forget them. He must not only see and remember them, but direct and overrule them all in such a manner as shall cause them to work together for the accomplishment of his own purposes and for the good of those who love him. He must also foresee, and be able to foretell, every thing which will take place, with the time and manner in which it will occur. In fine, he must be continually working in every place; and the past and the future—heaven, earth, and hell—all time and all space, with all which they contain—must be constantly present to his view. And O, what a mind must that be which, without effort and without confusion, can attend at once to such an infinite variety of objects and events, and direct and control them all in the wisest and best possible manner!

"Equally wonderful is the display of moral excellences which God's works of providence exhibit. We admire the bounty of a man who feeds a hundred poor families from his table. But God every day feeds the whole family of man, together with all the inferior animals, besides bestowing on them numberless additional blessings. We admire the magnanimity and generosity of an earthly monarch who forgives rebels and traitors when they lie at his mercy. But God has forgiven millions of the worst of rebels, adopted them as his children, and made them his heirs. We extol the condescension of a sovereign who, on one day in the week, orders his palace gates to be thrown open for the admission of petitioners. But the ear of the King of kings is every moment open to the petitions of the meanest slave who crawls upon his footstool. We justly admire and venerate St. Paul, who was the instrument of converting and saving some thousands of immortal souls. But God, as the sole efficient agent, has converted and saved many millions of our race, and is still daily converting and saving more.

"There is another point of view in which the superiority of the works of God to those of men appears, if possible, still more evident. He is the real author of all the admirable and excellent works which men perform. He gave them all the abilities by which these works are performed, prompted them to attempt the performance, and then crowned their attempts with success. All the writers who have enlightened the world were but as a pen guided by him. All the great men who have delivered their countrymen from oppression were but a sword in his hand to cut off oppressors. All the inventors and improvers of useful arts were indebted to him for all their inventions and improvements. And all the good men who have blessed the world by their example and their exertions owed all their goodness and all their success to him. He is also the author, the dispenser of all the happiness which has ever been enjoyed on earth or in heaven. He gave us senses capable of being gratified, and provided for them their appropriate gratifications. He gave us our intellectual faculties, and placed before them objects in the contemplation and acquisition of which they might find pleasure. He made us capable of affections which it is delightful to exercise, and gave relations and friends toward whom those affections may flow out. And all religious enjoyments, all the happiness of heaven, proceed directly from him.

In fine, he is constantly doing good, doing it on the largest scale, doing it not merely to individuals, families, and nations, but to whole worlds and systems at once.

"Now, if we would give God the glory which is due to him on account of his works, we must acknowledge that he performs all the works which have been mentioned, and, with suitable admiration and affection, render unto him the praises and thanksgivings which such works deserve. But what creature, or what combination of creatures, can give him all the praise and thanksgiving which such works deserve? If we praise the sculptor who merely forms the image of a man, how can we sufficiently praise Him who created not only the sculptor himself, but ten thousand thousand other forms glowing with life, and radiant in beauty! If we admire the painter who skillfully delineates a landscape or a human countenance, what admiration is due to the divine Artist who spreads out his canvas over the whole earth, and, with colors dyed in heaven, makes it all one grand landscape, in which all that is beautiful and all that is sublime are exhibited in contrast or harmoniously blended! If we extol the historian, the poet, the orator, the philosopher, how can we sufficiently extol Him who created and gave them all their powers! If we admire the astronomer who discovers the motions of the heavenly bodies, how shall we sufficiently admire Him who lighted up the firmament with suns and planets, and guides Arcturus with his suns! If we applaud the man who preserves the life of a single fellow-creature, what applauses are due to that God who daily preserves all creatures and all worlds in being! If no praises are thought too great for the patriot who delivers his country from temporal bondage, what praises are sufficient for Him who offers to a ruined and enslaved world deliverance from sin and misery, and death and hell? O, never, never can any creature, nor all creatures combined, give God the whole glory which his works deserve; not though they should spend an eternity in praising him! All they can do is, to give him all that they have, to acknowledge that he alone is worthy to be praised, that all glory and honor are his due, and to combine all their powers and all their affections and exertions in forming one refulgent, unequaled crown, not to be placed on his head, for it would be unworthy, but to be cast at his feet!"

A Deluge of Blessings.

"As soon as the world was created, see the windows of heaven opened above it, and all the fullness of the Godhead gushing forth, and pouring down upon it in a torrent a flood of blessings—rich, various, inestimable blessings. Without cessation or diminution this flood has ever since continued to flow, as if all heaven were to be poured out upon earth; while, in its descent, the deluge divides into as many streams as there are individuals in our world a constant stream falls upon each. My hearers, were God's blessings waters, they would long ere this have risen more than fifteen cubits above the summits of the highest mountains. Now look at the returns which men have made for all this deluge of blessings. From a comparatively small number of families and individuals scattered here and there, see a few clouds of incense, a few imperfect offerings, praises, and thanksgivings, slowly ascending to heaven. And is this all? Yes, my hearers, this is all; all the returns which men have made to God for blessings without number and without measure; and for the unspeakable gift of his Son."

Transient Emotions.

"In the spring of the year, when God seems to repeat his work of creation, and, in the language of the Psalmist, renews the face of the earth; when his unseen but swiftly-moving pencil repairs the ravages of winter—restores to faded nature the colors, the bloom, the freshness of youth, and adorns with unrivaled tints the forest and the field;—when all is mildness and serenity; when the whole landscape smiles, and happy warblers give it a thousand tongues, making every grove resound with the expressions of their joy; who has not felt his breast swell with emotions which resembled, and which he, perhaps, fondly called, love and gratitude to the Creator, admiration of his works, and delight in his perfections? But, alas, how transient, how unproductive of salutary effects, have all these emotions proved! Appetite and passion, though hushed for a moment, soon renewed their importunities; the glitter of wealth, and distinction, and power eclipsed, in our view, the glories of Jehovah; we sunk from that heaven toward which we seemed rising, to plunge afresh into the vortex of earthly pleasures and pursuits; we neglected and disobeyed Him whom we had been ready to adore, and continued to live without God, in a world which we had just seen to be full of his glory. The rays of that glory, darting upon our minds, enkindled, indeed, a sudden flame; and the flame thus kindled flashed up toward heaven, but sunk and expired with the flash. Thus we sang God's praise, but soon forgot his works. Our emotions were of precisely the same nature with those which are excited by some grand display of human powers; and, like them, they produce no reformation of conduct, no amelioration of the heart."

God's Works of Grace Soon Forgotten.

"God's works of grace most clearly display not only the natural but the moral perfections of Jehovah. Here his character shines, full-orbed and complete. Here all the fullness of the Godhead, all the insufferable splendors of Deity, burst at once upon our 'aching sight.' Here the manifold perfections of Jehovah—holiness and goodness, justice and mercy, truth and grace, majesty and condescension, hatred of sin and compassion for sinners—are harmoniously blended, like the many colored rays of solar light, in one pure blaze of dazzling whiteness. Here every thing that is suited to arrest the attention, to enlighten and convince the understanding, to seize the imagination or to melt the heart, is made to bear upon us with an energy which it would seem impossible to resist. That an exhibitition of these wonders should make, at least, a temporary impression upon our minds, is no more than might naturally be expected. When the glorious glad tidings of the blessed God are proclaimed in our ears; when the riches of his grace, the fullness of his condescension, compassion, and love are poured out before us from a heart which has felt their influence, by 'lips which have been touched as with a live coal from the altar of God;' when with a pencil dipped in the vivid colors which inspiration affords, he is drawn in the attitude of an affectionate father, grieved at once by the sins and the miseries of his children, beseeching them in the kindest language of entreaty to return, and giving them a Saviour in the Son of his love; when the beauties, the glories, and the sufferings of that Saviour are portrayed by one who has sat at the foot of the cross, and seen the glory of God in the face of Jesus Christ; when, with a countenance full of invitation, compassion, and love, this divine Friend of sinners stands and woos them to himself, assuring all who will come of a kind reception, and freely offering rewards such as eye has not seen nor ear heard;—when these rewards are displayed; when the immortal glories of an opening heaven are made to shine around us; when the echo of its triumphant songs vibrates upon our ears; when kingdoms, crowns, and thrones, eternal as their Bestower, are presented to our view; it is almost impossible that even our obdurate hearts should be always unaffected, or retain their characteristic insensibility. For a moment they seem to be melted. We feel, and are ready to acknowledge, that God is good; that the

Saviour is kind; that his love ought to be returned; that heaven is desirable. Like a class of hearers described by our great Teacher, we receive the word with joy; a joy not unmingled with something which resembles gratitude; and we sing, or feel as if we could with pleasure sing, God's praises. But we leave his house; the emotions there excited subside; like the earth when partially softened by a wintry sun, our hearts soon regain their icy hardness; the wonders of divine grace are forgotten; and God has reason to say in sorrow and in displeasure, Your goodness is as the morning cloud; and as the early dew it goeth away."

The Character of Our National Religion.

"Little as there appears to be of religion in the world, there is much less in reality than in appearance. In men who possess some real goodness, a single grain of gold gilds a large surface of baser materials; while in other men, varnish and tinsel supply the place of the gold. Much of the religion even of good men consists of merely animal emotions and natural affections, baptized by a Christian name; and all the religion of other men, if we except external forms, is of the same character of our national religion, if we can be said to have any. As a nation we treat Jehovah very much as heathen nations treat their gods, only with less apparent respect and veneration. We compliment him, as they do their gods, with the name and attributes of divinity. We publicly implore his aid, as they do that of their idols, when evils oppress or dangers threaten us. When relief is obtained, we, like them, have public seasons of thanksgiving and offerings of praise; and our festivals, like theirs, are marked by sensual indulgences, and followed by no reformation of national sins. What, then, are we to think of our annual seasons of thanksgiving? In what light must we suppose they are regarded by Him whose judgment is according to truth? Must he not, in view of every thing by which they are attended and followed, regard them as a mere empty form; as the copy of a heathen festival; or, at best, as only a repetition of the insincere praises of Israel? Must he not regard them as an earthly monarch would regard a book inscribed to him on the title-page, and preceded by a preface filled with flattery, but containing on every following page a gross libel on his character and government? Like such a book, this day is dedicated to God. Like such a preface, it is filled with his praise; while every other day of the year, like every other page of the book, speaks a language most offensive to his ear. Mistake me not, however. I would be far from insinuating or entertaining a wish, that this custom, established by our pious fathers, should be discontinued. I only wish that its original character may be restored; that it may become the preface to a whole volume of praise; that the stream of gratitude which seems to burst forth so copiously on this day may continue to flow, though more silently, through the year."

The Existence of the World Accounted For.

"One of the most acute philosophical authors of antiquity, writing on this subject, informs us that an infinite number of atoms had existed from all eternity; that somehow or other these atoms were put in motion, and that while moving about they happened to come together and form a world, out of which plants, animals, and men spontaneously sprang up. But perhaps some will say, These were the sentiments of men in the early and ignorant ages of the world. Since reason has been more cultivated and learning has increased men know better than to believe such absurdities. We will reply to this remark, by giving you a modern theory respecting the formation of the world; a theory which has been invented, published, and defended within a few years, by some of the most learned philosophers of the age. According to this theory, the sun had either existed from all eternity or was formed nobody knows how, and a comet, made and put in motion in a similar way, passing by the sun struck off a large piece of it by a blow of its tail, and by the same blow communicated to the piece thus struck off a rotary motion, which caused it to revolve till it acquired a globular form. All this happened many millions of years ago, and during this period the new-made world, being made to revolve round the sun, collected all the particles of dust which came in its way, till it had acquired soil sufficient to support plants, animals, and men, which sprang up upon it, one after the other. In a similar way all other planets were formed. As to the moon, that was once a part of this world, and was blown out of it by a tremendous volcano, whose fires are now quenched. Indeed, others suppose that this world and all the planets were, in a similar manner, blown out of the sun. Such are the theories of those whom the world styles philosophers; such the absurdities into which grave and learned men are left to fall when they renounce the Scriptures. And if we renounce the Scriptures what can we do better than adopt some of these theories? Human reason, unenlightened by revelation, can invent no better, no more plausible way of accounting for the creation of the world and its inhabitants. If you ask, Why cannot men without the Bible allow that there is a God, who created all things? I answer, I am not obliged to show why they cannot. It is sufficient for me to show, that without a revelation they do not, and never have done this. This it is easy to show. It is easy to prove, by appealing to history and to facts, that no nation under heaven, either in the first ages or the present day, has been able to form a rational or even a plausible conjecture respecting the origin of the world; much less to arrive at any thing that could be called knowledge on this subject."

"*If the Bible Be Not True.*"

"If we were without the Bible, or if the Bible could be proved to be false, we should know nothing of a future state or of the immortality of the soul. Reason can never prove that the soul is immortal, or that the body will be raised again. This is evident from the facts, that she never has been able to discover either of these truths, and that even at the present day many learned men deny them both. It is not long since the representatives of a numerous civilized nation ordered the words, 'death is an eternal sleep,' to be inserted over the portals of their grave-yards. Indeed, if there be a future state, an eternal world, into which the soul enters after death, no one but an inhabitant of that world can assure us of the fact; for it is not an object of our senses, nor can it be discovered by reasoning. All that men ever have done, all that they can do, without a revelation from God, is to conjecture, or at most to suppose it probable, that there is a future state, and that the soul is immortal. But these conjectures and surmises are of no use. They are too weak to build upon. In fact, they only serve to produce uneasiness and anxiety in the prospect of death; for while they lead men to suspect that there possibly may be a future state, they can afford them no shadow of information respecting that state. They cannot tell us whether we shall be happy or miserable there. And if we reflect calmly on the subject, we shall find much more reason to fear misery than to hope for happiness in a future state. We find this world full of evils. We suffer much in passing through it; we find the causes of these evils and sufferings deeply rooted in our nature. We see most of those who die appear to die in pain. Who, then, can assure us, or what reason have we to hope, that the other world will be less full of evil than this; that we shall not suffer there as much or more than we suffer here; that the seeds of sorrow and suffering which are sown in our nature will be eradicated; that those who die in pain will, after death, taste nothing but pleasure? Without the Bible we can have no reason to hope for happiness after death. The best we can rationally hope for, if the Bible be false, is to die like the brutes, to plunge into the gulf of annihilation. In fact, this is all which those who reject the Bible usually do hope for; and even their hope of this, if that may be called hope which seems more like despair, is not unfrequently mingled with distressing fears of something worse. And as annihilation is the best fate we can rationally expect for ourselves if the Bible be false, so it is the best which we can suppose to have happened to our departed friends. Yes, if the Bible be not true, you may well sorrow over their remains as those that have no hope. You will never see them again. Their minds as well as their bodies are dead. All that once pleased and delighted you, all that excited your admiration or engaged your affections, is put out like last night's lamp, quenched in everlasting night. This, too, if the Bible be not true, is, for aught you can tell, the fate of all who have gone before us. They who have fallen asleep in Christ are perished. The good and the bad, they who while alive ravaged, and they who blessed, the world; they who expired uttering the language of execration and despair, and they whose expiring lips poured forth the seraphic strains of that heaven which they saw opening to their view, have all sunk down alike into eternal darkness and insensibility. But why do I talk of heaven? If the Bible be not true there is no heaven—none for us, none of which we know any thing. Life and immortality have never been brought to light. He who professed to reveal them, and who called himself the Saviour of the world, was an impostor; the Gospel of salvation, the only real glad tidings which ever vibrated upon mortal man, is a cheat; the apostles who preached it, and the martyrs who sealed it with their blood, were deluded; and all the apparent holiness which it has produced in life, and all the joy and triumph which its disciples have expressed at death, were nothing but the effects of superstition and enthusiasm. But this is not all; for if the Bible be not true, then we have no ground to hope that good will ever be brought out of evil, or that any of our afflictions will be productive of the smallest advantage either to ourselves or to others. Then we have no Father, no Saviour, no Friend above to pity our sorrows, to hear our complaints, to support us by his power, or to guide us by his wisdom. What is still more discouraging, we have no reason to hope that the situation of our wretched race will ever be ameliorated, or their miseries ever come to an end. Nothing can be rationally anticipated but an endless succession of the same crimes, wars, revolutions, and convulsions which have so long filled the world with blood, and the hearts of its inhabitants with anguish; for there is not the smallest reason to suppose that mankind are really wiser or better now than they were thirty centuries ago. If at present any appearances which encourage us to hope for the prevalence of peace are to be seen, they are occasioned solely by the influence of the Bible. But if this be false its influence cannot long continue to operate. Men will burst its bands and go on as before. Despair, then, you who sorrow, for you never will be comforted. Despair ye who weep for the miseries of man, for there is no hope that they will ever end. Despair ye who are looking with anxious eyes for the dawn of a brighter day, for no day is ever to dawn on this wretched world. There is no Star of Bethlehem, no Sun of righteousness, to rise and shine upon it with healing in his beams. No; it is destined to be shrouded for ever in sevenfold night, a night without a star, without a moon, without a morning! Rejoice, then, ye wicked, for ye will never be punished! Despair, ye good, for ye will never be rewarded!"

The Certainty of a Future Judgment—Argument.

"No proposition of natural or revealed religion, not even that which regards the existence of a God, is accompanied with more convincing evidence than this. They are indeed truths necessarily and inseparably connected; for it is evident almost to demonstration, that he who created must govern, and that he who governs must judge, the world. We cannot possibly suppose that an infinitely wise Being would create man and then leave him to himself, or to the sport of blind accident. No, he must have had some suitable design in his creation; and the only design of a Being infinitely holy, just, and good, of which we can form any conception, is his own glory as connected with the greatest possible happiness of his creatures. To accomplish this design, certain laws and regulations are necessary; and if his creatures disobey these regulations, all his perfections join in requiring that they should be restrained and punished. Experience, however, abundantly shows that in this world no adequate punishment is inflicted; that there is little or no apparent distinction between the bad and the good, but that all things come alike to all; that there is one event to the righteous and to the wicked, to him that serveth God and him that serveth him not. Hence it appears that there must be a future day of recompense and retribution, when God will vindicate his own character, reward his faithful friends, and convince the assembled world that his righteous laws are not to be violated with impunity."

Christ Coming to Judgment.

"It is certainly highly fit and proper that He who made and redeemed should also judge the world; and that he who humbled himself below all creatures should also be exalted above all, so that to him every knee shall bow and every tongue confess him Lord, to the praise and glory of God the Father. Then will his exaltation be complete. Every thing will then manifestly appear to be put under him. The glory in which he will then appear will be greater than he has ever yet assumed, greater than we could support the sight of, while clothed with mortality. At the creation he was surrounded by hosts of morning stars, who sang together, and the sons of God, who shouted for joy; and at the dispensation of the law on Sinai he was arrayed in all the majesty and terror which the elements could afford. But on this still more awful occasion he will come, not in his own glory only, but in that of his Father and the holy angels. Heaven will pour forth all her armies to grace his triumph, and spread around him all her ineffable glories in one unremitted blaze of splendor, before which the sun will fade away, and even archangels vail their faces; while,

> 'From his keen glance affrighted worlds retire;
> He speaks in thunder and he breathes in fire.'

His countenance, like the pillar of cloud between the Israelites and Egyptians, will present a double appearance; and though clothed with the rainbow of peace toward his friends, it will lower on his enemies like a stormy sky; and while his eye, at every glance, pours upon the former a flood of joy, it will flash lightnings on the latter, which will scorch their inmost souls, and fill them with unutterable, inconceivable anguish. Then shall he come in the clouds of heaven, and every eye shall see him. Then shall all the tribes of the earth mourn, and they who condemned him as guilty of blasphemy will find—to their eternal shame and confusion will find—that he uttered a solemn truth when he said, 'Hereafter ye shall see the Son of man sitting on the right hand of power, and coming in the clouds of heaven to judge the world at the last day.' Then shall his murderers find that he whom they buffeted, scourged, mocked, and crucified, was indeed the Lord of life and glory; and they, with all who have since despised and all who are now despising his offered grace, will then be convinced by their own sad experience that whosoever falls on this stone shall be broken, and that on whomsoever it shall fall it will grind him to powder."

The Persons to Be Judged.

"The persons who will be judged are the whole human race, for we must all appear. There will be no exceptions. In vain shall any call upon the mountains to fall on them and the hills to cover them. Flight, resistance, threats, and entreaties will alike be vain. There must appear rulers, with their subjects; parents, with their children; ministers, with their people; masters, with their servants; and blind guides, with their blinded followers. There will be present all who have lived in the world, from creation down to the present day; there our first parents will contemplate, with various emotions, the long line of their descendants, while they, on the other hand, will behold their common father. There will be found the inhabitants of the old world, the men of Sodom and Gomorrah, the host of Pharaoh, with their proud king, and the ancient inhabitants of Canaan, with the Israelites, their rebellious and idolatrous successors. There will be seen Noah and Abraham, Isaac and Jacob, Enoch and Elijah, Joseph and Moses, with all the other patriarchs and prophets, in a long succession. There will also be assembled the proud, cruel, hypocritical pharisees, with the priests and rulers who, with such inveterate malice, persecuted Him who will then be their Judge. There Pilate, with Herod, shall appear before Him who once stood at his iniquitous tribunal, and receive the reward of his injustice and cowardice. There will be found all of whom we read in profane and sacred history; the apostles and martyrs, with their persecutors; the famous heroes and conquerors, who have so often deluged the world with blood, and were highly esteemed among men, but were an abomination in the sight of the Lord; the statesmen, the philosophers, and great ones of the earth, with all that is noble, all that is vile among mankind.

"Further, there will be present all who are now on the earth, they who now fill the mouths of men with their greatness, and think this world too narrow for their fame; they who are now envied for their beauty, wealth, honors, or accomplishments; they who now excite the love or hatred, the hopes or fears, the admiration or contempt of mankind, will then stand out in their naked characters. All disguises will then be stripped off, all human distinctions will be destroyed, and the only difference which will then be of any avail is the grand, the eternal distinction between saints and sinners. The scoffers who are now asking Where is the promise of his coming? who have wasted their lives and abused their talents in neglecting or denying a future judgment, will find to their cost, that, verily there is a God who judgeth in the earth, and that while they have been following lying vanities, they have forsaken their own mercies and destroyed themselves, with all their disciples."

The Things for Which Men are to Be Judged.

"The things for which this innumerable multitude will be called to give an account are, as we learn from our text, all the things done here in the body, whether good or bad. By the things done in the body, are intended not only external actions, but also words and the thoughts and intents of the heart. Of every idle word that men shall speak, says the Judge, shall they give an account in the day of judgment. God shall bring every secret thing into judgment, and will judge the secrets of men by Christ Jesus. The great rule by which these things will be tried is the divine law; and how this law will be interpreted our Saviour has himself informed us. He has declared that every sinful desire is no less a breach of its requirements, and no less exposes us to its dreadful curse, than the most open violation; and he will condemn as breakers of the sixth command, not only all actual murderers, but all who have at any time indulged feelings of malice, hatred, envy, or revenge against their neighbors. Not only all adulterers and adulteresses, but all who have not maintained the strictest purity in thought, word, and deed, will also fall under his just condemnation. He who has coveted, as well as he who has actually stolen, his neighbor's property will be found guilty. Nay more; not only they who hate God and their neighbor, but they who do not love God with all their heart, soul, strength, and mind, and their neighbor as themselves, must be condemned by the law of God. It is highly worthy of notice, that in all the descriptions which our Saviour has given of the day of judgment he represents himself as dooming sinners to the fire prepared for the devil and his angels, not for what the world call crimes—not for injuring their fellow-creatures or disturbing the peace of society—but for being unprofitable servants, for neglecting to feed the hungry, clothe the naked, to receive the stranger, and visit the sick. It is not so much against sins of commission that threatenings are denounced in the word of God. He that believeth not shall be damned. Except ye repent, ye shall all likewise perish. Not only every tree that bringeth forth bad fruit, but every tree that does not bring forth good fruit, shall be hewn down and cast into the fire. These regulations may seem, and, indeed, must seem to the unhumbled heart too rigid and severe; but if the word of God be true, if Christ the Judge abide by his own positive declarations, by these regulations must every thought, word, and action be tried. To this standard must the conduct of every individual be brought. In this balance must every individual be weighed."

The First Object that will Rush upon the Mind at Death.

"The soul when it leaves the body will find itself in a moment in the presence of the great Sun of the universe, whose beams, like a torrent, pervade immensity and eternity. Sun, moon, and stars will all have vanished. Earth and its objects will appear to have been suddenly annihilated, and God, God alone, will rush in upon the mind and fill every faculty, occupy every thought. Above and below, behind and before, wherever the mind can turn itself or whithersoever roam, it will still find itself in the immediate presence of God; nor, if I may so express it, can the eyelids of the soul ever close for an instant to shut out the dazzling refulgence of his glory. As companions in admiring, or in shrinking with despair from, these glories, the soul will perceive itself to be surrounded by myriads of created spirits of opposite characters, and will quickly find that the same God who, to holy spirits, is a refreshing, animating light, is, to the unholy, a consuming fire; that what is heaven to the one, is hell to the other."

Mortal, Yet Immortal.

"My brethren, through the great change we have been considering you must all pass. Your bodies must be changed. In a few years, of all the bodies which now fill this house nothing but a few hands-full of dust will remain. Your mode of existence will be changed. Your disembodied, but still living, spirits will pass into a new and untried state of being. Your place of residence will be changed. The places which now know you will soon know you no more. Another assembly will fill this house. Other inhabitants will dwell in your habitations. Other names will glitter over the marts of business, and yours will be transferred to the tombstone. And when this world has lost you another will have received you. After you are dead and forgotten here, you will be alive, and capable of exquisite happiness or misery elsewhere. After you are removed from all the objects which now affect you, a new world, new objects, new beings will rise upon you, and affect you in a manner far more powerful than you are or can be now affected. Above all, when this world and all that it contains sink from your view, God, that Being of whom you have heard so much and, perhaps, thought so little—that Being who formed and now invisibly surrounds and upholds you will burst in upon and fill your mind, fill it with delight inconceivable or agony unutterable, according to the state of your moral character. And as it affects you the moment after death, so it will continue to affect you forever; for neither his character nor yours will ever change. Long after all remembrance of you shall have been blotted from the earth, during all the remaining centuries which the sun may measure out to succeeding generations of mortals, you will still be bathing with delight or writhing in agony in the beams of Jehovah's presence. And even after this world shall have ceased to exist, when sun and stars are quenched in endless night, you will still continue the same individual, conscious being that you now are, and will still bear, and through eternity will continue to bear, that stamp of moral character with all its consequences in which you are found, and in which you will be unchangeably fixed, by death."

THE END.

OPINIONS OF THE PRESS.

WESLEY HIS OWN HISTORIAN.

Illustrations of his Character, Labors, and Achievements. From his own Diaries. By Rev. E. L. JANES. 12mo. $1 50.

AMONG the testimonials of the value of this book is the following from the venerable and highly-esteemed Dr. SPRAGUE, of the Presbyterian Church:

"MY DEAR MR. JANES: I was certainly very sincere in my expressions of thanks to you when you gave me the volume which you had compiled from the works of John Wesley, but I confess I had no adequate appreciation of the favor until I had an opportunity of reading it. You make us feel that we are verily in contact with the illustrious man, hearing his deliverances and witnessing his movements; and though as a Presbyterian I might not be able to indorse every word that I find in the book, yet, as a Christian, I can cordially recommend the volume, and I am sure it will be most gratefully welcomed by every evangelical denomination."

"We give it up. A diary is at last made into one of the most readable of books. Wesley's Journals are served up anew, and make a delicious *ragout*. . . . Whoever would catch a glimpse of the labors, cheerfulness, devotion, steadfastness, and wisdom—every thing that seemed to shine in his character and career—should read this volume." —*Zion's Herald*.

"Mr. Janes has here executed a most happy thought, and he might have styled his book, 'Wesley's Journals, *Abridged*.' He has, with excellent judgment and tact, made such selections as exhibit the real Wesley, himself speaking, writing, preaching, traveling, and making his own record of the facts and of his impressions."—*Chris. Advocate*.

"This work has been selected with great care and arranged with skill, and makes a most interesting volume."—*Northwestern Advocate*.

CHARACTER & CAREER OF FRANCIS ASBURY.

Illustrated by Numerous Selections from his Journal, arranged in Chronological Order. By Rev. E. L. JANES. 12mo., pp. 615. $2.

Rev. Bishop Haven, in *Zion's Herald* of May 23, has devoted more than a column in giving a notice of this work. He says: "Rev. Mr. Janes has done for Asbury what he did so well for Wesley—made him his own historian. He has taken his Journals and gone over them, uniting, arranging, and harmonizing them. This book is crowded with interest; every page is alive."

"The Journal of Bishop Asbury, taken as a whole, form rather dry reading, being often the bare recital of his immense horseback tours of apostolic service, with the scenes and texts of his almost daily preaching. To cull the incidents of permanent interest and value out of many pages of unimportant details is work that has long awaited some loving hand among the thousands of the spiritual children of this consecrated man. That reverent and affectionate disciple has been found.—Rev. B. K. PEIRCE, D.D., Editor *Zion's Herald*."

www.ingramcontent.com/pod-product-compliance
Lightning Source LLC
Chambersburg PA
CBHW032354230426
43672CB00007B/693